AS

American Vistas
1607-1877

Fifth Edition

Edited by

LEONARD DINNERSTEIN
UNIVERSITY OF ARIZONA

and

KENNETH T. JACKSON
COLUMBIA UNIVERSITY

New York   Oxford
OXFORD UNIVERSITY PRESS
1987

OXFORD UNIVERSITY PRESS

Oxford   New York   Toronto
Delhi   Bombay   Calcutta   Madras   Karachi
Petaling Jaya   Singapore   Hong Kong   Tokyo
Nairobi   Dar es Salaam   Cape Town
Melbourne   Auckland
and associated companies in
Beirut   Berlin   Ibadan   Nicosia

Published by Oxford University Press, Inc.
200 Madison Avenue, New York, New York 10016

Oxford is a registered trademark of Oxford University Press

Library of Congress Cataloging-in-Publication Data
American vistas.
   Bibliography: p.
   Contents: [1] 1607-1877—[2] 1877 to the present.
   1. United States—History.   I. Dinnerstein,
Leonard.   II. Jackson, Kenneth T.
E178.6.A426   1987   973   86-8454
ISBN 0-19-504136-4 (pbk. : v. 1 : alk. paper)
ISBN 0-19-504137-2 (pbk. : v. 2 : alk. paper)

10 9 8 7 6 5 4 3 2 1

Printed in the United States of America
on acid-free paper

For Barbara Jackson
and
To the bright, enduring memory of our son,
Kenneth Gordon Jackson II
(1968–1984)

O my son Absalom,
my son, my son Absalom!
would God I had died for thee
2 Samuel 18

PREFACE TO THE FIFTH EDITION

It is now almost two decades since we first embarked on our project of bringing together a series of historical essays that combined interest with readability and which could be used in conjunction with a survey text or a wide variety of other books. We have been gratified by the initial reader response as well as the enthusiasm with which our subsequent editions were received. The testaments that we have read indicate that there are a large number of instructors who find the combination of traditional and off-beat essays on the American past suitable to their own teaching styles. We are particularly pleased that *American Vistas* has been used by a wide diversity of people in every region of the country as well as in Canada and overseas. It reaffirms our belief that the American past can be both enlightening and instructive to all people who are fascinated by the development of societies.

For this revision we have made a searching reexamination of the contents and have kept only those essays that we believe have been particularly successful in the past. Letters from users and comments from other colleagues and scholars clearly indicated which pieces were most suitable for college classes. We have tried to follow this collective advice whenever possible. Many of our selections were so highly praised that we felt it would be an injustice to students and teachers alike if we eliminated them. On the other hand, more recent scholarship and the changing emphasis of societal and classroom interests have resulted in new selections on Benjamin Franklin's sister, the Confederation period, the Dartmouth College case and its implications, the efforts to obtain Oregon territory, Abraham Lincoln and the idea of equality, and an essay on the experience of Black people in the South after the Civil War ended.

As in the past, the office staff at the University of Arizona His-

tory Department facilitated the preparation of the manuscript
with its usual aplomb. For this we would like to thank Dawn
Polter, Nikki Matz, Dorothy Donnelly, Linda Garcia, Janey
Campbell, and Marita Coburn.

Finally, both of us would be grateful for individual comments
and suggestions from readers. We also hope that articles included
in this edition are as useful for classes as those that were chosen
for earlier editions.

L.D.
K.T.J.

June 1986

CONTENTS

I COLONIAL ORIGINS

II THE YOUNG REPUBLIC

I COLONIAL ORIGINS

I

The Man Behind Columbus

EDWARD T. STONE

• Christopher Columbus, a weaver's son, was born in Genoa
in 1451. He took to the sea as a boy and remained a mariner
for the rest of his life. Although he was in Portugal in 1488
when Bartholomeu Días returned from his voyage around the
southern tip of Africa with the sensational news that there
was an eastern water route to the Indies, Columbus was convinced that a western route as well was feasible. When King
John II of Portugal refused to finance an exploratory voyage,
Columbus turned to the Spanish Court. He finally persuaded
Queen Isabella to equip a tiny fleet, and he set out from the
port of Palos in August 1492. A little more than two months
later, on the morning of October 12, a lookout on the Pinta,
one of his vessels, shouted: "Tierra! Tierra!" That discovery is
generally regarded as the most important event in the history of Western civilization since the birth of Christ.

Columbus's reputation has not fared especially well in recent years. We now concede that he was a mediocre administrator and an impractical dreamer who never realized that he
had found anything more than a new route to the Orient.
We also believe that it was Leif Ericson, who reached the
shores of Labrador about the year 1000, who was the first
European to set foot in the New World—though there are
other contenders for the honor, St. Brendan the Navigator
and Madoc the Welshman among them.

The following article continues this tradition by suggesting
that if Columbus had been left to his own devices his ships
would never have sailed. According to its author, it was the
Pinzón brothers, and especially Martín, who enlisted a crew
and who got things moving. If only Martín Pinzón had lived

From *American Heritage* 27 (October 1976): 46–53. Copyright © 1976 by
American Heritage Publishing Co., Inc. Reprinted by permission.

a bit longer (Stone suggests), historians might have credited him with his critical role in the Columbus expedition.

As you approach the village of Palos de la Frontera, some fifty miles west of Seville in Spain's Andalusía, the squat little church of San Jorge looms in the foreground at the base of a rocky cliff that overlooks the tidal flats created by the mingling of the rivers Tinto and Odiel. The shallow estuary where the two rivers converge, known of old as the Saltés, is undistinguished scenically, an obscure corner of Spain virtually unknown to American tourists.

But a visitor mounting the steps to the plaza of the seven-hundred-year-old church from the road below soon becomes aware of a dusty marble plaque affixed to the crumbling brown façade of the sanctuary. Now chipped and broken, it is a sad remnant of a long-forgotten burst of civic pride. Chiseled on it are these words:

A LOS PINZONES

IMORTALES HIJOS DE ESTA VILLA

CODESCUBRIDORES CON COLON

DEL NUEVO MUNDO

3 AGOSTO 1910 EL PUEBLO DE PALOS

(to the Pinzóns: Immortal sons of this town, codiscoverers with Columbus of the New World; August 3, 1910; the community of Palos).

But didn't Columbus discover America all by himself? And who were the Pinzóns anyway? Good questions—and not one American in ten thousand probably knows the correct answers. Yet the role of the brothers Pinzón in the discovery of America, and particularly that of the eldest, their redoubtable leader, Martín Alonso Pinzón, can fairly be equated with that of Columbus himself.

Pinzón organized the expedition of 1492 after Columbus had failed to enlist a crew. Pinzón not only helped to finance the voyage but also advanced funds from his own pocket to the families of the sailors so they would not be in need during the absence of their breadwinners. One of the great sailors and navigators of his day, he contributed the maritime skill and knowledge necessary for the success of the expedition.

The *Pinta,* under Pinzón's command, invariably led the fleet, and it was her crew who first sighted land in the predawn hours of October 12. Pinzón was the discoverer of the island of Haiti, where the Spaniards established their first New World colony, and he was the first European to strike gold in America.

Pinzón was, in fact, the de facto leader of the expedition, since the crews looked to him for direction rather than to Columbus, whom they mistrusted as a foreigner.

It is not difficult to assess the reasons for history's neglect of Martín Pinzón. He died obscurely in Palos within two weeks after the return of the fleet of discovery on March 15, 1493. (Only two ships returned; Columbus's flagship was wrecked on the north shore of Haiti on Christmas Eve.) Columbus and Pinzón quarreled bitterly in the West Indies, and only Columbus's own version of the voyage has survived in conventional histories of the Discovery. He was a prolific writer of journals and letters; even if he and Pinzón had not quarreled, his incessant portrayal of himself as the lone discoverer of the New World would have prevailed because there was no other version.

After the quarrel Columbus's complaints against his fellow argonauts were endless: the seamen of Palos were a bad lot, lawless and disobedient; the Pinzón brothers were greedy and insolent. The theme was picked up by two major contemporary historians, Father Bartolomé de Las Casas, an ardent admirer of Columbus, and Ferdinand Columbus, the illegitimate son of Christopher, who wrote a laudatory biography of his father. Subsequent histories of the Discovery were based almost exclusively on these three sources—Columbus himself, his son Ferdinand, and the partisan Las Casas.

But lying virtually forgotten for nearly three hundred years in the Archive of the Indies in Seville was a mass of unique historical data that revealed the great part Martín Pinzón played in the discovery of America. Preserved in the cramped handwriting of sixteenth-century court reporters are hundreds of thousands of words of sworn testimony about the first voyage that offer a considerably different view of the Enterprise of the Indies from that of the Columbus tradition.

Only gradually, in the last century and this, has this mine of historical evidence yielded its treasure through the work of successive Spanish scholars. Known as the *Pleitos de Colón* (litigation of Columbus), the transcripts of these extraordinary proceedings embody the eyewitness recollections of nearly a hundred residents of the *comarca*, or countryside, of the Tinto-Odiel, men who had been personally acquainted with both Pinzón and Columbus and who had witnessed or participated in

the events in Palos immediately before the departure of the expedition
of 1492 and after its return seven months later. At least five of the witnesses had been on the voyage.

The *Pleitos* were initiated by Diego Columbus, elder son of Christopher and the latter's successor as admiral of the Indies. Diego brought
suit in 1508, two years after his father's death, to have restored to the
Columbus family the titles and authority of viceroy and governor of
the New World colonies, which King Ferdinand and Queen Isabella
had revoked in 1499, deposing Columbus and appointing a new governor. Defending the case for the Crown, the *fiscal*, or royal attorney,
chose to base his defense not on the grounds of Columbus's dubious
record as governor but on the allegation that he was not the exclusive
discoverer of America.

Testimony was presented in an attempt to prove that not only did
Martín Pinzón organize and lead the expedition but that it was his idea
in the first place. The latter claim, however, had so little evidence to
support it that the Council of the Indies, before which the suit was
tried, rejected it out of hand.

But the depositions relating to Pinzón's predominant part in organizing the fleet and his role as partner and collaborator in the Discovery were abundant and explicit and were never challenged or denied by
the attorney, and witnesses for Diego. Indeed, at least one witness for
the plaintiff, Juan Rodríguez de Mafra, a veteran pilot, volunteered in
his sworn statement, made in 1515, that if it had not been for Pinzón,
Columbus never could have enlisted a crew.

The proceedings dragged on for twenty-five years, with periodic hear-
ings over wide intervals of time and in widely separated places. In the
end Luis Colón, wastrel grandson of Columbus, was conceded a duke-
dom in lieu of the viceroyalty demanded in the suit. Meanwhile descendants of Martín Pinzón were granted a coat of arms by the em-
peror Charles V in belated recognition of Pinzón's contribution to the
Discovery.

Thus but for the court records of the *Pleitos* the knowledge of
Pinzón's great role would have vanished forever. Aside from those records the documentary history of the Pinzón family is scanty.

Traditionally 1441 is given as the year of Martín's birth in Palos.
Nothing is known of his parents, but evidently the family had been
settled in the Palos area for generations. Martín and his younger broth-

ers, Vicente Yáñez and Francisco Martín, lived together in a large house on Calle de la Nuestra Señora de la Rábida, the main street of Palos. Presumably they had inherited the house together with a *finca*, or farm estate, located upriver near Moguer.

Over the years Pinzón built up a prosperous deep-sea shipping business in which his brothers participated. His ships—he owned as many as three at a time—ranged far into the Atlantic and Mediterranean, particularly in the Guinea trade down the West African coast.

Las Casas, whose father later accompanied Columbus on the second voyage in 1493, described the Pinzón brothers as "wealthy mariners and principal persons to whom nearly everyone in their town deferred." And Martín Pinzón, he went on, was the "chief and most wealthy and most honored, very courageous and well versed in matters of the sea."

But it is in abundant testimony presented in the *Pleitos* that the full measure of Pinzón's influence in his community is realized. Witness after witness, without a dissenting voice, told of the admiration and respect in which he was held by his fellow citizens as a sea captain and as a civic leader. And it was precisely Pinzón's influence in the Tinto-Odiel *comarca* that was to be decisive in the discovery of America.

The declaration of Francisco Medel, *regidor* (magistrate) of Huelva, made in Seville in 1535, is typical of many:

> The said Martín Alonso Pinzón was very knowledgeable in the art of navigation in all the seas and was a man than whom in all the kingdom there was no other more courageous in warfare nor more determined . . . for whatever he set his mind to, and at times he had one ship and at others two or three and this witness saw that he had them . . . and he had many honorable relatives and friends and superb equipment . . . to make the said discovery.

From the *Pleitos* we learn the name of Pinzón's wife, María Alvarez, but little else about her. She was probably the daughter of one of the deep-sea mariners of Palos who formed an elite fraternity in a town devoted to the sea. The men who sailed the swift caravels of Andalusía to the far ports of Europe and Africa considered themselves a cut above the humbler fishermen whose daily forays into salt water were confined to the immediate area.

The couple were probably married in 1469, when Pinzón was about twenty-eight. This may be inferred from the testimony of their eldest son, Arias Pérez Pinzón, who was forty-five years old when he testified in 1515.

The world in which Martín and María began their married life was not a tranquil one. Palos was a tough little frontier seaport in a turbulent land. Andalusía was the bloody battleground for the hatreds and ambitions of feudal nobles who maintained private armies and even fleets of war. Bands of robbers nested in strongholds in the mountains and made periodic forays on villages and towns, returning with impunity to their lairs. Also, along the Andalusían coast the towns were prey to raids by Moslem corsairs from North Africa. The area around Palos, situated at the head of the estuary of the Saltés, an open door to the ocean, was particularly vulnerable to forays.

According to tradition in Palos, Pinzón's two younger brothers continued to live with him on Calle de la Rábida after María moved in as a bride, and she kept house for all three. At the end of her first confinement she and Martín, attired in their Sabbath best and accompanied by two sponsors, carried their infant son to the baptismal font in the church of San Jorge, where a friar from the monastery of La Rábida solemnly christened him Arias Pérez Pinzón. In subsequent years came Juan Martín, Catalina, Diego Martín, Mayor, Leonor, and Francisco Martín.

Most of the children were reasonably healthy, but there was a distressing exception. One of the little girls—which one is not known—was subject to violent convulsions. Her malady was diagnosed as the dreaded *gota coral*—epilepsy in its most acute form. This melancholy ordeal in the married life of the Pinzóns is revealed in a curious document brought to light by the Spanish historian Navarrete. Couched in archaic Castilian legalese, it is a mandate issued by Ferdinand and Isabella on December 5, 1500, ordering the authorities of Palos to act on a petition by Arias Pérez Pinzón that his brothers be compelled to take their turns in caring for their epileptic sister in their respective homes.

Martín and María had been married five years when the wretched reign of Enrique IV, the last of the Trasámara dynasty, which had ruled Castile for a hundred years, ended with his death in Madrid in 1474. The throne was seized immediately by his young half sister Isabella and Prince Ferdinand of Aragon, whom she had secretly married five years before. Isabella had the support of a powerful faction of Castilian·nobles who were profoundly disturbed by the moral degeneracy of Enrique's court.

Their accession precipitated a war with Portugal, whose king, Afonso V, claimed the Castilian throne on behalf of his niece, Juana. Afonso sent an invading army into Castile to enforce her claim, but it was routed by the forces of Ferdinand and Isabella in a battle on the Duero River in 1476.

Afonso did not attempt a second invasion, but the war continued at sea with singular ferocity. Martín Pinzón and his fellow seamen of Palos were in the forefront of the naval fighting that ranged up and down the Atlantic coast from Lisbon to Guinea in West Africa. In the *Pleitos* a number of witnesses testified to Pinzón's personal prowess. Commanding his own ship on privateering expeditions, he won the admiration of his contemporaries by his valor and daring.

"At the time of the war with Portugal, all the Portuguese feared him because each day he captured some of them," declared Gonzalo Martín of Huelva in his deposition in 1532. Fernando Iáñes Montiel, also of Huelva, said that "he knew very well the said Martín Alonso Pinzón and he was the most valorous man in all this land and with his ship he was feared by the Portuguese." Ferrán Yáñez described Pinzón as being "as courageous a man as there was in this land . . . and there was no Portuguese ship that dared face him."

Because of past irritations the fighting was especially bitter. The Spanish seamen resented the Portuguese claim to a monopoly of the African trade; the Portuguese were incensed by the Spaniards' incursions into what they considered their exclusive domain. The war finally ended with the Treaty of Alcáçovas in September 1479. Afonso gave up his claim to the Castilian throne; Ferdinand and Isabella recognized the exclusive right of the Portuguese to West African trade.

This last provision put a severe crimp in the economy of Palos. The shipowners and their crews henceforth had to depend largely on less lucrative trade with the Canaries and with Mediterranean and northern European ports.

So things went until one day in the winter of 1484–85 an indigent foreigner appeared at the gate of the monastery of La Rábida and begged for bread and water for his small son. It was a minor event that later was to have unimaginable consequences for Pinzón and for the whole world: the stranger was Christopher Columbus.

It was probably two or three years after this that María died and Pinzón took a second wife, Catalina Alonso, who was hated by her new stepchildren. There is no surviving record as such either of María's death or of the second marriage. But both events are implicit in two curious documents in the royal archives of Spain, both bearing the same date and marking another intervention by the Catholic sovereigns in the Pinzón family affairs.

They were discovered by the American scholar Alicia B. Gould y Quincy in the archive of Simancas. Both documents, signed by Ferdinand and Isabella, bear the date October 12, 1493, exactly one year after the discovery of America and six and a half months after the death of Pinzón. The first is a mandate to the authorities of Palos to take appropriate action on a petition by five of the Pinzón children—Arias Pérez, Juan Martín, Mayor, Catalina, and Leonor—to have their stepmother evicted from the family home. The second, directed to the woman herself, instructs her to comply with the wishes of the Pinzón heirs or show cause to the royal magistrates in Palos why she should not.

Thus when Pinzón first met Columbus some time in the latter half of 1491, the Pinzón household, with an epileptic daughter and with a second wife at swords' points with her stepchildren, was anything but happy.

Columbus had spent six bitter years, much of the time in dire poverty, trying to persuade the sovereigns to underwrite his expedition. They were mildly interested, but they were engaged in a costly war with the kingdom of Granada, the last stronghold of the Moors in Spain. Moreover, a commission appointed to examine Columbus's proposal, headed by the queen's most trusted adviser, Father Talavera, reported on it unfavorably. The queen informed Columbus he could not count on royal support.

Heartsick, Columbus returned to La Rábida, where, several years earlier, he had been too poor to care for his son and had left him in the care of the monks. He was determined to try his fortunes in France. But the guardian of the monastery, Father Juan Pérez, had become interested in the project and persuaded him to delay his departure until a new appeal could be made to the queen. Father Pérez at one time had been a *contador* (accountant) in the queen's household and had served as her confessor.

It is clear from testimony in the *Pleitos* that the new application to the queen was contingent on inducing Martín Pinzón to join the enterprise. The shrewd priest must have suspected that a weak point in Columbus's case was the lack of an experienced navigator and fleet organizer.

Unfortunately, at the moment Pinzón was on a voyage to Italy with a cargo of sardines. Once there, he and his twenty-one-year-old son, Arias Pérez, visited Rome and were taken on a tour of the library of Pope Innocent VIII. Their host is described as a "familiar" of the pope and an old acquaintance of Pinzón. He is not otherwise identified, but it is likely that he had once been a monk àt La Rábida.

In the *Pleitos* the legal battery for the Crown made much of this visit of the Pinzóns to the Vatican in attempting to prove that Pinzón and not Columbus had initiated the voyage of discovery. Responding to Question XI in the interrogatory of October 15, 1515, Arias testified to the conversation he and his father had had with the papal servant, whom he described as a "great cosmographer."

"And there this witness and his said father were informed of these lands that awaited discovery," Arias continued. He further said that his father was so impressed by the evidence of undiscovered lands that he was determined to go in search of them himself.

There is a great deal of eyewitness testimony relating to the first meeting between Columbus and Pinzón on the latter's return from Italy. Typical was that of Hernando de Villareal, who said that he "knows that on arrival of the said Martín Alonso from Rome, the said Admiral [Columbus] reached an agreement with him and the said Admiral sent to court a friar of La Rábida and he made relation thereof to Their Highnesses. . . ."

The evidence in the *Pleitos* dovetails with the accounts of the renewed negotiations between Columbus and the sovereigns as related by Father Las Casas and Ferdinand Columbus in their respective histories. Father Pérez wrote to the queen from La Rábida. His letter was so effective that she replied within two weeks, summoning both Pérez and Columbus to the royal encampment of Santa Fe on the *vega*, or lowland, of Granada, where the Spanish armies were besieging the Alhambra. The queen sent 20,000 maravedis (about $140) to Columbus so he could shed his threadbare clothes and make a decent appearance at court.

The Alhambra surrendered on January 2, 1492. Three and a half months later the monarchs signed the Capitulations of Santa Fe, authorizing the voyage and making extraordinary grants of titles and perquisites to Columbus. By a stroke of their pens the erstwhile Knight of the Ragged Cape, as some of the courtiers had scoffingly dubbed Columbus in his years of travail, was transformed into the Very Magnificent Lord, Don Cristóbal Colón, Admiral of the Ocean Sea. Along with the Capitulations the sovereigns issued a directive to the town authorities of Palos to furnish and equip two caravels and to supply the necessary manpower for them.

Columbus returned in triumph to Palos, and the royal directives were read in the church plaza to a small knot of Palos officialdom. Unfortunately for Columbus, his new admiral's uniform and the decrees from the sovereigns did little for him in the jaundiced eyes of the local citizens. To them he was still the indigent foreigner without money or credit who was trying to force them to go on a desperate journey to God knew where.

To Alonso Pardo, town notary of Moguer, fell the task of seeking two caravels in accordance with the royal mandate. He managed to commandeer a couple of ships of dubious vintage whose owners were either unlucky or indifferent. Pardo, a witness years later in the Columbus family litigation, testified that "this witness saw that everyone scorned the said Christopher Columbus and believed he would die and everyone who went with him."

The hostile state of mind of the people of Palos is abundantly revealed in uncontroverted testimony presented in the *Pleitos*. Witness after witness, in interrogatories taken over a period of twenty years and in widely separated places, testified to the universal lack of confidence in Columbus when he tried to man and equip the fleet on his own.

"Everyone said the enterprise of the said Don Cristóbal was vain and they made a mockery of it," declared Martín Gonzalo Bisochero in the 1515 hearing in Moguer.

The villagers' hostility toward Columbus was even confirmed by witnesses sympathetic to Diego Columbus. One of them was Juan Rodríguez de Cabezudo, a Moguer farmer who had rented a donkey to Columbus when the latter went to court after his first interview with Pinzón. "Many persons made fun of the said Admiral," Cabezudo testified. "They . . . even reproached this witness for lending him a mule and publicly they scorned the enterprise."

Week after week the embargoed caravels swung idly at anchor in the Rio Tinto while Columbus strove in vain to enlist a crew. Apparently he must have given the sovereigns the idea that the villagers' stolid resistance portended a full-scale revolt. On June 20, nearly a month after the reading of the ordinance impounding the caravels, Their Highnesses sent a stern letter to the Palos authorities ordering Columbus's ships manned by any means necessary. And they sent an officer of the royal household named Juan de Peñalosa to see that the order was carried out. At the same time the *alcaide* (governor) of the castle was summarily ousted and replaced by the *corregidor* (royal magistrate), Juan de Cepeda, who armed it to repel any rebellion.

These drastic measures only hardened the passive resistance of the villagers. The boycott was complete.

The reader may well wonder whatever happened to the understanding Columbus had reached with Pinzón. The question has never been satisfactorily answered. There is only one reasonable conclusion: with the mandates of the sovereigns in hand, Columbus had decided he had no need for Pinzón's collaboration, no necessity to share the glory and profits of the expedition. Professor Manuel Sales Ferre of the University of Seville, who did extensive research in the transcripts of the *Pleitos*, believes the boycott was actively abetted by a resentful Pinzón, who used his powerful influence in the community to thwart Columbus at every turn. Thus the enterprise was caught in a riptide of contention between two stubborn wills—the one armed with the authority of the Crown, the other with Pinzón's moral authority in the *comarca*.

In the end Columbus had to go to Pinzón. Father Pérez was probably an active mediator in the impasse. Once Columbus had accepted the reality that all the king's horses and all the king's men couldn't put together a crew for him, there remained the task of winning Pinzón to a reconciliation. This probably was not as difficult as it might seem. Pinzón was now fifty years old, well past the life expectancy of those days. Undoubtedly he yearned for one more great adventure to crown his distinguished maritime career. Even more compelling, perhaps, was his longing to escape from his unhappy household.

It is not difficult to imagine the scene as the two protagonists faced each other, Columbus now conciliatory and expansive in his promises, Pinzón dour and still suspicious as he stated his conditions for undertaking the voyage. What were those conditions? No one knows for sure. If there was a written agreement, it has not survived. However, there was considerable testimony by witnesses in the *Pleitos* on this point.

The import of the sworn evidence is that the two partners agreed to share equally the rewards of the expedition. Obviously such an understanding could relate only to the material profits and not to grants of high office made to Columbus by the sovereigns.

The eldest of the Pinzón sons, Arias Pérez and Juan Martín, testified that Columbus had pledged half. So did Diego Hernández Colmenero, who after the voyage married Pinzón's daughter Catalina. Their testimony might be considered suspect because of their close relationship. On the other hand, unless one makes the gratuitous assumption that they were lying, who would be in a better position to know the facts than the immediate members of the Pinzón family?

However, there was strong corroboration from other witnesses. Alonso Gallego of Huelva said he heard Columbus tell Pinzón: "Señor Martín Alonso we will go on this voyage and if God grants that we discover land, I promise you . . . I will share with you as I would my own brother." Gallego added that he heard Columbus make that pledge "many times." Francisco Medel, *regidor* (alderman) of Huelva, testified that "Martín Alonso Pinzón said to this witness that Columbus agreed . . . to give him all that he asked for and wanted."

Father Las Casas, who was strongly partial to Columbus, nevertheless has left a fair assessment of the situation. "Christopher Columbus began his negotiation with Martín Alonso Pinzón," Las Casas wrote in the *Historia de las Indias*,

> begging that he come with him and bring along his brothers and relatives and friends and without doubt he made some promises because no one is moved except in his own interest. . . . We believe that Martín Alonso principally and his brothers aided Christopher Columbus greatly . . . because of their wealth and abundant credit, mainly Martín Alonso Pinzón who was very courageous and well experienced in seamanship . . .
>   . . . And as Christopher Columbus had left the court in a very needy condition . . . it appears from accounts of expenses

made before a notary public in the said town of Palos that the
said Martín Alonso . . . himself advanced to Christopher Columbus a half million [maravedis], or he and his brothers . . .

With the decisive intervention of Pinzón, most of Columbus's difficulties vanished. Time was short if the expedition was to sail that
summer, and the energetic Pinzón went all out in organizing the voyage. He discarded the embargoed caravels and substituted two of his
own choice, the *Pinta* and the *Niña*. For a third vessel he and Columbus chartered a somewhat larger ship from the Bay of Biscay that happened to be in the Palos harbor with her owner, Juan de la Cosa of
Santona. Columbus chose her for his flagship. Although she has gone
down in history by the name *Santa María*, Columbus himself never referred to her by that name in his *Journal of the First Voyage*, invariably calling her *La Capitana*, or "the flagship."

With the ships in hand, Pinzón began the task of manning them.
His recruiting was little short of spectacular. He had a vast reservoir of
friends and relatives in the *comarca*, most of them seamen. When
word got out that the Pinzón brothers themselves would sail on the
voyage, many volunteers came to the recruiting table.

But Pinzón didn't leave it at that. He went up and down the little
main street and the waterfront of Palos, exhorting his fellow citizens
with all the fervor of a street evangelist. "Friends, you are in misery
here; go with us on this journey," he exclaimed to the men who gathered around him. "We will, with the aid of God, discover land in
which, according to report, we will find houses with roofs of gold and
everything of wealth and good adventure."

This lively eyewitness account of Pinzón's recruiting was given in a
deposition by Fernan Iáñes Montiel of Huelva. Alonso Gallego testified that Pinzón advanced money out of his own pocket to some of the
families of the sailors he induced to go on the voyage so they would not
be in need.

In the faint light of predawn on August 3, 1492, the little fleet glided
slowly down the Tinto toward the wide ocean and its rendezvous with
history. Columbus commanded the flagship, Martín Pinzón the *Pinta*,
and Vicente Pinzón the *Niña*, smallest of the three.

Twice during the outward crossing Pinzón again came to the rescue
of the expedition. As the voyage grew longer and longer a crisis oc-

curred on the flagship. A disgruntled and fearful crew openly threatened a mutiny.

Testimony concerning this episode is copious and explicit, much of it bearing an air of credibility. The consensus is that it was Martín Pinzón who silenced the grumblers and encouraged Columbus to continue the voyage. One of the most circumstantial of the many witnesses was Hernán Péres Mateos, a veteran pilot of Palos and a cousin of the Pinzóns, who said:

> . . . Having sailed many days and not discovered land those who came with the said Colón wanted to rebel . . . saying they would be lost and the said Colón told the said Martín Alonso what went on and asked what he should do and the said Martín Alonso Pinzón responded: "Señor, your grace should hang a half dozen or throw them into the sea and if you do not venture to do so I and my brothers will come alongside and do it for you, that the fleet which left with the mandate of such exalted princes should not return without good news."

Probably Pinzón bellowed his advice from the rail of his own ship in the hearing of everyone on the flagship. Whatever threat of mutiny may have existed promptly subsided. Mateos added that he had the story of the crisis from the Pinzóns themselves.

Perhaps even more important was the testimony of Francisco García Vallejos of Palos, who was a seaman on the *Pinta*.

"The said Admiral conferred with all the captains," Vallejos explained, "and with the said Martín Alonso Pinzón and said to them 'What shall we do?' [This was the sixth day of October of 92.] 'Captains, what shall we do since my people complain so bitterly to me? How does it appear to you that we should proceed?' And then said Vicente Yáñez [Pinzón]: 'We should keep on, Señor, for two thousand leagues and if by then we have not found what we have come to seek, we can turn back from there.' And then responded Martín Alonso Pinzón 'How, Señor? We have only just left and already your grace is fretting. Onward, Señor, that God may give us the victory in discovering land; never would God wish that we turn back so shamefully.' Then responded the said Admiral: 'Blessings on thee.' "

After the crisis had ended on the flagship and the *Pinta* had resumed her usual position far in advance of the other ships, Pinzón wondered if their due westerly course along the 28th parallel was the right one. Then, as sunset approached on October 6, there came a clear indication: birds.

They were land birds that foraged at sea by day and nested on shore at night, and they were flying over the caravel on what appeared to be a homing course—but not in the direction in which the ship was going. They were on the port side, headed southwesterly.

Pinzón reduced sail and waited for the flagship to catch up. As Columbus came alongside, Pinzón shouted his advice for a change of course toward the south. Columbus demurred and that night stubbornly adhered to his westerly course. But the next day he changed his mind and signaled a divergence toward the southwest. Columbus's journal entry for October 6 mentions Pinzón's advice and his rejection of it. The October 7 entry records the change of course, but characteristically it is now Columbus's own idea.

Pinzón's initiative in urging a change of course was confirmed by Seaman Vallejos of the *Pinta* in his testimony later in the *Pleitos*. Vallejos's version differs in minor detail from that of Columbus:

> He [the witness] knows and saw that [Pinzón] said on the said voyage: "It appears to me and my heart tells me that if we deviate toward the southwest we will find land sooner" and that then responded the said admiral don xtóbal colón "Be it so . . . that we shall do" and that immediately as suggested . . . they changed a quarter to the southwest . . .

Within five days after the change of course the fleet made its landfall on the tiny island of Guanahani in the outer Bahamas.

Had it continued due west along the 28th parallel, the voyage would have required many more days to reach the coast of what is now Florida. There is a good question whether the crews' patience would have endured that long.

Pinzón was mortally ill when the fleet returned to Palos on March 15, 1493. He was borne from his ship to the Pinzón family estate near Moguer, where he could rest in seclusion. But he wanted to spend his last days in the sacred precincts of the monastery of La Rábida among his friends the monks. Sorrowing relatives and friends bore him to the sanctuary of his wish, and there he died in the waning days of March.

2

The Puritans and Sex

EDMUND S. MORGAN

• In 1630, after an arduous Atlantic crossing aboard the
Arabella, John Winthrop and a small band of followers established the Massachusetts Bay Colony. In their "Holy
Commonwealth" the Puritans emphasized hard work, severe
discipline, and rigid self-examination and self-denial. Ministers had great political influence in the theocratic government, and profanation of the Sabbath day, blasphemy, fornication, drunkenness, and participation in games of chance
or theatrical performances were among their many penal
offenses. Even today the term "puritanical" suggests narrow-
mindedness and excessive strictness in matters of morals and
religion. Yet, as Daniel Boorstin and others have observed, the
Puritans were not simply an ascetic group of fanatics who
prohibited all earthly pleasures. Actually the severity of their
code of behavior has frequently been exaggerated. The Puritans were subject to normal human desires and weaknesses,
and they recognized that "the use of the marriage bed" is
"founded in Man's nature." Moreover, numerous cases of
fornication and adultery in the law courts of New England
belie the notion that all Puritans lived up to their rigid moral
ideology. In the following essay, Professor Edmund S. Morgan cites numerous examples of men and women, youths and
maids, whose natural urges recognized no legal limits. In
viewing their enforcement of laws and their judgments of
human frailty, we may find that the Puritans do not always
conform to their conventional stereotype as over-precise mor-
alists.

Henry Adams once observed that Americans have "ostentatiously
ignored" sex. He could think of only two American writers who
touched upon the subject with any degree of boldness—Walt Whit-

From *New England Quarterly*, XV (1942), 591–607. Reprinted by
permission of the author and the publisher.

man and Bret Harte. Since the time when Adams made this pene-
trating observation, American writers have been making up for lost
time in a way that would make Bret Harte, if not Whitman, blush.
And yet there is still more truth than falsehood in Adams's statement.
Americans, by comparison with Europeans or Asiatics, are squeamish
when confronted with the facts of life. My purpose is not to account
for this squeamishness, but simply to point out that the Puritans, those
bogeymen of the modern intellectual, are not responsible for it.

At the outset, consider the Puritans' attitude toward marriage and
the role of sex in marriage. The popular assumption might be that
the Puritans frowned on marriage and tried to hush up the physical
aspect of it as much as possible, but listen to what they themselves
had to say. Samuel Willard, minister of the Old South Church in the
latter part of the seventeenth century and author of the most complete textbook of Puritan divinity, more than once expressed his horror at "that Popish conceit of the Excellency of Virginity." Another
minister, John Cotton, wrote that

> Women are Creatures without which there is no comfortable
> Living for man: it is true of them what is wont to be said of
> Governments, *That bad ones are better than none*: They are a
> sort of Blasphemers then who dispise and decry them, and call
> them *a necessary Evil*, for they are *a necessary Good*.

These sentiments did not arise from an interpretation of marriage as
a spiritual partnership, in which sexual intercourse was a minor or
incidental matter. Cotton gave his opinion of "Platonic love" when
he recalled the case of

> one who immediately upon marriage, without ever approaching
> the *Nuptial Bed*, indented with the *Bride*, that by mutual con-
> sent they might both live such a life, and according did seques-
> tring themselves according to the custom of those times, from
> the rest of mankind, and afterwards from one another too, in
> their retired Cells, giving themselves up to a Contemplative life;
> and this is recorded as an instance of no little or ordinary Ver-
> tue; but I must be pardoned in it, if I can account it no other

than an effort of blind zeal, for they are the dictates of a blind mind they follow therein, and not of that Holy Spirit, which saith *It is not good that man should be alone.*

Here is as healthy an attitude as one could hope to find anywhere. Cotton certainly cannot be accused of ignoring human nature. Nor was he an isolated example among the Puritans. Another minister stated plainly that "the Use of the Marriage Bed" is "founded in mans Nature," and that consequently any withdrawal from sexual intercourse upon the part of husband or wife "Denies all reliefe in Wedlock vnto Human necessity: and sends it for supply vnto Beastiality when God gives not the gift of Continency." In other words, sexual intercourse was a human necessity and marriage the only proper supply for it. These were the views of the New England clergy, the acknowledged leaders of the community, the most Puritanical of the Puritans. As proof that their congregations concurred with them, one may cite the case in which the members of the First Church of Boston expelled James Mattock because, among other offenses, "he denied Coniugall fellowship vnto his wife for the space of 2 years together vpon pretense of taking Revenge upon himself for his abusing of her before marryage." So strongly did the Puritans insist upon the sexual character of marriage that one New Englander considered himself slandered when it was reported, "that he Brock his deceased wife's hart with Greife, that he would be absent from her 3 weeks together when he was at home, and wold never come nere her, and such Like."

There was just one limitation which the Puritans placed upon sexual relations in marriage: sex must not interfere with religion. Man's chief end was to glorify God, and all earthly delights must promote that end, not hinder it. Love for a wife was carried too far when it led a man to neglect his God:

> . . . sometimes a man hath a good affection to Religion, but the love of his wife carries him away, a man may bee so transported to his wife, that hee dare not bee forward in Religion, lest hee displease his wife, and so the wife, lest shee displease her husband, and this is an inordinate love, when it exceeds measure.

Sexual pleasures, in this respect, were treated like other kinds of pleasure. On a day of fast, when all comforts were supposed to be foregone in behalf of religious contemplation, not only were tasty food and drink to be abandoned but sexual intercourse, too. On other occasions, when food, drink, and recreation were allowable, sexual intercourse was allowable too, though of course only between persons who were married to each other. The Puritans were not ascetics; they never wished to prevent the enjoyment of earthly delights. They merely demanded that the pleasures of the flesh be subordinated to the greater glory of God: husband and wife must not become "so transported with affection, that they look at no higher end than marriage it self." "Let such as have wives," said the ministers, "look at them not for their own ends, but to be fitted for Gods service, and bring them nearer to God."

Toward sexual intercourse outside marriage the Puritans were as frankly hostile as they were favorable to it in marriage. They passed laws to punish adultery with death, and fornication with whipping. Yet they had no misconceptions as to the capacity of human beings to obey such laws. Although the laws were commands of God, it was only natural—since the fall of Adam—for human beings to break them. Breaches must be punished lest the community suffer the wrath of God, but no offense, sexual or otherwise, could be occasion for surprise or for hushed tones of voice. How calmly the inhabitants of seventeenth-century New England could contemplate rape or attempted rape is evident in the following testimony offered before the Middlesex County Court of Massachusetts:

> The examination of Edward Wire taken the 7th of october and alsoe Zachery Johnson. who sayeth that Edward Wires mayd being sent into the towne about busenes meeting with a man that dogd hir from about Joseph Kettles house to goody marshes. She came into William Johnsones and desired Zachery Johnson to goe home with her for that the man dogd hir. accordingly he went with her and being then as far as Samuell Phips his house the man over tooke them. which man caled himselfe by the name of peter grant would have led the mayd but she oposed itt three times: and coming to Edward Wires house the said grant would have kist hir but she refused itt: wire being at prayer grant dragd the mayd between the said wiers and Nathanill frothinghams house. hee then flung the mayd downe in the streete and got atop hir; Johnson seeing it hee caled vppon the fellow to be sivill and not abuse the mayd then Edward wire came forth and ran to the said grant and took hold of him asking him what he did

to his mayd, the said grant asked whether she was his wife for
he did nothing to his wife: the said grant swearing he would
be the death of the said wire. when he came of the mayd; he
swore he would bring ten men to pul down his house and soe ran
away and they followed him as far as good[y] phipses house
where they mett with John Terry and George Chin with clubs in
there hands and soe they went away together. Zachy Johnson
going to Constable Heamans, and wire going home. there came
John Terry to his house to ask for beer and grant was in the
streete but afterward departed into the towne, both Johnson and
Wire both aferme that when grant was vppon the mayd she
cryed out severall times.

Deborah hadlocke being examined sayth that she mett with
the man that cals himselfe peeter grant about good prichards
that he dogd hir and followed hir to hir masters and there threw
hir downe and lay vppon hir but had not the use of hir body but
swore several othes that he would ly with hir and gett hir with
child before she got home.

Grant being present denys all saying he was drunk and did not
know what he did.

The Puritans became inured to sexual offenses, because there were
so many. The impression which one gets from reading the records of
seventeenth-century New England courts is that illicit sexual intercourse was fairly common. The testimony given in cases of fornication and adultery—by far the most numerous class of criminal cases in
the records—suggests that many of the early New Englanders possessed a high degree of virility and very few inhibitions. Besides the
case of Peter Grant, take the testimony of Elizabeth Knight about the
manner of Richard Nevars's advances toward her:

The last publique day of Thanksgiving (in the year 1674) in
the evening as I was milking Richard Nevars came to me, and
offered me abuse in putting his hand, under my coates, but I
turning aside with much adoe, saved my self, and when I was
settled to milking agen took me by the shoulder and pulled
me backward almost. but I clapped one hand on the Ground and
held fast the Cows teatt with the other hand, and cryed out, and
then came to mee Jonathan Abbot one of my Masters Servants,
whome the said Never asked wherefore he came, the said Abbot
said to look after you, what you doe unto the Maid, but the said
Never bid Abbot goe about his businesse but I bade the lad to
stay.

One reason for the abundance of sexual offenses was the number of men in the colonies who were unable to gratify their sexual desires in marriage. Many of the first settlers had wives in England. They had come to the new world to make a fortune, expecting either to bring their families after them or to return to England with some of the riches of America. Although these men left their wives behind, they brought their sexual appetites with them; and in spite of laws which required them to return to their families, they continued to stay, and more continued to arrive, as indictments against them throughout the seventeenth century clearly indicate.

Servants formed another group of men, and of women too, who could not ordinarily find supply for human necessity within the bounds of marriage. Most servants lived in the homes of their masters and could not marry without their consent, a consent which was not likely to be given unless the prospective husband or wife also belonged to the master's household. This situation will be better understood if it is recalled that most servants at this time were engaged by contract for a stated period. They were, in the language of the time, "covenant servants," who had agreed to stay with their masters for a number of years in return for a specified recompense, such as transportation to New England or education in some trade (the latter, of course, were known more specifically as apprentices). Even hired servants who worked for wages were usually single, for as soon as a man had enough money to buy or build a house of his own and to get married, he would set up in farming or trade for himself. It must be emphasized, however, that anyone who was not in business for himself was necessarily a servant. The economic organization of seventeenth-century New England had no place for the independent proletarian workman with a family of his own. All production was carried on in the household by the master of the family and his servants, so that most men were either servants or masters of servants; and the former, of course, were more numerous than the latter. Probably most of the inhabitants of Puritan New England could remember a time when they had been servants.

Theoretically no servant had a right to a private life. His time, day or night, belonged to his master, and both religion and law required that he obey his master scrupulously. But neither religion nor law could restrain the sexual impulses of youth, and if those impulses could not be expressed in marriage, they had to be given vent outside marriage. Servants had little difficulty in finding the occasions. Though they might be kept at work all day, it was easy enough to slip away at night. Once out of the house, there were several ways of meeting with a maid. The simplest way was to go to her bedchamber, if she was so fortunate as to have a private one of her own. Thus Jock, Mr. Solomon Phipps's Negro man, confessed in court

> that on the sixteenth day of May 1682, in the morning, betweene 12 and one of the clock, he did force open the back doores of the House of Laurence Hammond in Charlestowne, and came in to the House, and went up into the garret to Marie the Negro.
>
> He doth likewise acknowledge that one night the last week he forced into the House the same way, and went up to the Negro Woman Marie and that the like he hath done at severall other times before.

Joshua Fletcher took a more romantic way of visiting his lady:

> Joshua Fletcher . . . doth confesse and acknowledge that three severall nights, after bedtime, he went into Mr Fiskes Dwelling house at Chelmsford, at an open window by a ladder that he brought with him the said windo opening into a chamber, whose was the lodging place of Gresill Juell servant to mr. Fiske. and there he kept company with the said mayd. she sometimes having her cloathes on, and one time he found her in her bed.

Sometimes a maidservant might entertain callers in the parlor while the family were sleeping upstairs. John Knight described what was perhaps a common experience for masters. The crying of his child awakened him in the middle of the night, and he called to his maid, one Sarah Crouch, who was supposed to be sleeping with the child. Receiving no answer, he arose and

> went downe the stayres, and at the stair foot, the latch of doore was pulled in. I called severall times and at the last said if shee would not open the dore, I would breake it open, and when she opened the doore shee was all undressed and Sarah Largin with her undressed, also the said Sarah went out of doores and Dropped some of her clothes as shee went out. I enquired of Sarah Crouch what men they were, which was with them. Shee made mee no answer for some space of time, but at last shee told me Peeter Brigs was with them, I asked her whether Thomas Jones was not there, but shee would give mee no answer.

In the temperate climate of New England it was not always necessary
to seek out a maid at her home. Rachel Smith was seduced in an open
field "about nine of the clock at night, being darke, neither moone nor
starrs shineing." She was walking through the field when she met a
man who

> asked her where shee lived, and what her name was and shee told
> him. and then shee asked his name, and he told her Saijing that
> he was old Good-man Shepards man. Also shee saith he gave her
> strong liquors, and told her that it was not the first time he had
> been with maydes after his master was in bed.

Sometimes, of course, it was not necessary for a servant to go outside his master's house in order to satisfy his sexual urges. Many cases
of fornication are on record between servants living in the same house.
Even where servants had no private bedroom, even where the whole
family slept in a single room, it was not impossible to make love. In
fact many love affairs must have had their consummation upon a bed
in which other people were sleeping. Take for example the case of
Sarah Lepingwell. When Sarah was brought into court for having an
illegitimate child, she related that one night when her master's brother,
Thomas Hawes, was visiting the family, she went to bed early. Later,
after Hawes had gone to bed, he called to her to get him a pipe of tobacco. After refusing for some time,

> at the last I arose and did lite his pipe and cam and lay doune
> one my one bead and smoaked about half the pip and siting vp
> in my bead to giue him his pip my bead being a trundell bead
> at the sid of his bead he reached beyond the pip and Cauth me
> by the wrist and pulled me on the side of his bead but I biding
> him let me goe he bid me hold my peas the folks wold here me
> and if it be replyed come why did you not call out I Ansar I was
> posesed with fear of my mastar least my mastar shold think I
> did it only to bring a scandall on his brothar and thinking thay
> wold all beare witnes agaynst me but the thing is true that he did
> then begete me with child at that tim and the Child is Thomas
> Hauses and noe mans but his.

In his defense Hawes offered the testimony of another man who was
sleeping "on the same side of the bed," but the jury nevertheless accepted Sarah's story.

The fact that Sarah was intimidated by her master's brother suggests that maidservants may have been subject to sexual abuse by their masters. The records show that sometimes masters did take advantage of their position to force unwanted attentions upon their female servants. The case of Elizabeth Dickerman is a good example. She complained to the Middlesex County Court,

> against her master John Harris senior for profiring abus to her by way of forsing her to be naught with him: . . . he has tould her that if she tould her dame: what cariag he did show to her shee had as good be hanged and shee replyed then shee would run away and he sayd run the way is befor you: . . . she says if she should liwe ther shee shall be in fear of her lif.

The court accepted Elizabeth's complaint and ordered her master to be whipped twenty stripes.

So numerous did cases of fornication and adultery become in seventeenth-century New England that the problem of caring for the children of extra-marital unions was a serious one. The Puritans solved it, but in such a way as to increase rather than decrease the temptation to sin. In 1668 the General Court of Massachusetts ordered:

> that where any man is legally convicted to be the Father of a Bastard childe, he shall be at the care and charge to maintain and bring up the same, by such assistance of the Mother as nature requireth, and as the Court from time to time (according to circumstances) shall see meet to Order: and in case the Father of a Bastard, by confession or other manifest proof, upon trial of the case, do not appear to the Courts satisfaction, then the Man charged by the Woman to be the Father, shee holding constant in it, (especially being put upon the real discovery of the truth of it in the time of her Travail) shall be the reputed Father, and accordingly be liable to the charge of maintenance as aforesaid (though not to other punishment) notwithstanding his denial, unless the circumstances of the case and pleas be such, on the behalf of the man charged, as that the Court that have the cognizance thereon shall see reason to acquit him, and otherwise dispose of the Childe and education thereof.

As a result of this law a girl could give way to temptation without the fear of having to care for an illegitimate child by herself. Furthermore, she could, by a little simple lying, spare her lover the expense of sup-

porting the child. When Elizabeth Wells bore a child, less than a year
after this statute was passed, she laid it to James Tufts, her master's
son. Goodman Tufts affirmed that Andrew Robinson, servant to Goodman Dexter, was the real father, and he brought the following testimony as evidence:

> Wee Elizabeth Jefts aged 15 ears and Mary tufts aged 14 ears
> doe testyfie that their being one at our hous sumtime the last
> winter who sayed that thear was a new law made concerning
> bastards that If aney man wear aqused with a bastard and the
> woman which had aqused him did stand vnto it in her labor that
> he should bee the reputed father of it and should mayntaine it
> Elizabeth Wells hearing of the sayd law she sayed vnto vs that
> If shee should bee with Child shee would bee sure to lay it vn to
> won who was rich enough abell to mayntayne it wheather it wear
> his or no and shee farder sayed Elizabeth Jefts would not you doe
> so likewise If it weare your case and I sayed no by no means for
> right must tacke place: and the sayd Elizabeth wells sayed If it
> wear my Caus I think I should doe so.

A tragic unsigned letter that somehow found its way into the files of
the Middlesex County Court gives more direct evidence of the practice which Elizabeth Wells professed:

> der loue i remember my loue to you hoping your welfar and i
> hop to imbras the but now i rit to you to let you nowe that i am
> a child by you and i wil ether kil it or lay it to an other and you
> shal have no blame at al for I haue had many children and none
> have none of them. . . . [*i.e.*, none of their fathers is support-
> ing any of them.]

In face of the wholesale violation of the sexual codes to which all
these cases give testimony, the Puritans could not maintain the severe penalties which their laws provided. Although cases of adultery
occurred every year, the death penalty is not known to have been
applied more than three times. The usual punishment was a whipping
or a fine, or both, and perhaps a branding, combined with a symbolical
execution in the form of standing on the gallows for an hour with a
rope about the neck. Fornication met with a lighter whipping or a
lighter fine, while rape was treated in the same way as adultery. Though
the Puritans established a code of laws which demanded perfection—

which demanded, in other words, strict obedience to the will of God, they nevertheless knew that frail human beings could never live up to the code. When fornication, adultery, rape, or even buggery and sodomy appeared, they were not surprised, nor were they so severe with the offenders as their codes of law would lead one to believe. Sodomy, to be sure, they usually punished with death; but rape, adultery, and fornication they regarded as pardonable human weaknesses, all the more likely to appear in a religious community, where the normal course of sin was stopped by wholesome laws. Governor Bradford, in recounting the details of an epidemic of sexual misdemeanors in Plymouth, wrote resignedly:

> it may be in this case as it is with waters when their streames are stopped or damned up, when they gett passage they flow with more violence, and make more noys and disturbance, then when they are suffered to rune quietly in their owne chanels. So wickednes being here more stopped by strict laws, and the same more nerly looked unto, so as it cannot rune in a comone road of liberty as it would, and is inclined, it searches every wher, and at last breaks out wher it getts vente.

The estimate of human capacities here expressed led the Puritans not only to deal leniently with sexual offenses but also to take every precaution to prevent such offenses, rather than wait for the necessity of punishment. One precaution was to see that children got married as soon as possible. The wrong way to promote virtue, the Puritans thought, was to "ensnare" children in vows of virginity, as the Catholics did. As a result of such vows, children, "not being able to contain," would be guilty of "unnatural pollutions, and other filthy practices in secret: and too oft of horrid Murthers of the fruit of their bodies," said Thomas Cobbett. The way to avoid fornication and perversion was for parents to provide suitable husbands and wives for their children:

> Lot was to blame that looked not out seasonably for some fit matches for his two daughters, which had formerly minded marriage (witness the contract between them and two men in *Sodom*, called therfore for his Sons in Law, which had married his daughters, Gen. 19. 14.) for they seeing no man like to come into them in a conjugall way . . . then they plotted that incestuous course, whereby their Father was so highly dishonoured. . . .

As marriage was the way to prevent fornication, successful marriage was the way to prevent adultery. The Puritans did not wait for
adultery to appear; instead, they took every means possible to make
husbands and wives live together and respect each other. If a husband
deserted his wife and remained within the jurisdiction of a Puritan
government, he was promptly sent back to her. Where the wife had
been left in England, the offense did not always come to light until
the wayward husband had committed fornication or bigamy, and of
course there must have been many offenses which never came to light.
But where both husband and wife lived in New England, neither had
much chance of leaving the other without being returned by order of
the county court at its next sitting. When John Smith of Medfield
left his wife and went to live with Patience Rawlins, he was sent home
poorer by ten pounds and richer by thirty stripes. Similarly Mary
Drury, who deserted her husband on the pretense that he was impo-
tent, failed to convince the court that he actually was so, and had to
return to him as well as to pay a fine of five pounds. The wife of
Phillip Pointing received lighter treatment: when the court thought
that she had overstayed her leave in Boston, they simply ordered her
"to depart the Towne and goe to Tanton to her husband." The courts,
moreover, were not satisfied with mere cohabitation; they insisted that
it be peaceful cohabitation. Husbands and wives were forbidden by
law to strike one another, and the law was enforced on numerous occasions. But the courts did not stop there. Henry Flood was required
to give bond for good behavior because he had abused his wife simply
by "ill words calling her whore and cursing of her." The wife of Christopher Collins was presented for railing at her husband and calling
him "Gurley gutted divill." Apparently in this case the court thought
that Mistress Collins was right, for although the fact was proved by
two witnesses, she was discharged. On another occasion the court
favored the husband: Jacob Pudeator, fined for striking and kicking
his wife, had the sentence moderated when the court was informed
that she was a woman "of great provocation."

Wherever there was strong suspicion that an illicit relation might
arise between two persons, the authorities removed the temptation by
forbidding the two to come together. As early as November, 1630, the
Court of Assistants of Massachusetts prohibited a Mr. Clark from "co-
habitacion and frequent keepeing company with Mrs. Freeman, vnder

paine of such punishment as the Court shall thinke meete to inflict."
Mr. Clark and Mr. Freeman were both bound "in XX£ apeece that
Mr. Clearke shall make his personall appearance att the nexte Court
to be holden in March nexte, and in the meane tyme to carry himselfe
in good behaviour towards all people and espetially towards Mrs. Freeman, concerning whome there is stronge suspicion of incontinency."
Forty-five years later the Suffolk County Court took the same kind of
measure to protect the husbands of Dorchester from the temptations
offered by the daughter of Robert Spurr. Spurr was presented by the
grand jury

> for entertaining persons at his house at unseasonable times both
> by day and night to the greife of theire wives and Relations &c
> The Court having heard what was alleaged and testified against
> him do Sentence him to bee admonish't and to pay Fees of
> Court and charge him upon his perill not to entertain any mar-
> ried men to keepe company with his daughter especially James
> Minott and Joseph Belcher.

In like manner Walter Hickson was forbidden to keep company with
Mary Bedwell, "And if at any time hereafter hee bee taken in company of the saide Mary Bedwell without other company to bee forth-
with apprehended by the Constable and to be whip't with ten stripes."
Elizabeth Wheeler and Joanna Peirce were admonished "for theire
disorderly carriage in the house of Thomas Watts being married women
and founde sitting in other mens Laps with theire Armes about theire
Necks." How little confidence the Puritans had in human nature is
even more clearly displayed by another case, in which Edmond Mad-
dock and his wife were brought to court "to answere to all such matters
as shalbe objected against them concerning Haarkwoody and Ezekiell
Euerells being at their house at unseasonable tyme of the night and
her being up with them after her husband was gone to bed." Haarkwoody and Everell had been found "by the Constable Henry Bridg-
hame about tenn of the Clock at night sitting by the fyre at the house
of Edmond Maddocks with his wyfe a suspicious weoman her husband
being on sleepe [*sic*] on the bedd." A similar distrust of human ability
to resist temptation is evident in the following order of the Connecticut Particular Court:

James Hallett is to returne from the Correction house to his master Barclyt, who is to keepe him to hard labor, and course dyet during the pleasure of the Court provided that Barclet is first to remove his daughter from his family, before the sayd James enter therein.

These precautions, as we have already seen, did not eliminate fornication, adultery, or other sexual offenses, but they doubtless reduced the number from what it would otherwise have been.

In sum, the Puritan attitude toward sex, though directed by a belief in absolute, God-given moral values, never neglected human nature. The rules of conduct which the Puritans regarded as divinely ordained had been formulated for men, not for angels and not for beasts. God had created mankind in two sexes; He had ordained marriage as desirable for all, and sexual intercourse as essential to marriage. On the other hand, He had forbidden sexual intercourse outside of marriage. These were the moral principles which the Puritans sought to enforce in New England. But in their enforcement they took cognizance of human nature. They knew well enough that human beings since the fall of Adam were incapable of obeying perfectly the laws of God. Consequently, in the endeavor to enforce those laws they treated offenders with patience and understanding, and concentrated their efforts on prevention more than on punishment. The result was not a society in which most of us would care to live, for the methods of prevention often caused serious interference with personal liberty. It must nevertheless be admitted that in matters of sex the Puritans showed none of the blind zeal or narrow-minded bigotry which is too often supposed to have been characteristic of them. The more one learns about these people, the less do they appear to have resembled the sad and sour portraits which their modern critics have drawn of them.

3

The White Indians of Colonial America

JAMES AXTELL

• Although the Indians encountered at Jamestown and at
Plymouth and at a score of other sites along the East Coast
were unlettered, unwashed, unclothed, and "uncivilized," the
European settlers quickly discovered that they were also "of
a tractable, free, and loving nature, without guile or treachery"—to quote a seventeenth-century eyewitness. These native peoples were especially open with their knowledge and
experience. For example, after the first desperate winter at
Plymouth, during which time half the Pilgrims died, the Indians gave the survivors food and taught them to grow corn
under primitive conditions. The following November, after a
bountiful harvest, the two groups jointly celebrated America's
first Thanksgiving.

Initially, many of the colonists believed that the Indians
were descendants of the lost tribes of Israel, and the Europeans made honest, if somewhat misguided, efforts to Chris-
tianize them. But red-white relations deteriorated rapidly during the seventeenth century. Pressed by increasing numbers
and eager to provide more space for their expanding society,
the white settlers pushed farther and farther inland, thus
forcing the Indians to battle for their very existence. As the
struggle took on more violent dimensions—King Philip's War
(1675–1676) was particularly bloody—myths of the worth-
lessness and brutality of the Indians had to be fabricated to
justify the slaughter that ensued. Past experiences contradict-
ing the image of the Indian as a savage tended to be forgotten.

The following article by James Axtell, which suggests that
the simplicity, harmony, and cooperative spirit of Indian life

From the *William and Mary Quarterly* 32 (January 1975): 55–88. Reprinted
with permission from the author and the publisher.

had greater appeal to colonists than the benefits of "civilization" had to the Indians, should be read in the context of the
suspicion, fear, and contempt which the white society was beginning to feel toward the Indian. We often think of the appeal of native culture as a recent phenomenon; yet those few
European settlers who were intimately exposed to it often
chose to remain "white Indians."

The English, like their French rivals, began their colonizing ventures
in North America with a sincere interest in converting the Indians to
Christianity and civilization. Nearly all the colonial charters granted by
the English monarchs in the seventeenth century assigned the wish to
extend the Christian Church and to redeem savage souls as a principal,
if not the principal, motive for colonization. This desire was grounded
in a set of complementary beliefs about "savagism" and "civilization."
First, the English held that the Indians, however benighted, were capable of conversion. "It is not the nature of men," they believed, "but
the education of men, which make them barbarous and uncivill."
Moreover, the English were confident that the Indians would want to
be converted once they were exposed to the superior quality of English
life. The strength of these beliefs was reflected in Cotton Mather's astonishment as late as 1721 that

> Tho' they saw a People Arrive among them, who were Clothed in
> *Habits* of much more Comfort and Splendour, than what there
> was to be seen in the *Rough Skins* with which they hardly cov-
> ered themselves; and who had *Houses full of Good Things*, vastly
> out-shining their squalid and dark *Wigwams*; And they saw this
> People Replenishing their *Fields*, with *Trees* and with *Grains*,
> and useful *Animals*, which until now they had been wholly Stran-
> gers to; yet they did not seem touch'd in the least, with any *Am-
> bition* to come at such Desireable Circumstances, or with any
> *Curiosity* to enquire after the *Religion* that was attended with
> them.

The second article of the English faith followed from their fundamental belief in the superiority of civilization, namely, that no civilized
person in possession of his faculties or free from undue restraint would
choose to become an Indian. "For, easy and unconstrained as the sav-

age life is," wrote the Reverend William Smith of Philadelphia, "certainly it could never be put in competition with the blessings of improved life and the light of religion, by any persons who have had the happiness of enjoying, and the capacity of discerning, them."

And yet, by the close of the colonial period, very few if any Indians had been transformed into civilized Englishmen. Most of the Indians who were educated by the English—some contemporaries thought *all* of them—returned to Indian society at the first opportunity to resume their Indian identities. On the other hand, large numbers of Englishmen had chosen to become Indians—by running away from colonial society to join Indian society, by not trying to escape after being captured, or by electing to remain with their Indian captors when treaties of peace periodically afforded them the opportunity to return home.

Perhaps the first colonist to recognize the disparity between the English dream and the American reality was Cadwallader Colden, surveyor-general and member of the King's council of New York. In his *History of the Five Indian Nations of Canada*, published in London in 1747, Colden described the Albany peace treaty between the French and the Iroquois in 1699, when "few of [the French captives] could be persuaded to return" to Canada. Lest his readers attribute this unusual behavior to "the Hardships they had endured in their own Country, under a tyrannical Government and a barren Soil," he quickly added that "the *English* had as much Difficulty to persuade the People, that had been taken Prisoners by the *French Indians*, to leave the *Indian* Manner of living, though no People enjoy more Liberty, and live in greater Plenty, than the common Inhabitants of *New-York* do." Colden, clearly amazed, elaborated:

> No Arguments, no Intreaties, nor Tears of their Friends and Relations, could persuade many of them to leave their new *Indian* Friends and Acquaintance[s]; several of them that were by the Caressings of their Relations persuaded to come Home, in a little Time grew tired of our Manner of living, and run away again to the *Indians*, and ended their Days with them. On the other Hand, *Indian* Children have been carefully educated among the *English*, cloathed and taught, yet, I think, there is not one Instance, that any of these, after they had Liberty to go among their own People, and were come to Age, would remain with the *English*, but returned to their own Nations, and became as fond of the *Indian* Manner of Life as those that knew nothing of a

civilized Manner of living. What I now tell of Christian Prisoners among *Indians* [he concluded his history], relates not only to what happened at the Conclusion of this War, but has been found true on many other Occasions.

Colden was not alone. Six years later Benjamin Franklin wondered how it was that

> When an Indian Child has been brought up among us, taught our language and habituated to our Customs, yet if he goes to see his relations and makes one Indian Ramble with them, there is no perswading him ever to return. [But] when white persons of either sex have been taken prisoners young by the Indians, and lived a while among them, tho' ransomed by their Friends, and treated with all imaginable tenderness to prevail with them to stay among the English, yet in a Short time they become disgusted with our manner of life, and the care and pains that are necessary to support it, and take the first good Opportunity of escaping again into the Woods, from whence there is no reclaiming them.

In short, "thousands of Europeans are Indians," as Hector de Crèvecoeur put it, "and we have no examples of even one of those Aborigines having from choice become Europeans!"

The English captives who foiled their countrymen's civilized assumptions by becoming Indians differed little from the general colonial population when they were captured. They were ordinary men, women, and children of yeoman stock, Protestants by faith, a variety of nationalities by birth, English by law, different from their countrymen only in their willingness to risk personal insecurity for the economic opportunities of the frontier. There was no discernible characteristic or pattern of characteristics that differentiated them from their captive neighbors who eventually rejected Indian life—with one exception. Most of the colonists captured by the Indians and adopted into Indian families were children of both sexes and young women, often the mothers of the captive children. They were, as one captivity narrative observed, the "weak and defenceless."

The pattern of taking women and children for adoption was consistent throughout the colonial period, but during the first century and one-half of Indian-white conflict, primarily in New England, it coexisted with a larger pattern of captivity that included all white colo-

nists, men as well as women and children. The Canadian Indians who
raided New England tended to take captives more for their ransom
value than for adoption. When Mrs. James Johnson gave birth to a
daughter on the trail to Canada, for example, her captor looked into
her makeshift lean-to and "clapped his hands with joy, crying two
monies for me, two monies for me." Although the New England legislatures occasionally tried to forbid the use of public moneys for "the
Ransoming of Captives," thereby prolonging the Indians' "diabolical
kidnapping mode of warfare," ransoms were constantly paid from both
public and private funds. These payments became larger as inflation
and the Indians' savvy increased. Thus when John and Tamsen Tib-
betts redeemed two of their children from the Canadian Indians in
1729, it cost them £105 10s. (1,270 livres). "Being verry Poore,"
many families in similar situations could ill afford to pay such high
premiums even "if they should sell all they have in the world."

When the long peace in the Middle Atlantic colonies collapsed in
1753, the Indians of Pennsylvania, southern New York, and the Ohio
country had no Quebec or Montreal in which to sell their human chattels to compassionate French families or anxious English relatives. For
this and other reasons they captured English settlers largely to replace
members of their own families who had died, often from English mus-
ketballs or imported diseases. Consequently, women and children—the
"weak and defenceless"—were the prime targets of Indian raids.

According to the pattern of warfare in the Pennsylvania theater, the
Indians usually stopped at a French fort with their prisoners before
proceeding to their own villages. A young French soldier captured by
the English reported that at Fort Duquesne there were "a great number of English Prisoners," the older of whom "they are constantly
sending . . . away to Montreal" as prisoners of war, "but that the Indians keep many of the Prisoners amongst them, chiefly young People
whom they adopt and bring up in their own way." His intelligence was
corroborated by Barbara Leininger and Marie LeRoy, who had been
members of a party of two adults and eight children captured in 1755
and taken to Fort Duquesne. There they saw "many other Women
and Children, they think an hundred who were carried away from the
several provinces of P[ennsylvania] M[aryland] and V[irginia]." When
the girls escaped from captivity three years later, they wrote a narrative
in German chiefly to acquaint "the inhabitants of this country . . .

with the names and circumstances of those prisoners whom we met, at the various places where we were, in the course of our captivity." Of the fifty-two prisoners they had seen, thirty-four were children and fourteen were women, including six mothers with children of their own.

The close of hostilities in Pennsylvania came in 1764 after Col. Henry Bouquet defeated the Indians near Bushy Run and imposed peace. By the articles of agreement reached in October, the Delawares, Shawnees, and Senecas were to deliver up "all the Prisoners in [their] Possession, without any Exception, Englishmen, Frenchmen, Women, and Children, whether adopted in your Tribes, married, or living amongst you, under any Denomination, or Pretence whatever." In the weeks that followed, Bouquet's troops, including "the Relations of [some of] the People [the Indians] have Massacred, or taken Prisoners," encamped on the Muskingum in the heart of the Ohio country to collect the captives. After as many as nine years with the Indians, during which time many children had grown up, 81 "men" and 126 "women and children" were returned. At the same time a list was prepared of 88 prisoners who still remained in Shawnee towns to the west: 70 were classified as "women and children." Six months later, 44 of these prisoners were delivered up to Fort Pitt. When they were captured, all but 4 had been less than sixteen years old, while 37 had been less than eleven years old.

The Indians obviously chose their captives carefully so as to maximize the chances of acculturating them to Indian life. To judge by the results, their methods were hard to fault. Even when the English held the upper hand militarily, they were often embarrassed by the Indians' educational power. On November 12, 1764, at his camp on the Muskingum, Bouquet lectured the Shawnees who had not delivered all their captives: "As you are now going to Collect all our *Flesh*, and *Blood*, . . . I desire that you will use them with Tenderness, and look upon them as Brothers, and no longer as Captives." The utter gratuitousness of his remark was reflected—no doubt purposely—in the Shawnee speech when the Indians delivered their captives the following spring at Fort Pitt. "Father—Here is your *Flesh*, and *Blood* . . . they have been all tied to us by Adoption, although we now deliver them up to you. We will always look upon them as Relations, whenever the *Great Spirit* is pleased that we may visit them . . . Father—we have taken as much Care of these Prisoners, as if they were [our] own Flesh, and blood; they are become unacquainted with your Customs, and manners, and therefore, Father we request you will use them tender, and kindly, which will be a means of inducing them to live contentedly with you."

The Indians spoke the truth and the English knew it. Three days after his speech to the Shawnees, Bouquet had advised Lt.-Gov. Francis Fauquier of Virginia that the returning captives "ought to be treated by their Relations with Tenderness and Humanity, till Time and Reason make them forget their unnatural Attachments, but unless they are closely watch'd," he admitted, "they will certainly return to the Barbarians." And indeed they would have, for during a half-century of conflict captives had been returned who, like many of the Ohio prisoners, responded only to Indian names, spoke only Indian dialects, felt comfortable only in Indian clothes, and in general regarded their white saviors as barbarians and their deliverance as captivity. Had they not been compelled to return to English society by militarily enforced peace treaties, the ranks of the white Indians would have been greatly enlarged.

From the moment the Indians surrendered their English prisoners, the colonists faced a series of difficult problems. The first was the problem of getting the prisoners to remain with the English. When Bouquet sent the first group of restored captives to Fort Pitt, he ordered his officers there that "they are to be closely watched and well Secured" because "most of them, particularly those who have been a long time among the Indians, will take the first Opportunity to run away." The young children especially were "so completely savage that they were brought to the camp tied hand and foot." Fourteen-year-old John McCullough, who had lived with the Indians for "eight years, four months, and sixteen days" (by his parents' reckoning), had his legs tied "under the horses belly" and his arms tied behind his back with his father's garters, but to no avail. He escaped under the cover of night and returned to his Indian family for a year before he was finally carried to Fort Pitt under "strong guard." "Having been accustomed to look upon the Indians as the only connections they had, having been tenderly treated by them, and speaking their language," explained the Reverend William Smith, the historian of Bouquet's expedition, "it is no wonder that [the children] considered their new state in the light of a captivity, and parted from the savages with tears."

Children were not the only reluctant freedmen. "Several women eloped in the night, and ran off to join their Indian friends." Among them undoubtedly were some of the English women who had married Indian men and borne them children, and then had been forced by the English victory either to return with their half-breed children to a country of strangers, full of prejudice against Indians, or to risk escaping under English guns to their husbands and adopted culture. For Bouquet had "reduced the Shawanese and Delawares etc. to the most Humiliating Terms of Peace," boasted Gen. Thomas Gage. "He has Obliged them to deliver up even their Own Children born of white women." But even the victorious soldier could understand the dilemma into which these women had been pushed. When Bouquet was informed that the English wife of an Indian chief had eloped in the night with her husband and children, he "requested that no pursuit should be made, as she was happier with her Chief than she would be if restored to her home."

Although most of the returned captives did not try to escape, the emotional torment caused by the separation from their adopted families deeply impressed the colonists. The Indians "delivered up their beloved captives with the utmost reluctance; shed torrents of tears over them, recommending them to the care and protection of the commanding officer." One young woman "cryed and roared when asked to come and begged to Stay a little longer." "Some, who could not make their escape, clung to their savage acquaintance at parting, and continued many days in bitter lamentations, even refusing sustenance." Children "cried as if they should die when they were presented to us." With only small exaggeration an observer on the Muskingum could report that "every captive left the Indians with regret."

Another problem encountered by the English was the difficulty of communicating with the returned captives, a great many of whom had replaced their knowledge of English with an Algonquian or Iroquoian dialect, and their baptismal names with Indian or hybrid ones. This immediately raised another problem—that of restoring the captives to their relatives. Sir William Johnson, the superintendent of Indian affairs, "thought it best to advertise them [in the newspapers] immediately, but I believe it will be very difficult to find the Friends of some of them, as they are ignorant of their own Names, or former places of abode, nay cant speak a word of any language but Indian." The only recourse the English had in such instances was to describe them "more particularly . . . as to their features, Complexion etc. That by the Publication of Such descriptions their Relations, parents or friends may hereafter know and Claim them."

But if several colonial observers were right, a description of the captives' physiognomy was of little help after they had been with the Indians for any length of time. Peter Kalm's foreign eye found it difficult to distinguish European captives from their captors, "except by their color, which is somewhat whiter than that of the Indians," but many colonists could see little or no difference. To his Maine neighbors twelve-year-old John Durell "ever after [his two-year captivity] appeared more like an Indian than a white man." So did John Tarbell. After thirty years among the Indians in Canada, he made a visit to his relatives in Groton "in his Indian dress and with his Indian complexion (for by means of grease and paints but little difference could be discerned)." When O. M. Spencer returned after only eight months with the Shawnees, he was greeted with a newspaper allusion "to [his] looks and manners, as slightly resembling the Indians" and by a gaggle of visitors who exclaimed "in an under tone, 'How much he looks like an Indian!' " Such evidence reinforced the environmentalism of the time, which held that white men "who have incorporated themselves with any of [the Indian] tribes" soon acquire "a great resemblance to the savages, not only in their manners, but in their colour and the expression of the countenance."

The final English problem was perhaps the most embarrassing in its manifestations, and certainly was so in its implications. For many Indians who had adopted white captives, the return of their "own Flesh, and Blood" to the English was unendurable. At the earliest opportunity, after bitter memories of the wars had faded on both sides, they journeyed through the English settlements to visit their estranged children, just as the Shawnee speaker had promised Bouquet they would. Jonathan Hoyt's Indian father visited him so often in Deerfield, sometimes bringing his captive sister, that Hoyt had to petition the Massachusetts General Court for reimbursement for their support. In 1760 Sir William Johnson reported that a Canadian Indian "has been since down to Schenectady to visit one Newkirk of that place, who was some years a Prisoner in his House, and sent home about a year ago with this Indians Sister, who came with her Brother now purely to see Said Newkirk whom she calls her Son and is verry fond of."

Obviously the feelings were mutual. Elizabeth Gilbert, adopted at the age of twelve, "always retained an affection toward John Huston, her Indian father (as she called him), for she remembered his kindness to her when in captivity." Even an adult who had spent less than six months with the Indians honored the chief who had adopted him. In 1799, eleven years after Thomas Ridout's release, his friend and father, Kakinathucca, "accompanied by three more Shawanese chiefs, came to pay me a visit at my house in York town (Toronto). He regarded myself and family with peculiar pleasure, and my wife and children contemplated with great satisfaction the noble and good qualities of this worthy Indian." The bond of affection that had grown in the Indian villages was clearly not an attachment that the English could dismiss as "unnatural."

Children who had been raised by Indian parents from infancy could be excused perhaps for their unwillingness to return, but the adults who displayed a similar reluctance, especially the women who had married Indian men and borne them children, drew another reaction. "For the honour of humanity," wrote Smith, "we would suppose those persons to have been of the lowest rank, either bred up in ignorance and distressing penury, or who had lived so long with the Indians as to forget all their former connections. For, easy and unconstrained as the savage life is, certainly it could never be put in competition with the blessings of improved life and the light of religion, by any persons who have had the happiness of enjoying, and the capacity of discerning, them." If Smith was struck by the contrast between the visible impact of Indian education and his own cultural assumptions, he never said so.

To find a satisfactory explanation for the extraordinary drawing power of Indian culture, we should begin where the colonists themselves first came under its sway—on the trail to Indian country. For although the Indians were known for their patience, they wasted no time in beginning the educational process that would transform their hostile or fearful white captives into affectionate Indian relatives.

Perhaps the first transaction after the Indians had selected their prisoners and hurried them into cover was to replace their hard-heeled shoes with the footwear of the forest—moccasins. These were universally approved by the prisoners, who admitted that they traveled with "abundant more ease" than before. And on more than one occasion the knee-deep snows of northern New England forced the Indians to make snowshoes for their prisoners in order to maintain their pace of twenty-five to thirty miles a day. Such an introduction to the superbly adapted technology of the Indians alone would not convert the English, but it was a beginning.

The lack of substantial food supplies forced the captives to accommodate their stomachs as best they could to Indian trail fare, which ranged from nuts, berries, roots, and parched corn to beaver guts, horse-flank, and semi-raw venison and moose, eaten without the customary English accompaniments of bread or salt. When there was nothing to eat, the Indians would "gird up their loins with a string," a technique that at least one captive found "very useful" when applied to himself. Although their food was often "unsavory" and in short supply, the Indians always shared it equally with the captives, who, being hungry, "relished [it] very well."

Sometimes the lessons learned from the Indians were unexpectedly vital. When Stephen Williams, an eleven-year-old captive from Deerfield, found himself separated from his party on the way to Canada, he "Hellowed" for his Indian master. When the boy was found, the Indian threatened to kill him because, as Williams remembered five years later, "the Indians will never allow anybody to Hollow in the woods. Their manner is to make a noise like wolves or any other wild creatures, when they call to one another." The reason, of course, was that they did not wish to be discovered by their enemies. To the young neophyte Indian this was a lesson in survival not soon forgotten.

Two other lessons were equally unexpected but instrumental in preparing the captives for even greater surprises when they reached the Indian settlements. Both served to undermine the English horror of the Indians as bloodthirsty fiends who defile "any Woman they take alive" before "putting her to Death." Many redeemed prisoners made a point of insisting that, although they had been completely powerless in captivity, "the Indians are very civil towards their captive women, not offering any incivility by any indecent carriage." Thomas Ridout testified that "during the whole of the time I was with the Indians I never once witnessed an indecent or improper action amongst any of the Indians, whether young or old." Even Smith admitted that "from every enquiry that has been made, it appears—that no woman thus saved is preserved from base motives, or need fear the violation of her honour." If there had been the least exception, we can be sure that this champion of civilization would have made the most of it.

One reason for the Indians' lack of sexual interest in their female captives was perhaps aesthetic, for the New England Indians, at least, esteemed black the color of beauty. A more fundamental reason derived from the main purpose of taking captives, which was to secure new members for their families and clans. Under the Indians' strong incest taboos, no warrior would attempt to violate his future sister or cousin. "Were he to indulge himself with a captive taken in war, and much more were he to offer violence in order to gratify his lust, he would incur indelible disgrace." Indeed, the taboo seems to have extended to the whole tribe. As George Croghan testified after long acquaintance with the Indians, "they have No [J]uri[s]diction or Laws butt that of Nature yett I have known more than onest thire Councils, order men to be putt to Death for Committing Rapes, wh[ich] is a Crime they Despise." Since murder was a crime to be revenged by the victim's family in its own way and time, rape was the only capital offense punished by the tribe as a whole.

Captive testimony also chipped away at the stereotype of the Indians' cruelty. When Mrs. Isabella M'Coy was taken from Epsom, New Hampshire, in 1747, her neighbors later remembered that "she did indeed find the journey [to Canada] fatiguing, and her fare scanty and precarious. But in her treatment from the Indians, she experienced a very agreeable disappointment. The kindness she received from them was far greater than she had expected from those who were so often distinguished for their cruelties." More frequent still was recognition of the Indians' kindness to children. Thomas Hutchinson told a common story of how "some of the children who were taken at Deerfield, they drew upon slays; at other times they have been known to carry them in their arms or upon their backs to Canada. This tenderness," he noted, "has occasioned the beginning of an affection, which in a few years has been so rivetted, that the parents of the children, who have gone to Canada to seek them, could by no means prevail upon them to leave the Indians and return home." The affections of a four-year-old Pennsylvania boy, who became Old White Chief among the

Iroquois, seem to have taken even less time to become "rivetted." "The last I remember of my mother," he recalled in 1836, "she was running, carrying me in her arms. Suddenly she fell to the ground on her face, and I was taken from her. Overwhelmed with fright, I knew nothing more until I opened my eyes to find myself in the lap of an Indian woman. Looking kindly down into my face she smiled on me, and gave me some dried deer's meat and maple sugar. From that hour I believe she loved me as a mother. I am sure I returned to her the affection of a son."

When the returning war parties approached the first Indian village, the educational process took on a new complexion. As one captive explained, "Whenever the warriors return from an excursion against an enemy, their return to the tribe or village must be designated by warlike ceremonial; the captives or spoils, which may happen to crown their valor, must be conducted in a triumphant form, and decorated to every possible advantage." Accordingly, the cheek, chin, and forehead of every captive were painted with traditional dashes of vermilion mixed with bear's grease. Belts of wampum were hung around their necks, Indian clothes were substituted for English, and the men and boys had their hair plucked or shaved in Indian fashion. The physical transformation was so effective, said a twenty-six-year-old soldier, "that I began to think I was an Indian." Younger captives were less aware of the small distance between role-playing and real acceptance of the Indian lifestyle. When her captor dressed Frances Slocum, not yet five years old, in "beautiful wampum beads," she remembered at the end of a long and happy life as an Indian that he "made me look, as I thought, very fine. I was much pleased with the beautiful wampum."

The prisoners were then introduced to a "new school" of song and dance. "Little did we expect," remarked an English woman, "that the accomplishment of dancing would ever be taught us, by the savages. But the war dance must now be held; and every prisoner that could move must take its awkward steps. The figure consisted of circular motion round the fire; each sang his own music, and the best dancer was the one most violent in motion." To prepare for the event each captive had rehearsed a short Indian song on the trail. Mrs. Johnson recalled many years later that her song was "danna witchee natchepung; my son's was nar wiscumpton." Nehemiah How could not master the Indian pronunciation, so he was allowed to sing in English "I don't know where I go." In view of the Indians' strong sense of ceremonial propriety, it is small wonder that one captive thought that they "Seem[e]d to be Very much a mind I Should git it perfect."

Upon entering the village the Indians let forth with some distinctive music of their own. "When we came near the main Body of the Enemy," wrote Thomas Brown, a captive soldier from Fort William Henry, "the *Indians* made a Live-Shout, as they call it when they bring in a Prisoner alive (different from the Shout they make when they bring in Scalps, which they call a Dead-Shout)." According to another soldier, "their Voices are so sharp, shrill, loud and deep, that when they join together after one has made his Cry, it makes a most dreadful and horrible Noise, that stupifies the very Senses," a noise that naturally frightened many captives until they learned that it was not their death knell.

They had good reason to think that their end was near when the whole village turned out to form a gauntlet from the entrance to the center of the village and their captors ordered them to run through it. With ax handles, tomahawks, hoop poles, clubs, and switches the Indians flogged the racing captives as if to beat the whiteness out of them. In most villages, significantly, "it was only the more elderly People both Male and Female wh[ic]h rece[iv]ed this Useage—the young prisoners of Both Sexes Escaped without it" or were rescued from any serious harm by one or more villagers, perhaps indicating the Indian perception of the captives' various educability. When ten-year-old John Brickell was knocked down by the blows of his Seneca captors, "a very big Indian came up, and threw the company off me, and took me by the arm, and led me along through the lines with such rapidity that I scarcely touched the ground, and was not once struck after he took me."

The purpose of the gauntlet was the subject of some difference of opinion. A French soldier who had spent several years among the northeastern Indians believed that a prisoner "so unfortunate as to fall in the course of the bastonnade must get up quickly and keep on, or he will be beaten to death on the spot." On the other hand, Pierre de Charlevoix, the learned traveler and historian of Canada, wrote that "even when they seem to strike at random, and to be actuated only by fury, they take care never to touch any part where a blow might prove mortal." Both Frenchmen were primarily describing the Indians' treatment of other Indians and white men. Leininger and LeRoy drew a somewhat different conclusion from their own treatment. Their welcome at the Indian village of Kittanning, they said, "consisted of three blows each, on the back. They were, however, administered with great mercy. Indeed, we concluded that we were beaten merely in order to keep up an ancient usage, and not with the intention of injuring us."

William Walton came closest to revealing the Indians' intentions in his account of the Gilbert family's captivity. The Indians usually beat the captives with "great Severity," he said, "by way of Revenge for their Relations who have been slain." Since the object of taking captives was to satisfy the Indian families who had lost relatives, the gauntlet served as the first of three initiation rites into Indian society, a purgative ceremony by which the bereaved Indians could exorcise their anger and anguish, and the captives could begin their cultural transformation.

If the first rite tried to beat the whiteness out of the captives, the second tried to wash it out. James Smith's experience was typical.

> The old chief, holding me by the hand, made a long speech, very loud, and when he had done he handed me to three squaws, who led me by the hand down the bank into the river until the water was up to our middle. The squaws then made signs to me to plunge myself into the water, but I did not understand them. I thought that the result of the council was that I should be drowned, and that these young ladies were to be the executioners. They all laid violent hold of me, and I for some time opposed them with all my might, which occasioned loud laughter by the multitude that were on the bank of the river. At length one of the squaws made out to speak a little English (for I believe they began to be afraid of me) and said, 'No hurt you.' On this I gave myself up to their ladyships, who were as good as their word; for though they plunged me under water and washed and rubbed me severely, yet I could not say they hurt me much.

More than one captive had to receive similar assurance, but their worst fears were being laid to rest.

Symbolically purged of their whiteness by their Indian baptism, the initiates were dressed in new Indian clothes and decorated with feathers, jewelry, and paint. Then, with great solemnity, the village gathered around the council fire, where after a "profound silence" one of the chiefs spoke. Even a hostile captive, Zadock Steele, had to admit that although he could not understand the language spoken, he could "plainly discover a great share of native eloquence." The chief's speech, he said, was "of considerable length, and its effect obviously manifested weight of argument, solemnity of thought, and at least human sensibility." But even this the twenty-two-year-old New Englander could not appreciate on its own terms, for in the next breath he denigrated the ceremony as "an assemblage of barbarism, assuming the appearance of civilization."

A more charitable account was given by James Smith, who through an interpreter was addressed in the following words:

> My son, you are now flesh of our flesh and bone of our bone. By the ceremony that was performed this day, every drop of white blood was washed out of your veins. You are taken into the Caughnewaga nation and initiated into a war-like tribe. You are adopted into a great family and now received with great seriousness and solemnity in the room and place of a great man. After what has passed this day you are now one of us by an old strong law and custom. My son, you have now nothing to fear. We are now under the same obligations to love, support and defend you that we are to love and to defend one another. Therefore you are to consider yourself as one of our people.

"At this time," admitted the eighteen-year-old Smith, "I did not believe this fine speech, especially that of the white blood being washed out of me; but since that time I have found that there was much sincerity in said speech; for from that day I never knew them to make any distinction between me and themselves in any respect whatever until I left them . . . we all shared one fate." It is a chord that sounds through nearly every captivity narrative: "They treated me . . . in every way as one of themselves."

When the adoption ceremony had ended, the captive was taken to the wigwam of his new family, who greeted him with a "most dismal howling, crying bitterly, and wringing their hands in all the agonies of grief for a deceased relative." "The higher in favour the adopted Prisoners [were] to be placed, the greater Lamentation [was] made over them." After a threnodic memorial to the lost member, which may have "added to the Terror of the Captives," who "imagined it to be no other than a Prelude to inevitable Destruction," the mood suddenly shifted. "I never saw . . . such hug[g]ing and kissing from the women and crying for joy," exclaimed one young recipient. Then an interpreter introduced each member of the new family—in one case "from brother

to seventh cousins"—and "they came to me one after another," said
another captive, "and shook me by the hand, in token that they considered me to stand in the same relationship to them as the one in
whose stead I was placed."

Most young captives assumed the place of Indian sons and daughters,
but occasionally the match was not exact. Mary Jemison replaced a
brother who had been killed in "Washington's war," while twenty-six-
year-old Titus King assumed the unlikely role of a grandfather. Although their sex and age may not always have corresponded, the
adopted captives succeeded to all the deceased's rights and obligations—
the same dignities, honors, and often the same names. "But the one
adopted," reported a French soldier, "must be prudent and wise in his
conduct, if he wants to make himself as well liked as the man he is
replacing. This seldom fails to occur, because he is continually reminded of the dead man's conduct and good deeds."

So literal could the replacement become at times that no amount of
exemplary conduct could alter the captive's reception. Thomas Peart, a
twenty-three-year-old Pennsylvanian, was adopted as an uncle in an
Iroquois family, but "the old Man, whose Place [he] was to fill, had
never been considered by his Family as possessed of any Merit." Accordingly, Peart's dress, although in the Indian style, was "in a meaner
Manner, as they did not hold him high in Esteem after his Adoption."
Since his heart was not in becoming an Indian anyway, and "observing
that they treated him just as they had done the old worthless Indian
. . . he therefore concluded he would only fill his Predecessor's Station, and used no Endeavours to please them."

When the prisoners had been introduced to all their new relatives
and neighbors, the Indians proceeded to shower them with gifts. Luke
Swetland, taken from Pennsylvania during the Revolution, was unusually feted with "three hats, five blankets, near twenty pipes, six
razors, six knives, several spoons, gun and ammunition, fireworks, several Indian pockets [pouches], one Indian razor, awls, needles, goose
quills, paper and many other things of small value"—enough to make
him the complete Indian warrior. Most captives, however, settled for a
new shirt or dress, a pair of decorated moccasins, and abundant promises of future kindness, which later prompted the captives to acknowledge once again that the Indians were "a[s] good as their word." "All
the family was as kind to me," related Thomas Gist, "as if I had really

been the nearest of relation they had in the world." The two women who adopted Jemison were no less loving. "I was ever considered and treated by them as a real sister," she said near the end of a long life with them, "the same as though I had been born of their mother."

Treatment such as this—and it was almost universal—left an indelible mark on every captive, whether or not they eventually returned to English society. Although captives like Mrs. Johnson found their adoption an "unnatural situation," they had to defend the humanity of the practice. "Those who have profited by refinement and education," she argued, "ought to abate part of the prejudice, which prompts them to look with an eye of censure on this untutored race. . . . Do they ever adopt an enemy," she asked, "and salute him by the tender name of brother?" It is not difficult to imagine what effect such feelings must have had in younger people less habituated to English culture, especially those who had lost their own parents.

The formalities, purgations, and initiations were now completed. Only one thing remained for the Indians: by their daily example and instruction to "make an Indian of you," as the Delawares told Brickell. This required a steady union of two things: the willingness and gratitude of the captives, and the consistent love and trust of the Indians. By the extraordinary ceremonies through which they had passed, most captives had had their worst fears allayed. From a state of apprehension or even terror they had suddenly emerged with their persons intact and a solemn invitation to begin a new life, as full of love, challenge, and satisfaction as any they had known. For "when they [the Indians] once determine to give life, they give every thing with it, which, in their apprehension, belongs to it." The sudden release from anxiety into a realm of affirmative possibility must have disposed many captives to accept the Indian way of life.

According to the adopted colonists who recounted the stories of their new lives, Indian life was more than capable of claiming their respect and allegiance, even if they eventually returned to English society. The first indication that the Indians were serious in their professions of equality came when the adopted captives were given freedom of movement within and without the Indian villages. Naturally the degree of freedom and its timing depended on the captive's willingness to enter into the spirit of Indian life.

Despite his adult years, Ridout had earned his captor's trust by the

third night of their march to the Shawnee villages. Having tied his prisoner with a rope to himself the first two nights, the Indian "never afterwards used this precaution, leaving me at perfect liberty, and frequently
during the nights that were frosty and cold," Ridout recalled, "I found
his hand over me to examine whether or not I was covered." As soon
as seventeen-year-old John Leeth, an Indian trader's clerk, reached his
new family's village, "my father gave me and his two [Indian] sons our
freedom, with a rifle, two pounds of powder, four pounds of lead, a
blanket, shirt, match-coat, pair of leggings, etc. to each, as our freedom
dues; and told us to shift for ourselves." Eleven-year-old Benjamin
Gilbert, "considered as the [Indian] King's Successor," was of course
"entirely freed from Restraint, so that he even began to be delighted
with his Manner of Life." Even Steele, a somewhat reluctant Indian at
twenty-two, was "allowed the privilege of visiting any part of the village, in the day time, and was received with marks of fraternal affection,
and treated with all the civility an Indian is capable to bestow."

The presence of other white prisoners complicated the trust relationship somewhat. Captives who were previously known to each other,
especially from the same family, were not always allowed to converse
"much together, as [the Indians] imagined they would remember their
former Situation, and become less contented with their present Manner of Life." Benjamin Peart, for example, was allowed the frequent
company of "Two white Men who had been taken Prisoners, the one
from Susquehanna, the other from Minisinks, both in Pennsylvania,"
even though he was a Pennsylvanian himself. But when he met his
captive wife and infant son by chance at Fort Niagara, the Indians
"separated them again the same Day, and took [his] Wife about Four
Miles Distance."

Captives who were strangers were permitted not only to visit frequently but occasionally to live together. When Gist suddenly moved
from his adopted aunt's house back to her brother's, she "imajined I
was affronted," he wrote, and "came and asked me the reason why I
had left her, or what injury she or any of the family had done me that
I should leave her without so much as leting her know of it. I told her
it was the company of my fellow prisoners that drew me to the town.
She said that it was not so far but I mite have walked to see them every
two or three days, and ask some of them to come and see me those days
that I did not chuse to go abroad, and that all such persons as I thought

proper to bring to the house should be as welcom[e] as one of the family, and made many promises how kind she would be if I would return. However," boasted the twenty-four-year-old Gist, "I was obstinate and would not." It is not surprising that captives who enjoyed such autonomy were also trusted under the same roof. John Brickell remarked that three white prisoners, "Patton, Johnston, and Mrs. Baker [of Kentucky] had all lived with me in the same house among the Indians, and we were as intimate as brothers and sisters."

Once the captives had earned the basic trust of their Indian families, nothing in Indian life was denied them. When they reached the appropriate age, the Indians offered to find them suitable marriage partners. Understandably, some of the older captives balked at this, sensing that it was calculated to bind them with marital ties to a culture they were otherwise hesitant to accept. When Joseph Gilbert, a forty-one-year-old father and husband, was adopted into a leading family, his new relatives informed him that "if he would marry amongst them, he should enjoy the Privileges which they enjoyed; but this Proposal he was not disposed to comply with, . . . as he was not over anxious to conceal his Dislike to them." Elizabeth Peart, his twenty-year-old married sister, was equally reluctant. During her adoption ceremony "they obliged her to sit down with a young Man an Indian, and the eldest Chieftain of the Family repeating a Jargon of Words to her unintelligible, but which she considered as some form amongst them of Marriage," she was visited with "the most violent agitations, as she was determined, at all events, to oppose any step of this Nature." Marie LeRoy's honor was even more dearly bought. When "it was at length determined by the [Indians] that [she] should marry one of the natives, who had been selected for her," she told a fellow captive that "she would sooner be shot than have him for her husband." Whether her revulsion was directed toward the act itself or toward the particular suitor was not said.

The distinction is pertinent because the weight of evidence suggests that marriage was not compulsory for the captives, and common sense tells us that any form of compulsion would have defeated the Indians' purpose in trying to persuade the captives to adopt their way of life. Mary Jemison, at the time a captive for two years, was unusual in implying that she was forced to marry an Indian. "Not long after the Delawares came to live with us, at Wiisho," she recalled, "my sisters told me that I must go and live with one of them, whose name was

She-nin-jee. Not daring to cross them, or disobey their commands, with
a great degree of reluctance I went; and Sheninjee and I were married
according to Indian custom." Considering the tenderness and kindness
with which most captives reported they were treated, it is likely that
she was less compelled in reality than in her perception and memory
of it.

For even hostile witnesses could not bring themselves to charge that
force was ever used to promote marriages. The Puritan minister John
Williams said only that "great *essays* [were] made to get [captives]
married" among the Canadian Indians by whom he was captured. Elizabeth Hanson and her husband "could by no means obtain from their
hands" their sixteen-year-old daughter, "for the squaw, to whom she
was given, had a son whom she intended my daughter should in time
be prevailed with to marry." Mrs. Hanson was probably less concerned
that her daughter would be forced to marry an Indian than that she
might "in time" want to, for as she acknowledged from her personal
experience, "the Indians are very civil towards their captive women, not
offering any incivility by any indecent carriage." An observer of the
return of the white prisoners to Bouquet spoke for his contemporaries
when he reported—with an almost audible sigh of relief—that "there
had not been a solitary instance among them of any woman having her
delicacy injured by being compelled to marry. They had been left liberty of choice, and those who chose to remain single were not sufferers
on that account."

Not only were younger captives and consenting adults under no compulsion, either actual or perceived, to marry, but they enjoyed as wide
a latitude of choice as any Indian. When Gist returned to his Indian
aunt's lodge, she was so happy that she "dress'd me as fine as she could,
and . . . told me if I wanted a wife she would get a pretty young girl
for me." It was in the same spirit of exuberant generosity that Spencer's
adopted mother rewarded his first hunting exploit. "She heard all the
particulars of the affair with great satisfaction," he remembered, "and
frequently saying, 'Enee, wessah' (that is right, that is good), said I
would one day become a great hunter, and placing her forefingers together (by which sign the Indians represent marriage) and then pointing to Sotonegoo" (a thirteen-year-old girl whom Spencer described as
"rather homely, but cheerful and good natured, with bright, laughing
eyes") "told me that when I should become a man I should have her

for a wife." Sotonegoo cannot have been averse to the idea, for when Spencer was redeemed shortly afterward she "sobbed loudly as [he] took her hand, and for the moment deeply affected, bade her farewell."

So free from compulsion were the captives that several married fellow white prisoners. In 1715 the priest of the Jesuit mission at Sault-au-Recollect "married Ignace shoetak8anni [Joseph Rising, aged twenty-one] and Elizabeth T8atog8ach [Abigail Nims, aged fifteen], both English, who wish to remain with the Christian Indians, not only renouncing their nation, but even wishing to live *en sauvages*." But from the Indians' standpoint, and perhaps from their own, captives such as John Leeth and Thomas Armstrong may have had the best of all possible marriages. After some years with the Indians, Leeth "was married to a young woman, seventeen or eighteen years of age; also a prisoner to the Indians; who had been taken by them when about twenty months old." Armstrong, an adopted Seneca, also married a "full blooded white woman, who like himself had been a captive among the Indians, from infancy, who unlike him, had not acquired a knowledge of one word of the English language, being essentially Indian in all save blood." Their commitment to each other deepened their commitment to the Indian culture of which they had become equal members.

The captives' social equality was also demonstrated by their being asked to share in the affairs of war and peace, matters of supreme importance to Indian society. When the Senecas who had adopted Thomas Peart decided to "make a War Excursion," they asked him to go with them. But since he was in no mood—and no physical condition —to play the Indian, "he determinately refused them, and was therefore left at Home with the Family." The young Englishman who became Old White Chief was far more eager to defend his new culture, but his origins somewhat limited his military activity. "When I grew to manhood," he recalled, "I went with them [his Iroquois kinsmen] on the warpath against the neighboring tribes, but never against the white settlers, lest by some unlucky accident I might be recognized and claimed by former friends." Other captives—many of them famous renegades—were less cautious. Charlevoix noticed in his travels in Canada that adopted captives "frequently enter into the spirit of the nation, of which they are become members, in such a manner, that they make no difficulty of going to war against their own countrymen." It was behavior such as this that prompted Sir William Johnson to praise Bouquet after his expedition to the Ohio for compelling the Indians to give up every white person, even the "Children born of White Women. That mixed Race," he wrote, referring to first-generation captives as well, "forgetting their Ancestry on one side are found to be the most Inveterate of any, and would greatly Augment their numbers."

It is ironic that the most famous renegade of all should have introduced ten-year-old Spencer to the ultimate opportunity for an adopted captive. When he had been a captive for less than three weeks, Spencer met Simon Girty, "the very picture of a villain," at a Shawnee village below his own. After various boasts and enquiries, wrote Spencer, "he ended by telling me that I would never see home; but if I should 'turn out to be a good hunter and a brave warrior I might one day be a chief.'" Girty's prediction may not have been meant to tease a small boy with impossible delusions of grandeur, for the Indians of the Northeast readily admitted white captives to their highest councils and offices.

Just after Ridout was captured on the Ohio, he was surprised to meet an English-speaking "white man, about twenty-two years of age, who had been taken prisoner when a lad and had been adopted, and now was a chief among the Shawanese." He need not have been surprised, for there were many more like him. John Tarbell, the man who visited his Groton relatives in Indian dress, was not only "one of the wealthiest" of the Caughnawagas but "the eldest chief and chief speaker of the tribe." Timothy Rice, formerly of Westborough, Massachusetts, was also made one of the clan chiefs of Caughnawaga [Québec], partly by inheritance from his Indian father but largely for "his own Super[io]r Talents" and "warlike Spirit for which he was much celebrated."

Perhaps the most telling evidence of the Indians' receptivity to adopted white leadership comes from Old White Chief, an adopted Iroquois.

> I was made a chief at an early age [he recalled in 1836] and as my sons grew to manhood they also were made chiefs. . . . After my youngest son was made chief I could see, as I thought, that some of the Indians were jealous of the distinction I enjoyed and it gave me uneasiness. This was the first time I ever entertained the thought of leaving my Indian friends. I felt sure that it was displeasing to the Indians to have three of my sons, as well as myself, promoted to the office of chief. My wife was well pleased to leave with me, and my sons said, "Father, we will go wherever you will lead us."

I then broke the subject to some of my Indian relatives, who were very much disturbed at my decision. They immediately called the chiefs and warriors together and laid the plan before them. They gravely deliberated upon the subject for some hours, and then a large majority decided that they would not consent to our leaving. They said, "We cannot give up our son and brother" (meaning myself) "nor our nephews" (meaning my children). "They have lived on our game and grown strong and powerful among us. They are good and true men. We cannot do without them. We cannot give them to the pale faces. We shall grow weak if they leave us. We will give them the best we have left. Let them choose where they will live. No one shall disturb them. We need their wisdom and their strength to help us. If they are in high places, let them be there. We know they will honor us."

"We yielded to their importunity," said the old chief, and "I have never had any reason to regret my decision." In public office as in every sphere of Indian life, the English captives found that the color of their skin was unimportant; only their talent and their inclination of heart mattered.

Understandably, neither their skill nor their loyalty was left to chance. From the moment the captives, especially the young ones, came under their charge, the Indians made a concerted effort to inculcate in them Indian habits of mind and body. If the captives could be taught to think, act, and react like Indians, they would effectively cease to be English and would assume an Indian identity. This was the Indians' goal, toward which they bent every effort in the weeks and months that followed their formal adoption of the white captives.

The educational character of Indian society was recognized by even the most inveterately English captives. Titus King, a twenty-six-year-old New England soldier, spent a year with the Canadian Indians at St. Francis trying—unsuccessfully—to undo their education of "Eight or tin young [English] Children." What "an awfull School this [is] for Children," he wrote. "When We See how Quick they will Fall in with the Indians ways, nothing Seems to be more takeing in Six months time they Forsake Father and mother Forgit thir own Land Refuess to Speak there own toungue and Seemin[g]ly be Holley Swollowed up with the Indians." The older the person, of course, the longer it took to become fully Indianized. Mary Jemison, captured at the age of twelve, took three or four years to forget her natural parents and the home she had once loved. "If I had been taken in infancy," she said, "I should have been contented in my situation." Some captives, commonly those over fifteen or sixteen years old, never made the transition from English to Indian. Twenty-four-year-old Gist, soldier and son of a famous scout and Indian agent, accommodated himself to his adoption and Indian life for just one year and then made plans to escape. "All curiosity with regard to acting the part of an Indian," he related, "which I could do very well, being througherly [thoroughly] satisfied, I was determined to be what I really was."

Children, however, took little time to "fall in with the Indians ways." Titus King mentioned six months. The Reverend John Williams witnessed the effects of eight or nine months when he stopped at St. Francis in February 1704. There, he said, "we found several poor children, who had been taken from the eastward [Maine] the summer before; a sight very affecting, they being in habit very much like Indians, and in manners very much symbolizing with them." When young Joseph Noble visited his captive sister in Montreal, "he still belonged to the St. François tribe of Indians, and was dressed remarkably fine, having forty or fifty broaches in his shirt, clasps on his arm, and a great variety of knots and bells about his clothing. He brought his little sister . . . a young fawn, a basket of cranberries, and a lump of sap sugar." Sometime later he was purchased from the Indians by a French gentleman who promptly "dressed him in the French style; but he never appeared so bold and majestic, so spirited and vivacious, as when arrayed in his Indian habit and associating with his Indian friends."

The key to any culture is its language, and the young captives were quick to learn the Indian dialects of their new families. Their retentive memories and flair for imitation made them ready students, while the Indian languages, at once oral, concrete, and mythopoeic, lightened the task. In less than six months ten-year-old Spencer had "acquired a sufficient knowledge of the Shawnee tongue to understand all ordinary conversation and, indeed, the greater part of all that I heard (accompanied, as their conversation and speeches were, with the most significant gestures)," which enabled him to listen "with much pleasure and sometimes with deep interest" to his Indian mother tell of battles, heroes, and history in the long winter evenings. When Jemima Howe was allowed to visit her four-year-old son at a neighboring Indian village in Canada, he greeted her "in the Indian tongue" with "Mother, are you come?" He too had been a captive for only six months.

The early weeks of captivity could be disquieting if there were no English-speaking Indians or prisoners in the village to lend the comfort of a familiar language while the captives struggled to acquire a strange one. If a captive's family left for their winter hunting camp before he could learn their language, he might find himself, like Gist, "without any com[p]any that could unders[t]and one word that I spake." "Thus I continued, near five months," he wrote, "sometimes reading, other times singing, never melancholy but when alone. . . . About the first of April (1759) I prevailed on the family to return to town, and by the last of the month all the Indians and prisoners returned, when I once more had the pleasure to talk to people that understood what I said."

Younger captives probably missed the familiarity of English less than the adult Gist. Certainly they never lacked eager teachers. Mary Jemison recalled that her Seneca sisters were "diligent in teaching me their language; and to their great satisfaction I soon learned so that I could understand it readily, and speak it fluently." Even Gist was the recipient of enthusiastic, if informal, instruction from a native speaker. One of his adopted cousins, who was about five or six years old and his "favorite in the family," was always "chattering some thing" with him. "From him," said Gist affectionately, "I learn'd more than from all the rest, and he learn'd English as fast as [I] did Indian."

As in any school, language was only one of many subjects of instruction. Since the Indians generally assumed that whites were physically inferior to themselves, captive boys were often prepared for the hardy life of hunters and warriors by a rigorous program of physical training. John McCullough, aged eight, was put through the traditional Indian course by his adoptive uncle. "In the beginning of winter," McCullough recalled, "he used to raise me by day light every morning, and make me sit down in the creek up to my chin in the cold water, in order to make me hardy as he said, whilst he would sit on the bank smoking his pipe until he thought I had been long enough in the water, he would then bid me to dive. After I came out of the water he would order me not to go near the fire until I would be dry. I was kept at that till the water was frozen over, he would then break the ice for me and send me in as before." As shocking as it may have been to his system, such treatment did nothing to turn him against Indian life. Indeed, he was transparently proud that he had borne up under the strenuous regimen "with the firmness of an Indian." Becoming an Indian was as much a challenge and an adventure for the young colonists as it was a "sore trial," and many of them responded to it with alacrity and zest. Of children their age we should not expect any less.

The captives were taught not only to speak and to endure as Indians but to act as Indians in the daily social and economic life of the community. Naturally, boys were taught the part of men and girls the part of women, and according to most colonial sources—written, it should be noted, predominantly by men—the boys enjoyed the better fate. An Ohio pioneer remembered that the prisoners from his party were "put into different families, the women to hard drudging and the boys to run wild with the young Indians, to amuse themselves with bow and arrow, dabble in the water, or obey any other notion their wild natures might dictate." William Walton, the author of the Gilbert family captivity narrative, also felt that the "Labour and Drudgery" in an Indian family fell to "the Share of the Women." He described fourteen-year-old Abner Gilbert as living a "dronish Indian life, idle and poor, having no other Employ than the gathering of Hickory-Nuts; and although young," Walton insisted, "his Situation was very irksome." Just how irksome the boy found his freedom from colonial farm chores was revealed when the ingenuous Walton related that "Abner, having no useful Employ, amused himself with catching fish in the Lake. . . . Not being of an impatient Disposition," said Walton soberly, "he bore his Captivity without repining."

While most captive boys had "nothing to do, but cut a little wood for the fire," draw water for cooking and drinking, and "shoot Blackbirds that came to eat up the corn," they enjoyed "some leisure" for "hunting and other innocent devertions in the woods." Women and girls, on the other hand, shared the burdens—onerous ones in English eyes—of their Indian counterparts. But Jemison, who had been taught English ways for twelve years before becoming an Indian, felt that the Indian women's labor "was not severe," their tasks "probably not harder than that [sic] of white women," and their cares "certainly . . . not half as numerous, nor as great." The work of one year was "exactly similar, in almost every respect, to that of the others, without that endless variety that is to be observed in the common labor of the white people. . . . In the summer season, we planted, tended and harvested our corn, and generally had all our children with us; but had no master to oversee or drive us, so that we could work as leisurely as we pleased. . . . In the season of hunting, it was our business, in addition to our cooking, to bring home the game that was taken by the [men], dress it, and carefully preserve the eatable meat, and prepare or dress the skins." "Spinning, weaving, sewing, stocking knitting," and like domestic tasks of colonial women were generally unknown. Unless Jemison was correct, it would be virtually impossible to understand why so many women and girls chose to become Indians. A life of unremitting drudgery, as the English saw it, could certainly hold no attraction for civilized women fresh from frontier farms and villages.

The final and most difficult step in the captives' transition from English to Indian was to acquire the ability to think as Indians, to share unconsciously the values, beliefs, and standards of Indian culture. From an English perspective, this should have been nearly an impossible task for civilized people because they perceived Indian culture as immoral and irreligious and totally antithetical to the civilized life they had known, however briefly. "Certainly," William Smith assumed, "it could never be put in competition with the blessings of improved life and the light of religion." But many captives soon discovered that the English had no monopoly on virtue and that in many ways the Indians were morally superior to the English, more Christian than the Christians.

As early as 1643 Roger Williams had written a book to suggest such a thing, but he could be dismissed as a misguided visionary who let the Narragansetts go to his head. It was more difficult to dismiss someone like Brickell, who had lived with the Indians for four and one-half years and had no ax to grind with established religion. "The Delawares are the best people to train up children I ever was with," he wrote. "Their leisure hours are, in a great measure, spent in training up their children to observe what they believe to be right. . . . [A]s a nation they may be considered fit examples for many of us Christians to follow. They certainly follow what they are taught to believe right more closely, and I might say more honestly, in general, than we Christians do the divine precepts of our Redeemer. . . . I know I am influenced to good, even at this day," he concluded, "more from what I learned among them, than what I learned among people of my own color." After many decades with them, Jemison insisted that "the moral character of the Indians was . . . uncontaminated. Their fidelity was perfect, and became proverbial; they were strictly honest; they despised deception and falsehood; and chastity was held in high veneration." Even the tory historian Peter Oliver, who was no friend to the Indians, admitted that "they have a Religion of their own, which, to the eternal Disgrace of many Nations who boast of Politeness, is more influential on their Conduct than that of those who hold them in so great Contempt." To the acute discomfort of the colonists, more than one captive maintained that the Indians were a "far more moral race than the whites."

In the principled school of Indian life the captives experienced a decisive shift in their cultural and personal identities, a shift that often fostered a considerable degree of what might be called "conversion zeal." A French officer reported that "those Prisoners whom the Indians keep with them . . . are often more brutish, boisterous in their Behaviour and loose in their Manners than the Indians," and thought that "they affect that kind of Behaviour thro' Fear of and to recommend themselves to the Indians." Matthew Bunn, a nineteen-year-old soldier, was the object of such behavior when he was enslaved—not adopted— by the Maumee in 1791. "After I had eaten," he related, "they brought me a little prisoner boy, that had been taken about two years before, on the river called Monongahela, though he delighted more in the ways of the savages than in the ways of Christians; he used me worse than any of the Indians, for he would tell me to do this, that, and the other, and if I did not do it, or made any resistance, the Indians would threaten to kill me, and he would kick and cuff me about in such a manner, that I hardly dared to say my soul was my own." What Bunn experienced was the attempt of the new converts to pattern their behavior after their young Indian counterparts, who, a Puritan minister observed, "are as much to be dreaded by captives as those of maturer years, and in many cases much more so; for, unlike cultivated people, they have no restraints upon their mischievous and savage propensities, which they indulge in cruelties."

Although fear undoubtedly accounted for some of the converts' initial behavior, desire to win the approval of their new relatives also played a part. "I had lived in my new habitation about a week," recalled Spencer, "and having given up all hope of escaping . . . began to regard it as my future home. . . . I strove to be cheerful, and by my ready obedience to ingratiate myself with Cooh-coo-cheeh [his Indian mistress], for whose kindness I felt grateful." A year after James Smith had been adopted, a number of prisoners were brought in by his new kinsmen and a gauntlet formed to welcome them. Smith "went and told them how they were to act" and then "fell into one of the ranks with the Indians, shouting and yelling like them." One middle-aged man's turn came, and "as they were not very severe on him," confessed the new Indian, "as he passed me I hit him with a piece of pumpkin— which pleased the Indians much." If their zeal to emulate the Indians sometimes exceeded their mercy, the captives had nonetheless fulfilled their new families' expectations: they had begun to act as Indians in spirit as well as body. Only time would be necessary to transform their conscious efforts into unconscious habits and complete their cultural conversion.

"By what power does it come to pass," asked Crèvecoeur, "that children who have been adopted when young among these people, . . . and even grown persons . . . can never be prevailed on to re-adopt European manners?" Given the malleability of youth, we should not be surprised that children underwent a rather sudden and permanent transition from English to Indian—although we might be pressed to explain why so few Indian children made the transition in the opposite direction. But the adult colonists who became Indians cannot be explained as easily, for the simple reason that they, unlike many of the children, were fully conscious of their cultural identities while they were being subjected to the Indians' assiduous attempts to convert them. Consequently, their cultural metamorphosis involved a large degree of personal choice.

The great majority of white Indians left no explanations for their choice. Forgetting their original language and their past, they simply disappeared into their adopted society. But those captives who returned to write narratives of their experiences left several clues to the motives of those who chose to stay behind. They stayed because they found Indian life to possess a strong sense of community, abundant love, and uncommon integrity—values that the English colonists also honored, if less successfully. But Indian life was attractive for other values—for social equality, mobility, adventure, and, as two adult converts acknowledged, "the most perfect freedom, the ease of living, [and] the absence of those cares and corroding solicitudes which so often prevail with us." As we have learned recently, these were values that were not being realized in the older, increasingly crowded, fragmented, and contentious communities of the Atlantic seaboard, or even in the newer frontier settlements. By contrast, as Crèvecoeur said, there must have been in the Indians' "social bond something singularly captivating." Whatever it was, its power had no better measure than the large number of English colonists who became, contrary to the civilized assumptions of their countrymen, white Indians.

4

Benjamin Franklin as Experimental Philosopher

SAMUEL DEVONS

• Benjamin Franklin will be remembered and revered by Americans as long as we seek to know how full and varied human existence can be. As a resident of Philadelphia, he did more than any person in the eighteenth century to make cities livable and urbane. As an author, he offered practical hints on how to improve thrift and productivity. As a diplomat in European capitals, he made the intellectual transition from defender of empire to signer of the Declaration of Independence. As a man, he led a dazzling romantic life and even after the age of seventy was the intimate companion of some of the most elegant ladies of Paris.

It was as a scientist, however, that Benjamin Franklin best revealed his true nature, and it was as a scientist that he learned a method of inquiry that would serve him well in other fields. We are inclined to think of Benjamin Franklin the experimenter with some amusement, perhaps because of his crude equipment or because of the oft-told tale of the kite and electricity. But Samuel Devons reminds us that Franklin's research put him at the cutting edge of knowledge in his time. In 1753, for example, the Royal Society recognized him with its highest scientific honor, the Copley Medal.

The essay below illustrates that Franklin's genius lay in his ability to find a simple uniform principle in a bewildering array of detail. Always curious, always aware of his own fallibility, and always willing to be instructed by observation and experience, Franklin summed up his philosophy during de-

This article was originally published in the *American Journal of Physics* (*Am. Journ. of Phys.* 45, 1148 [1977]). Permission to reprint this article has been granted by the *American Journal of Physics* and the American Association of Physics Teachers.

AUTHOR'S NOTE: I am happy to record my indebtedness to Professor I. B. Cohen for his comments on the present paper.

bate at the Constitutional Convention of 1787, when he urged members to vote for an imperfect document. "Having lived long," he said, "I have experienced many Instances of being obliged, by better Information, or fuller Consideration, to change Opinions even on Important Subjects, which I once thought right, but found to be otherwise." Each member, he urged, should "doubt a little of his own Infallibility."

In 1751, when Dr. William Watson, rich apothecary and amateur of science, and for a brief time Franklin's rival, presented to the Royal Society of London Franklin's newly published electrical discoveries, he felt compelled to excuse his inadequacy: "To give even the shortest account of all the experiments contained in Mr. Franklin's book," he sighed, "would exceed greatly the time allowed for these purposes by the Royal Society."

One can sympathize with Dr. Watson. He was reviewing Franklin's first scientific publication, a slim volume of but a few dozen pages, relating the outcome of the early Philadelphia experiments of 1747–50 (before the famous lightning experiments), but written with Franklin's unfeigned candor and unadorned lucidity, and with no words wasted. It was impossible to condense or to summarize or to improve upon. And how many times since has it seemed that what has been written about Franklin is no match for what he himself wrote?

And how indeed can one summarize, as our celebrations here demand, one aspect of a life so brimful of activity of every conceivable variety? "The most versatile genius that ever lived" is an encomium that has been applied to Franklin with some justification. A man of innumerable parts, but the parts are not separable. There is an essential integrity in all that he did: not so much that he applied experience gained in one sphere to activity in another, but rather that he expressed his whole incomparable self in every sphere. To present Benjamin Franklin as an "Experimental Philosopher," and more particularly as an explorer of electricity where his scientific genius found its fullest expression, is not so much to depict a particular part of Franklin, as to portray in a particular light the unique whole.

Franklin's electricity, like all Franklin's science, is so much in character with Franklin himself. It exemplifies his superb common sense—developed to a highly uncommon degree and expressed alike in practice and principle, in purpose and procedure. Its hallmarks are native wit coupled to a keen eye and skilled hands; leavened by wisdom born of experience and enriched by philosophical enlightenment, but never overburdened by a surfeit of sophistry or scholarship.

Franklin's science epitomizes Franklin, and Franklin his era in science: the age of the amateur—pursuing science to satisfy curiosity, for amusement, for enlightenment, possibly for benefit, but as a passion more than a profession. Electricity in the mid-18th century might have been made for Franklin and Franklin for electricity: their meeting, however accidental historically, seemed preordained!

Born in Boston, in 1706, "of humble stock" as the phrase goes—his father an emigrant soap-boiler and candle-maker—the sixth, youngest son of ten children, his "formal" school education began at eight and was completed at age ten. From then on he was not only self-taught in the practical, worldly sense; he diligently and systematically educated himself. He read widely—both classical and contemporary writings—and taught himself French, Italian, Spanish, and Latin. At twelve, he is an apprenticed printer; at fifteen he is not only reading, but writing, and publishing (with his brother) a "radical" newspaper. At eighteen, he is a seasoned journalist and printer; at twenty, having gained wide experience and traveled afar, he establishes his own printing-publishing business. He is now, and remains for the rest of his life, his own master, a citizen of his new home, Philadelphia.

Printing and publishing provide Franklin not only with a good living, but the opportunity to disseminate his ideas and ideals. Matching his skill as an artisan, his diligence in trade, and his acumen in business, is his powerful gift as a writer: equally able to inform, instruct, and to enlighten, to entertain and to influence.

And Franklin is never at a loss for subject matter. His curiosity is aroused, his mind stirred and pen moved by everything and everybody he encounters: from smokeless chimneys to the grand architecture of nature; from the cultivation of silkworms to the management of civic affairs. Thoughts, deeds, works, and words—all were ineluctably linked. Within a few years he had written articles on *Liberty and Necessity*; *Pleasure and Pain*; *On the Need for Paper Money*; and *On Pleasant Dreams*; he was publishing two newspapers, had started up that endless stream of advice, wit, and homespun philosophy—*Poor Richard's Almanac*—and had argued for the defense of the Colony in a pamphlet entitled *Plain Truth!* Concurrently he had organized the first lending library, was Grandmaster of the Freemasons, had established the first fire brigade, and was clerk to the Pennsylvania Assembly and a member of the City Council. He reorganized the mails, helped raise troops and erect blockhouses, and founded a moral-philosophical debating society—the Junto Club, the forerunner of the American Philosophical Society. With no exaggeration it was said of him that "he gave the impulse to nearly every measure or project for the welfare and prosperity of Philadelphia undertaken in his day."

It is impossible to conceive of Benjamin Franklin, more than 40 years old, prosperous citizen, husband and father, deeply immersed in business and civic affairs of every variety, devoting his whole attention or all his boundless energies to any one subject. Yet for a few years, from about 1747 to 1750, one subject—electricity—seems to have fully capitivated, if not captured, him. Early in 1747, he wrote his friend Collison in London: "I never was engaged in a study [electricity] that so totally engrossed my time as this has lately done."

Of course there had to be time off to attend to defending the colony from attacks by the Indians (or was it really the French?). Convincing Quakers of the need for a militia must have taxed even Franklin's energies and powers of persuasion! Nonetheless, it was his contributions to electrical science during those few years that earned for Franklin his immense reputation, in his day, as a natural philosopher and ensured his place, for all time, in the history of science.

Electricity in the mid-18th century, a favorite hunting ground for amateurs, was viewed with more than circumspection by the scientifically learned, particularly many of the great mathematical savants. The renowned Leonhard Euler, for example, in his celebrated letters to a German princess, writes: "The subject [electricity] . . . almost terrifies me. The variety it presents is immense, and the enumeration of its parts serves rather to confound than to inform—almost every day [there is] discovered some new phenomenon . . . the fatigue of wading through diffuse, long, tedious detail."

But this "tedious detail" did not daunt the amateurs—and Franklin was an amateur in the best and literal sense of the word. In the 18th century it was not unusual for a gentleman with sufficient leisure and money to dabble in science; but how many of the dilettantes could claim Franklin's distinction of having acquired his opportunities entirely by the efforts of his own hands and brain? Here Benjamin Franklin was, if not unique, certainly outstanding. Years as an artisan and entrepreneur had gained for him intimate practical insight into the vagaries of men and materials, and he knew how to coax the most out of both. And Nature, whether majestic or miniscule, was for him always fascinating; intriguing, perplexing, capricious, sometimes trying, perhaps. But tedious? Never!

How Benjamin Franklin became so absorbed with electricity at this particular time need not detain us: the story (or some story) has been told and retold. In any event, there was at this time a great surge of interest—both scientific and popular—in the subject, whose immediate climax was to be the discovery of the Leyden jar. Franklin was following, albeit at a distance, the main lines of scientific development in Europe and he must have already noticed the increasing prominence of electrical investigations. When the moment arrived, he set about the business with characteristic directness and dispatch. He did not wait to build grand apparatus: a simple glass tube from his friend Collison and common artifacts—personal, domestic, and from his trade—wine glasses, bottles, salt-cellars, gun-barrels, gilt-paper bookbindings, etc., were pressed into service. His "team" of co-workers was likewise spontaneous and opportune. It included: a local judge, a silversmith, and an "unemployed" Baptist minister.

With such naive paraphernalia, with such an odd group of collaborators, in a remote colony, far from the European centers of science and enlightenment, how could an unsophisticated tinkerer—as Franklin has often been dubbed—possibly probe the profundities of the new electrical science? Indeed, his contemporary and great opponent—the learned Abbé Nollet in Paris—was (at first!) convinced that no such *American* philosopher could possibly exist. He was a fiction fabricated by his enemies to torment him!

More persistent has been the assessment of Franklin's experiments in electricity as crude and qualitative, lacking proper instruments and therefore quantitative significance, successful only because of the simplicity of the phenomena he examined. What lack of appreciation of history and misunderstanding of the true nature of scientific discovery this betrays! The simplicity was not in the phenomena: these were attended by all the baffling complexities, all the capriciousness of real phenomena. It was the art of the experimenter that extracted from them the "simple" principles and made the experiments seem simple—afterwards! Simplicity was the antithesis of *confusion*, not of subtlety!

To find a simple uniform principle underlying and buried in the bewildering variety of detail was precisely Franklin's great achievement. It was the sort of principle which Franklin could recognize and appreciate *a priori*; and one whose role and significance in electricity he could demonstrate. His view of Nature, influenced no doubt by the current fashionable expositions of a simplified philosophical Newtonianism, included notions of permanent immutable "elements," the work of the great Architect and Lawgiver; and of endless variety and change in the actual world which only disguised, but did not destroy, the underlying permanence and order. In any event, he seems from the outset to have introduced this notion—of something *conserved*—into his interpretations. Very soon he made it the basic axiom of his electrical theory. The famous "single fluid" hypothesis—the subject of more than a century of controversy—is really a side issue. Conservation of two (or more) fluids could also have worked (as many later appreciated), but this would not only have complicated matters unnecessarily; it would also have made the significance of the essential feature—*conservation*—harder to perceive and therefore harder to demonstrate. One fluid was enough; a second would have been not so much wrong as superfluous.

A basic experimental language—with its own grammar and idiom—was essential both to demonstrate the principle and to pursue its implications. Stripped of some of its more archaic terminology—the electric "fires" and "atmospheres," the "pores" and the "effluvia," Franklin's basic grammar ran thus: ordinary "unelectrified" objects which produced no spark, shock, or attraction and repulsion were identified as bodies in which the electricity was in "equilibrium." Electrification consisted, then, in disturbing the equilibrium—not by *creating* electricity but by transferring it from one body to another, thereby producing a deficit $(-)$ in one and an excess $(+)$ in the other. Conversely, electricity is never destroyed; rather, equilibrium may be restored by the passage of electricity from the region of excess to that of deficit, and this may be signaled by the familiar spark or shock. It could be facilitated by the particular technique of discharge to or from sharp points.

This is Franklin's basic grammar. His experiments are models of clear conception, keen observation, and cogent analysis. For a century or so, since the experiments of Burgomeister von Guericke, glass, and many other materials, had been rubbed and the sparks and shocks witnessed. The new and decisive feature which Franklin introduces and exploits is the electrical isolation of both producer of electricity (silk, glass, and all) and its recipient. Here for the first time are deliberately arranged, clearly recognized and exploited "closed" electrical systems. For the rest, the experimental technique is ludicrously simple: one person standing on wax rubs the tube; another, similarly isolated, "draws the fire." A third, standing on the floor (unisolated), acts simply to register the extent of electrification of each of the other two, by taking a spark with his knuckle.

This procedure of "isolation" is soon skillfully exploited in Franklin's masterly elucidation of the new sensation: the Leyden jar. Born out of attempts to *store* (or literally to bottle!) electricity, and conceived of as such, its extraordinary powers were, and would have remained, a mystery. It was Franklin who perceived, clearly demonstrated, and emphatically asserted that there was *no* net charge of electricity in the Leyden jar—just the close proximity of a surplus on one side and a deficiency on the other! Wherein lay the particular merit of such a proximate combination? After all, *all* unelectrified bodies contain immense quantities of such surpluses and deficits in close proximity. This was a more subtle matter for which Franklin invented his own peculiar detailed theory (which later experiments compelled him to modify) based on the mystique of glass. Franklin's studies of the Leyden jar, so central in the development of his ideas, provided a splendid illustration of both the power and the limitations of his experimental procedures and electrical principles.

In experiments with the original, hand-held, water-filled Leyden jar, he showed by decanting the water from a "charged" jar that the electricity did not reside in the water, but rather that the electrification was, seemingly, associated with, and retained by, the glass separating the water from his hand outside. "Thus, the whole force of the bottle, and power of giving a shock, is in the *glass itself*; the nonelectrics [i.e., conductors] in contact with the two surfaces, serving only to *give* and *receive* to and from the several parts of the glass; that is, to give on one side and take away from the other."

But how could he be sure that the form of the glass, or indeed the nature of the conductors—the water, hand, etc.—did not play a significant role?

> To find, then, whether glass had this property merely as glass, or whether the form contributed anything to it, we took a pane of sash-glass, and, laying it on the hand, placed a plate of lead on its upper surface; then electrified that plate, and bringing a finger to it there was a spark and shock. We then took two plates of lead of equal dimensions, but less than the glass by two inches every way, and electrified the glass between them, by electrifying the uppermost lead; then separated the glass from the lead, in doing which that little fire might be in the lead was taken out, and the glass being touched in the electrified parts with a finger, afforded only very small pricking sparks, but a great number of them might be taken from different places. Then dexterously placing it again between the leaden plates, and completing a circle between the two surfaces, a violent shock ensued. Which demonstrates the power to reside in glass as glass.

Franklin's detecting instrument—his finger taking the spark and shock—was certainly rudimentary. Even his most sensitive detector—his suspended cork-balls—were capable of responding only to strongly charged objects (corresponding to potential differences of several kilovolts). Surely more sensitive and precise instruments would have enhanced his experiments, endowed them with more quantitative significance? Let us see then what might have ensued had Franklin performed this Leyden jar experiment using a more sensitive electrometer or gold-leaf electroscope, which proved such valuable tools a few decades later.

Here I use a demountable Leyden jar, similar to Franklin's glass and lead plate, but for convenience, cup-shaped, rather than plane. (It is a contemporary product made, I believe, to demonstrate Franklin's experiments, and assuming perhaps that their outcome is known!) We have a pair of such Leyden jars. Each comprises an outer metal cup (grounded), an insulating lining, and an inner metal cup. We charge the first, strongly, sufficient to give a shock, or to show on this crude detector—a suspended cork-ball, à-la-Franklin. The other jar is uncharged. Now we remove the inner metal cups from both jars and replace each by that from the other jar. We find—just as in Franklin's experiment—that the electrification does *not* follow the "charged" conductor, but remains with the insulator. Now we repeat the experiment, but with a much smaller charge, one which gives a barely perceptible shock but is readily detected by this gold-leaf electroscope. Now, in contrast, the electrification seems to follow not the insulator, but the conductors!

Perhaps Franklin was not completely and blissfully ignorant of the qualitative differences that could result from experimenting at widely different levels of electrification. (We notice how he seemed content to treat "what little fire might be in the lead" as insignificant!) Yet he does arrive at a simple, definite, and essentially quantitative conclusion. This he does not by accumulating a mass of detailed (and possibly meaningless) numerical data, but rather by multiplying the variety of experiments which can guide his perceptions towards what is significant. He neither pursues nor claims a numerical precision, one that could be illusory where the particular circumstances are little understood. As for enhanced sensitivity, the perceptions of the experimenter, like those of the nervous system, can suffer by being too indiscriminantly sensitive.

At the level of electrification which he employed, Franklin could find a certain uniformity which was, to him, significant. To relate his experiments to his general principles, he characteristically clothed the abstractions of the latter in picturesque detail. To be sure, this led him to an untenable, one might even say naive, view of the role of the glass (insulator) in the Leyden jar; but was not this a small price to pay for the discovery of the conservation of electric charge?

Franklin's discoveries and speculations greatly impressed the cognoscenti of the Royal Society in 1750, but the full impact of Franklin's electricity—on both the philosophical and lay world—came a year or two later, when the precise procedures he had laid down (based on a bold extrapolation of his experiments and his own principles, of course) for demonstrating the identity of lightning and electricity were successfully exploited; first by Dalibard at Paris. Franklin's fame spread rapidly; "Franklinism" and the "Philadelphia Experiments" became household terms.

In 1753, the Royal Society awarded him its highest scientific honor, the Copley Medal.

The law of conservation of charge, the principle of the Leyden jar (condenser), and the invention of the lightning conductor epitomize Franklin's lasting contributions to science. But for Franklin himself, in his own time and in his own wide circle of friends, electricity was but one part of his boundless interest in matters scientific. On the basis of theoretical principles and practical experiments, he designed and made fuel-saving fireplaces; devised cures for smoking chimneys and draughty rooms; proposed improved techniques of navigation; studied the resistance to motion of boats in canals, the cultivation of grass, and the husbandry of hedges; and he was actively involved in the promotion of silk production in America. His inventions ranged from a novel musical instrument, his "Armonica," to bifocal spectacles; his enquiries from the generation of cold by evaporation, and the causes of the common cold. His eminently sensible views on the heating and circulation of the blood, on gallstones, on lead poisoning, and atmospheric pollution, etc., earned the widespread respect of professional physicians.

Nothing, at any time or place, that caught Franklin's keen eye— and little escaped it—failed to stir his mind and as often as not move him to experiment.

And what matter if his boundless curiosity and endless speculation often outstripped his ability to resolve the innumerable problems which he energetically pursued? Posing questions seemed to give him as much satisfaction as answering them; and the answers he does essay are so often, as he readily acknowledges "but conjectures and suppositions, which ought always to give place when careful observation militates against them." Although Franklin can, and does, propound what he believes to be true with forceful eloquence, there is no trace of stubbornness in his defense of a belief simply because it is his own. Indeed, he makes a virtue of his errors and limitations: "A frank acknowledgement of one's ignorance is not only the easiest way to get rid of a difficulty, but the likeliest way to obtain information, and I therefore practice it."

With this complete unconcern about discovering, or disclosing his own ignorance, he can embark on a long trail of enquiry, seeking to learn from every circumstance and opportunity and listening to all who can proffer information, with little apparent concern about reaching the final destination of a definite conclusion.

A fascinating example of such a roving enquiry is one prompted by a chance observation on board ship between England and America. He describes the incident in a letter to his London friend, Dr. John Pringle:

> During our passage to Madeira, the weather being warm and the cabin windows constantly open for the benefit of air, the candles at night flared and run very much, which was an inconvenience. At Madeira, we got oil to burn, and with a common glass tumbler or beaker, slung in wire, and suspended to the ceiling of the cabin, and a little wire hoop for the wick, furnished with corks to float on the oil, I made an Italian lamp, that gave us very good light all over the table. The glass at bottom contained water to about one third of its height; another third was taken up with oil; the rest was left empty that the sides of the glass might protect the flame from the wind. There is nothing remarkable in all this; but what follows is particular. At supper, looking on the lamp, I remarked, that though the surface of the oil was perfectly tranquil, and duly preserved its position and distance with regard to the brim of the glass, the water under the oil was in great commotion, rising and falling in irregular waves, which continued during the whole evening. The lamp was kept burning as a watch-light all night, till the oil was spent, and the water only remained. In the morning I observed, that though the motion of the ship continued the same, the water was now quiet, and its surface as tranquil as that of the oil had been the evening before. At night again, when oil was put upon it, the water resumed its irregular motions, rising in high waves almost to the surface of the oil, but without disturbing the smooth level of that surface. And this was repeated every day during the voyage.

Franklin can scarcely believe his eyes; but what he cannot understand he does not forget. At home, on dry land, he soon reproduces the effect. It is indeed striking, as you can see by a reproduction of his experiments. Ten years later, Franklin is still puzzling over what he recalls as the "wonderful quietness of oil on agitated waters." But in the meantime, he has enquired far and wide about what may be similar oil-on-water phenomena, and some earlier observations and recollections of his own have been evoked. He recalls Pliny's mention of divers stilling water by oil; and his earlier experience at sea, in 1757, when he noticed that the wakes of some among a large fleet of ships were remarkably smooth. On enquiring, the captain told him that "the cooks have, I suppose, been just emptying greasy water through the scuppers." Another "old captain" informs him that the fishermen in Bermuda, and in Lisbon, practice calming ruffled water with oil, and confirms Pliny's account of the same practice by Mediterranean divers. From "a gentleman from Rhode Island" he learns that "the harbour of Newport was ever smooth while any whaling vessels were in it; which probably arose from hence, that the blubber which they sometimes bring loose in the hold, or the leakage of their barrels, might afford some oil, to mix with that water, which from time to time they pump out to keep their vessel free."

All this leads, inevitably, to experiment—performed on a pond on Clapham Common, London—which not only confirms the reality of the phenomenon, but leads to a new surprise—the remarkable spreading power of oil. A mere teaspoonful covers some half-an-acre of water!

Thereafter, Franklin tells us, whenever he went into the country he took with him "a little oil in the upper hollow of [his] bamboo cane" so that he can share the surprise and the pleasure of the experiment with others. The phenomenon of the swinging lamp which started all this train of enquiry remained unforgotten but unexplained; or Franklin remains skeptical of the proffered explanations:

> I have shown this experiment to a number of ingenious persons. Those who are but slightly acquainted with the principles of hydrostatics, and are apt to fancy immediately that they understand it, and readily attempt to explain it; but their explanations have been different, and to me not very intelligible. Others, more deeply skilled in those principles, seem to wonder at it, and promise to consider it.

Franklin made no pretensions of deep learning in fluid mechanics or of the mathematical subtleties involved. Of his theory of storms he confessed: "If my hypothesis is not the truth, it is at least as naked. For I have not, with some of our learned moderns, disguised my nonsense in Greek, cloyed it in algebra, or adorned it in fluxions."

But he was not unappreciative of the power of mathematics. When young, he had invented a mathematics of his own: a "moral or prudential algebra" in which, as in his electricity, an accounting could be made of good (positive) and bad (negative), and by their mutual cancellation, the net result estimated. And in later years, he displays, in his reply to Madame Brillon's accusations of inconstancy, a mellow sense of mathematical nicety. It is "as plain as Euclid that who ever was constant to several persons was more constant than he who was only constant to one."

Remarkably, this irrepressible interest in science continued unabated even as Franklin became ever more engrossed and burdened by affairs of state. From oil on troubled water, he could turn readily to political diplomacy; from the nature of atmospheric storms to warnings and prognostications of impending political disaster. Experimental science and practical politics, natural philosophy and political philosophy seemed barely separate.

Benjamin Franklin was the supreme amateur. Balzac could sum him up as the inventor of the lightning rod, the political hoax ("canard"), and the republic! His only profession—as he described himself in his own epitaph—was that of "printer." For the rest, he did what interested him, and what he believed necessary and good. He wrote and spoke as he felt, and what he felt to be true. Not a professional—either in science or letters or politics—he had no professional reputation to establish or to defend. He probably held more public offices than anyone before him, or since, and yet he could justly claim: "I never did, directly or indirectly, solicit any man's vote." His preeminence as a statesman was unquestioned, and yet it was through anonymous satire that he delivered some of his most influential political thrusts.

His electrical discoveries and ideas had immense influence; his theories were, for decades, exploited and developed by many who followed him; yet he could honestly assert: "I have never entered into any controversy in defense of my philosophical opinions. If they are right, trial and experience will support them; if wrong they ought to be refuted and rejected. . . . I have no private interest in the reception of my inventions, having never made, nor proposed to make, the least profit of them."

This willingness to let deeds speak for themselves, and to use words to convey ideas rather than to solicit acquiescence, is the more remarkable in one so gifted in the powers of persuasion. Franklin possessed this power to the highest degree—yet he never abused it. In all his writing, whether he is explaining some simple matter to the young Mary Stevenson, or to the sophisticated Madame Helvetius, whether expounding his views to the savants of his day, or denouncing the policies of King George's haughty ministers, or musing in his own autobiography, it is always the same voice: Franklin expressing lucidly, forcibly, but with natural ease, what he thinks and believes.

No pleading, no pretensions, no puffery. His experimental philosophy—his dialogue with Nature—has the same essential character. He does not try to teach Nature, to impose his views on it, but to converse with and learn from it. He has no illusions about the difference between a dialogue with Nature and a political debate. Yet in his approach to both, it is the same Franklin. It is not that he brings to his politics the standards of impartial truth he has learned from science. Rather he brings to both—science and politics—his own incomparable blend of honesty, insight, and imagination. He would have agreed with Bacon that "Nature to be commanded must first be obeyed."

A like motto would serve him in government, as a public servant: a people to be governed must first be served. In science one must assume that Nature already knows what we are trying to learn: in politics he would advise a similar stance. He would take his cue from Pope's lines: "Men must be taught as if you taught them not, / And things unknown, proposed as things forgot."

Franklin lived his philosophy; and his philosophy was a practical one. If truth was his goal, honesty was his constant guide that might with good fortune lead him there. Honest, practical utility prompts alike much of his scientific enterprise and his industrious diplomacy, but the ideals of scientific truth and social justice are never far absent. And if truth and justice are unattainable ideals, there remains the more modest task of combating error and injustice; in Michael Faraday's more solemn expression, "the high and pure philosophic desire to remove error as well as discover truth."

Franklin was no idealist, yet stirred by ideals; no pragmatist, though all he did was stamped with purpose. The truth was for him a natural by-product of honesty as the ideal was of the practical. He allegorizes his philosophy in a parable of a hard-working, prosperous farmer imparting his final advice to his heir: "My son, I gave thee now a valuable parcel of land; I assure you I have found a considerable quantity of gold by digging there. Thee mayest do the same: but thee must carefully observe this, *Never dig more than plough deep.*"

Finally, there is Franklin's own brand of humor and humility! The scale of his achievements rendered modesty unfitting and cynicism implausible. Yet he was quite aware of the world's and his own limitations. Poor Richard warns that "in a corrupt age, that putting the world in order would breed confusion." Truth (and justice) must remain unattainable ideals; but there was no monopoly of honesty (or honest purpose). Never did Franklin assume that office, rank, or reputation entitled his views to more respect than did their intrinsic merit. In the presumption of omnipotence he saw evil only compounded by the added conceit of omniscience. Nor did Franklin confuse the right to speak freely with the demand to be heard.

Minister Turgot portrays him, with Latin verve: "He snatched fire from the Heavens and the Sceptre from the Tyrant's hand." His Scottish admirer, Lord Kames, pays tribute in more sombre words: "A man who makes a great figure in the learned world, and one who would make a still greater figure, were virtue as much regarded in this declining age as knowledge." For Franklin himself, the search for knowledge was also the path to virtue. And just as at times we err in judgment so also we stray from the path of true virtue. Franklin was certainly no saint!

Franklin's style of experimental exploration, its spontaneity, its unsophisticated light-heartedness, its gaiety and its deceptive simplicity, even naivete, all seem to belong to a bygone age. His effluvia, electric fire, and atmospheres, his sparks and shocks—all are now historical curiosities. But his law of conservation of electricity—whether in its simple Franklinian form, or embodied in some highly sophisticated abstraction—remains: challenged from time to time, but still part of the bedrock of basic principles. But that is not the whole—or perhaps even the major part of Franklin's philosophical legacy. The apparent paradox of Franklin, at once the pragmatist and the idealist, the man of the world and the workshop, equally at home and at ease with printers, politicians, and philosophers, lies deep in Franklin's philosophy. If in the probing of Nature, truth remains undiscovered, if in the affairs of nations the final tasks remain unresolved, then this at least—or at best?—we may learn: the truth about ourselves!

So, of science he could write: "If there is no other Use discovered for Electricity, this, however, is something considerable: *that it may help make a vain man humble.*" And of politics: "The first mistake in public business is the going into it."

From innumerable finite accomplishments—practical, political, and philosophical—derive his assurance and authority; from the awareness of boundless unattained ideals—his humility. "Knowledge is proud that it has learnt so much / Wisdom is humble that it knows no more." Franklin's younger contemporary, William Cowper, might have written the lines for him!

But it is with his own clear voice that we should part company with Benjamin Franklin. His deeds were numberless, but his ideals he could sum up in three words: Truth, Sincerity, and Integrity.

5

Gender and Career Choices: The Case
of Benjamin Franklin's Sister

ANNE SCOTT

• *The importance of one's sex in determining the career opportunities of a lifetime is very well illustrated in this remarkable little essay. A younger sister of famed statesman and
inventor Benjamin Franklin, Jane Franklin Mecom grew up
in the same family, the same house, and the same city as the
boy who was to become the "first citizen of America." As
you read the story of Jane's marriage, when she was only a
teenager, and of her struggle to overcome persistent bad luck,
you might reflect on the frequent tragedies which punctuated
the lives of females two centuries ago. Seven of Jane Mecom's
twelve children died at an early age, and two of the four
grandchildren she raised did not reach adulthood. That this
remarkable individual maintained her sanity and her spirit
throughout her vale of tears is testimony to the strength,
faith, and resolve of generations of women who overcame
similarly devastating reverses. As Jane Mecom wrote toward
the end of her own life, "Every won has ther Trobles."*

Jane, youngest of Josiah Franklin's seventeen children, was born in
1712, six years after Benjamin. Because in later life she would become
her brother's favorite correspondent, we know more about her than
about any other woman of her social class in eighteenth-century Boston.

She was eleven when Benjamin made his famous getaway, breaking
his apprenticeship and embarking on the legendary career which would
make him the archetypal self-made American. In old age both looked
back with favor upon their early childhood: "It was indeed a Lowly

Dwelling we were brought up in but we were fed Plentifully, made comfortable with fire and cloathing, had sildom any contention among us, but all was Harmony: Especially betwen the Heads—and they were Universally Respected, & the most of the famely in good Reputation, this is still happier liveing than multituds Injoy."

Even allowing for the rosy glow the passage of time creates, the recollections of both brother and sister suggest that the parents were remarkable people, and that such education as children get at home, both had gotten. The things Jane Mecom singled out for recollection were central values all her life: a good reputation and the respect of the community. She always tried to "live respectable," and her fondest hope was that her children should do so.

At the age when her brother had run away to begin his climb to fame, Jane Franklin married a neighbor who was a saddler. Her brother sent a spinning wheel, an appropriate gift for a seventeenth child who could expect no dowry. The best efforts of both spouses would be required to keep up with a growing family, as—for a quarter of a century—every second year brought a new baby. Three died in infancy, but nine survived to be fed, clothed, and trained for self-support.

By the time we catch another glimpse of Jane Mecom she was already thirty, living in a house owned by her father, taking in lodgers, and caring for her aging parents. Her twelve-year-old son was learning the saddler's trade, and she was searching for appropriate apprenticeships for the younger ones. Between caring for parents, children, lodgers, and her husband's shop it is no wonder that the only written word of hers which survives from this period is a postscript to a letter her mother wrote to Benjamin. His letters to her began a pattern which would last a lifetime, as he spoke of sending "a few Things that may be of some Use perhaps in your Family."

His help was more than financial. Busy making his own way in Philadelphia, he took time to find an apprenticeship for his namesake, Benny Mecom, who gave some promise of talents similar to his own. There were problems "such as are commonly incident to boys of his years," although, Franklin added, "he has many good qualities, for which I love him." Diligence was not one of those qualities, and Jane Mecom was deeply concerned lest Benny never learn to work. He never did, at least not steadily, and would continue to cause his mother anxiety as long as he lived.

We get our next clear glimpse of Jane Mecom when she was fifty-one and entertaining her brother in her own house. While he was there, she enjoyed what would ever after be her measure of "suitable Conversation," and shone, however briefly, in the reflected glory of Dr. Franklin as Boston admirers paid court to him at her house. The fact that he chose to domicile himself with the Mecoms, rather than with the far more affluent and equally welcoming "cousen Williams," says something about the quality of her conversation, or, perhaps, about his sensitivity to her feelings.

That interval of pleasure was brief. Four of the twelve Mecom children were already dead; now Sarah, at twenty-seven a "Dear and Worthy child," died, leaving a husband and four children who promptly moved into Jane Mecom's house. Within six months two of the four grandchildren were dead. She was still grieving for them when Edward Mecom, her husband of thirty-eight years, also died. She wrote one of the two comments about him to be found in any of her letters: "It pleased God to call my Husband out of this Troblesom world where he had Injoyed Little and suffered much by Sin & Sorrow." Two years later she lost her youngest and favorite, Polly, at eighteen: "Sorrows roll upon me like the waves of the sea. I am hardly allowed time to fetch my breath. I am broken with breach upon breach, and I have now, in the first flow of my grief, been almost ready to say 'What have I more?' But God forbid, that I should indulge that thought. . . . God is sovereign and I submit."

In 1766 she was fifty-five. Of five surviving children the oldest was thirty-four and the youngest twenty-one, but none was in a position to support a widowed mother. Two sons had been bred to the saddler's trade; one had died and the other gone to sea. Peter, a soap-boiler like his grandfather, showed signs of the mental illness which would eventually incapacitate him, and the feckless Benjamin was not earning enough to support his own wife and children. Her son-in-law Flagg was an unskilled workman, hard put to take care of his two children. The one daughter who still lived with her was a melancholy and sickly young woman.

Jane Mecom's thoughts turned, therefore, to self-support. She continued to take in lodgers, and her brother sent from England a small stock of trading goods which arrived just as Bostonians decided to boycott English goods in protest of the Stamp Act. Poverty, she concluded, "is Intailed on my famely."

She was acutely aware of her dependence on her brother's help. She tried to repay him with reports of life in Boston. "The whol conversation of this Place turns upon Politices and Riligous contryverces," she wrote, adding that her own sentiments were for peace. With his reply he sent her a set of his philosophical papers, which she proudly read.

Somehow in 1769 she contrived a trip to Philadelphia, where Franklin's wife and daughter found her "verey a greabel"—so much so that he was moved to suggest, from London, that she consider staying on permanently. But Boston was home, and back she went into the midst of the rising conflict with Great Britain.

Her brother, though thoroughly engrossed in the same conflict in London, took time to write Jane Mecom asking for detailed instructions as to the making of "crown soap," a family secret which he feared might be lost if it were not preserved for the next generation. Here at last was something she could do in return for all his help; her instructions were given in minute detail.

At about this time her letters began to grow longer and more revealing. Perhaps her visit to Deborah Franklin had reduced her awe of her famous brother; perhaps confidence in her own capacities was growing. Whatever the reason, she began to speak more freely, range more widely, and fill out—for us—the scanty self-portrait belatedly begun.

An admirer of Thomas Hutchinson and a lover of peace, Jane Mecom was no early patriot. By 1774, however, "Proflegate soulders," making trouble and harassing citizens on the streets of Boston, pushed her closer to the rebel position. The battle of Lexington finished what the soldiers had begun, as she locked her house, packed such goods as she could carry, and took refuge in Rhode Island.

In some ways the war changed her life for the better. Catherine Ray Greene, with whom she stayed at first, became her good friend. Her [Jane's] granddaughter, Jenny Flagg, married Elihu Greene, brother of General Nathanael Greene, a solid farmer, merchant, and enterpreneur. A man of his standing could well have demanded a dowry, but his willingness to marry Jenny for love marked a change in the hitherto unbroken stream of Mecom bad luck.

In the fall of 1774 Franklin came home after a decade in England, and not long after took his sister for a prolonged stay in Philadelphia. His wife, Deborah, had died, and Jane was able to be helpful to him until he went off to France. In two years General William Howe's decision to occupy Philadelphia sent her back to Rhode Island to her granddaughter's house, where she was "much Exposed & . . . under constant Apprehensions" that the British would invade.

Yet the British were not as troublesome to her as a personal crisis brought on by wartime inflation. The country woman who cared for her son Peter suddenly demanded more money for that service than Jane Mecom had or could see any way to get. Dependence on her brother was galling enough when he anticipated her needs; now she had to ask for help. Her spirits felt "so deprest" that she could scarcely write, but what else could she do?

The war had disrupted communication, and her letter was a long time reaching him. Meanwhile, relief came in a painful guise: Peter died. Accustomed as she was to accepting God's will, Jane Mecom reflected that Peter had been "no comfort to any won nor capable of injoying any Himself for many years." His death was a blessing.

But at the same time she had heard nothing for five months from her daughter Jane Collas in Boston and began to worry lest this last remaining child might be going the way of her brothers into insanity. Apologizing for burdening a busy and important man, she wrote her fears to Franklin: "It gives some Relief to unbousom wons self to a dear friend as you have been & are to me."

Her daughter was, it turned out, physically rather than mentally ill, but sick or well she was never able to live up to her mother's standards of energy and enterprise. "You say you will endeavour to correct all your faults," Jane Mecom wrote in 1778 when Jane Collas was already in her thirties, and proceeded to outline in some detail what those faults were: a tendency to look on the dark side of "God's Providence," an inclination to despair and to extravagance, laziness, and a lack of ingenuity in working to meet her material needs, an unseemly fondness for a great deal of company. She also tended to lie abed late, which her mother found "a trouble to me on many accounts." To top it off, she aspired to gentility without the means to support her aspiration—a tendency Jane Mecom scorned whenever she encountered it.

Nine children had survived infancy, and none had fulfilled their mother's hopes. Most had died in early adulthood. Benjamin simply disappeared during the battle of Trenton, and no trace of him was ever found. Peter's tragic end has already been noted. The fate of her children pushed Jane Mecom to a rare moment of questioning God's will: "I think there was hardly Ever so unfortunate a Famely. I am not willing to think it is all owing to misconduct. I have had some children that seemed to be doing well till they were taken off by Death." But there was nothing to be done. One must accept these things or go mad.

In the late 1770s the long train of bereavement, displacement, and struggle abated for a while. Her granddaughter Jenny Greene, with whom she was living, was a most satisfactory young person whose conversation and attention to her comfort she much appreciated, and whose husband she respected. Though there was no neighbor for two miles, many visitors dropped in. She herself never left home unless someone sent a carriage (the Greenes owning none) since "I hant courage to ride a hors." She made and sent to Franklin several batches of crown soap, which he wanted for his friends in France, took care of Jenny Greene in her successive lyings-in, helped with the babies, supervised the household, and, from time to time, sold "some little matter" from the small store of goods she had brought from Boston in 1775. "My time seems to be filled up as the Famely I am in Increases fast," she wrote. She was sixty-eight and very energetic, though "as I grow older I wish for more Quiet and our Famely is more Incumbered as we have three children Born since I came & tho they give grat Pleasure . . . yet the Noise of them is sometimes troblesom." She knew "but little how the world goes Except seeing a Newspaper sometimes which contains Enough to give Pain but little satisfaction while we are in Armes against each other." In spite of the inflation and the losses the Greenes were suffering as many of their ships were captured, her life was pleasanter than it had been since childhood. "I contineu very Easey and happy hear," she wrote in 1781, "have no more to trroble me than what is Incident to human Nature & cant be avoided in any Place, I wrote now in my own litle chamber the window opening on won of the Pleasantest prospects in the country the Birds singing about me and nobod up in the house near me to Desturb me."

Life had taught Jane Mecom to be wary when things were going well. Ten months after that happy note her granddaughter died, giving birth to the fourth child in four years, and at seventy Jane Mecom was suddenly again the female head of a household of young children who needed, she thought, "some person more lively and Patient to watch over them continualy"; but since there was no one else, she did it anyway. Fortunately she found them a comfort as she grieved for her beloved grandchild, a sacrifice to the age's custom of unbroken childbearing. She was too busy to pine, though the war had cut off her communication with Franklin for three years.

His first postwar letter included a "grat, very grat, Present," for which she thanked him extravagantly, adding that his generosity would enable her to live "at Ease in my old Age (after a life of Care Labour & Anxiety)."

By 1784 she was back in Boston, in a house long owned by her brother, where she was able to "live all ways Cleen and Look Decent." It was a great comfort. She had leisure to read and write, a minister she respected with whom to discuss theology and other things, the care and companionship of her granddaughter Jenny Mecom, the regular attention of her nephew-in-law Jonathan Williams. Her grandchildren and great-grandchildren were often a source of pride and pleasure.

One grandchild, Josiah Flagg, turned up in Philadelphia and, as she saw it, presumed on his relationship to persuade Franklin to take him on as a secretary. He beseeched his grandmother to conceal the fact that he, Josiah, had once been a shoemaker, thus bringing down on himself the scorn she reserved for false pride. She lectured him severely, betraying trepidation lest her demanding relatives threaten her warm relationship with her brother. Fortunately Josiah turned out to be an excellent penman and behaved well in the Franklin family.

With her brother back in Philadelphia, correspondence quickened. He was still concerned that someone in the family be trained to carry on the tradition of the crown soap. Might she teach the younger Jonathan Williams, or even Josiah Flagg, how to make it? She would think about it. She had thought earlier of teaching her son-in-law Peter Collas, whose difficulties in earning a living had become almost ludicrous. Whenever he took berth on a ship, it was promptly captured. But she had decided that the soap required a man of "Peculiar Genius" and that Collas was not. Meanwhile she continued to make the soap herself, sending batch after batch to Franklin.

He felt the urge for some "cods cheeks and sounds," a favorite New

England delicacy. She managed to acquire a keg to send him. She wished him well in the enterprise of the federal convention, and when the Constitution arrived in Boston she reported that while some quarrelsome spirits opposed it, those of "Superior Judgement" were going to support it.

She assured him that she followed his advice about taking exercise and walked even when a chaise was available, "but I am so weak I make but a Poor Figure in the Street." She had her chamber painted and papered against the day she might be confined to it.

A ship captain friend took a favorable report of her to Philadelphia, for which she was grateful: "The Gratest Part of my time when I am sitting at home I am apt to Imagine as Samson did when He lost his Hare, that I can Arise & Shake my Self & Go forth as at other times but on Tryal Like him I am wofully disapointed & find my Feet cripling & my Breath short, but I am still chearful for that is my Natural Temper."

In January 1788, replying to his request for a "very peticular" account of how she lived, she provided a detailed description:

> I have a good clean House to Live in my Grandaughter constantly to atend me to do whatever I desier in my own way & in my own time, I go to bed Early lye warm & comfortable Rise Early to a good Fire have my Brakfast directly and Eate it with a good Apetite and then Read or Work or what Els I Pleas, we live frugaly Bake all our own Bread, brew small bear, lay in a little cyder, Pork, Buter, &c. & suply our selves with Plenty of other nesesary Provision Dayly at the Dore we make no Entertainments, but some Times an Intimate Acquaintance will come in and Pertake with us the Diner we have Provided for our selves & a Dish of Tea in the After Noon, & if a Friend sitts and chats a litle in the Evening we Eate our Hasty Puding (our comon super) after they are gone; It is trew I have some Trobles but my Dear Brother Does all in His Power to Aleviat them by Praventing Even a wish, that when I Look Round me on all my Acquaintance I do not see won I have reason to think Happier than I am and would not change my neighbour with my Self where will you Find one in a more comfortable State as I see Every won has ther Trobles and I sopose them to be such as fitts them best & shakeing off them might be only changing for the wors.

Six more years of life remained to her. The new Constitution was inaugurated, George Washington took office, merchants and politicians concerned themselves with their own and the nation's prosperity, foreign conflicts flamed and threatened. Jane Mecom, for her part, worried about Benjamin Franklin's illness with "the stone" and prayed for his tranquillity in the face of pain. Their correspondence ranged around topics mostly personal and family, and upon reflections on life as they had lived it. "I do not Pretend to writ about Politics," she said, "tho I Love to hear them."

Franklin's death in 1790 was a blow, but she was now seventy-eight herself and prepared to be philosophical about this, as she saw it, temporary separation from her best friend. In his will he provided for her, and when she died four years later this woman who had lived so frugally was able to leave an estate of a thousand pounds to Jane Collas (in trust—she still worried about her daughter's extravagance!) and to her fifteen grandchildren and great-grandchildren.

When the historians came to treat the years covered by her life, they dwelt on wars and politics, on the opening of land and trade and manufacture, on the economic development of a fertile wilderness, the rapid growth in population, the experiment in representative government.

That all these things shaped Jane Mecom's life experience there can be no doubt. Yet life as she perceived it was mostly made up of the small events of which great events are composed: of twenty-one years of pregnancy and childbirth which, multiplied by millions of women, created the rapid population growth; of the hard struggle to "git a living" and to make sure her children were prepared to earn theirs; of the constant procession of death which was the hallmark of her time; of the belated prosperity and happiness which came to her in old age. What added up to a wilderness conquered, a new nation created, was often experienced by individuals as a very hard life somehow survived. It is only in retrospect that all the separate experiences together create something we call "economic development," or "manifest destiny," or—simply—"history."

The events of Jane Mecom's life might have destroyed a weaker person, but some combination of natural resilience, good health, belief in the virtues of diligence, industry, and ingeniousness, and firm faith that God had good reasons for all the pain and sorrow which befell her carried her through. Perhaps her final judgment on the whole experience was summed up in that sentence: "Every won has ther Trobles and I sopose them to be such as fitts them best & shakeing off them might be only changing for the wors."

In chapter three of Virginia Woolf's *Room of One's Own* there is a clever and moving fantasy: what if Shakespeare had had a sister as gifted as himself? The end of the fantasy is tragic, for Shakespeare's imaginary sister, born with a great gift, was so thwarted and hindered by the confines of "woman's place" that she killed herself. In Jane Mecom we have a real-life case, for of the sixteen siblings of Benjamin Franklin, she alone showed signs of talent and force of character similar to his. At the age of fifteen one ran off to Philadelphia and by a combination of wit, luck, and carefully cultivated ability to get ahead began his rise to the pinnacle among the Anglo-American intelligentsia. At the same age the other married a neighbor and in a month was pregnant. From that time forward her life was shaped almost entirely by the needs of other people. Like her brother she had a great capacity for growth, though the opportunity came to her late and was restricted by her constant burden of family responsibilities. The Revolution broadened her experience as it did his, yet she was almost never without children to care for, even in her seventies. Her letters showed a steady improvement in vigor of style and even in spelling. Her lively intelligence kept Franklin writing her even when he was very busy. Perhaps she had herself half in mind when she wrote in 1786: "Dr. Price thinks Thousands of Boyles Clarks and Newtons have Probably been lost to the world, and lived and died in Ignorance and meanness, mearly for want of being Placed in favourable Situations, and Injoying Proper Advantages, very few we know is able to beat thro all Impedements and Arive to any Grat Degre of superiority in Understanding."

The "impedements" in her own life had been many, some might have thought insuperable, yet clearly by the age of eighty she had arrived at the "superiority in Understanding" which makes her letters a powerful chronicle of an eighteenth-century life.

6

Land of the Unfree: Legal Limitations on Liberty in Pre-Revolutionary America

LINDA GRANT DE PAUW

• In 1776, representatives of thirteen British colonies in North America boldly affixed their signatures to the Declaration of Independence. Arguing that all men were endowed by their creator with certain "inalienable" rights, they gave liberty as the purpose of the new United States. Based on the theory of natural rights, which had been espoused earlier by John Locke and Jean Jacques Rousseau, the Declaration of Independence is the most important of all American historical documents.

Actually, the notion of freedom was rather new in 1776. Until the twentieth century, in many parts of the world serfs were bound to the land, meaning that they lacked the freedom to come and go as they pleased without undue restraint. Freedom of religion, the right to worship with groups of one's own choosing, was unknown before the Protestant Reformation. The right to vote and to hold office was practically nonexistent before the nineteenth century, as was freedom of speech and of the press. Prior to the Habeas Corpus Act (1679) in England and for centuries thereafter in most countries, a person could be seized or kept in prison indefinitely without trial or hearing.

Even in the United States, long known as "the Land of the Free," the concept of liberty has expanded only gradually. The idea of equality, for example, has come only slowly to be associated with the idea of freedom. And for specific minorities, women and blacks being notable examples, many liberties are seen only as operative for white men. But whatever its shortcomings, the United States has usually come closer to

This article appeared originally in the *Maryland Historical Magazine* 68 (Winter 1973), published by the Maryland Historical Society, Baltimore. Reprinted by permission.

the ideals and spirit of the universal symbol of freedom, the
Statue of Liberty, than have other nations of the world.

The fortune that Thomas Jefferson pledged with his life and sacred honor in support of the declaration that all men are created equal and endowed with inalienable rights to life, liberty, and the pursuit of happiness included, in the summer of 1776, almost two hundred slaves. The incongruity of a slave-owning people basing their Revolution on such exalted doctrines did not escape remark by contemporaries any more than it has escaped notice by historians. "How is it" sneered Samuel Johnson, "that we hear the loudest *yelps* for liberty among the drivers of negroes?" The Loyalist Thomas Hutchinson dryly observed that there seemed to be some discrepancy between the declaration that all men were equal and a practice that deprived "more than a hundred thousand Africans of their rights to liberty."

Even those Englishmen who sympathized with the American cause were repelled by the paradox. "If there be an object truly ridiculous in nature," Thomas Day commented, "it is an American patriot signing resolutions of independence with the one hand, and with the other brandishing a whip over his affrighted slaves." And the patriots themselves were not insensitive to it. "I have sometimes been ready to think," Abigail Adams wrote to her husband, "that the passion for liberty cannot be equally strong in the breasts of those who have been accustomed to deprive their fellow creatures of theirs." Patrick Henry confessed amazement that men as sincerely "fond of liberty" and genuinely religious as himself tolerated slavery. "Would anyone believe," he asked, "I am the master of slaves of my own purchase!"

Historians writing about the age of the American Revolution have tended to ignore the paradox more frequently than they have attempted to resolve it, but in recent years serious attention has been given to the enslaved blacks, and such New Left historians as Jesse Lemish and Staughton Lynd have pointed out the limitations on the rights of such groups as merchant seamen and urban workers. Yet the full magnitude of the paradox is still unmeasured, for it appears that the contradiction between Lockean ideals and social practice in the year 1776 was not only more pronounced than contemporaries and traditional historians described but even exceeds the dimensions suggested by recent historians of the New Left. Had Lockean dicta been applied to all the human beings in British North America on the eve of the Revolution, and had all been permitted to enjoy the natural and legal rights of freemen, it would have been necessary to alter the status of more than 85 percent of the population. In law and in fact no more than 15 percent of the Revolutionary generation was free to enjoy life, liberty, and the pursuit of happiness unhampered by any restraints except those to which they had given their consent.

The unfree of Revolutionary America may be conveniently considered in five categories: Negroes, white servants, women, minors, and propertyless adult white males. These categories overlap and the proportion of the total population falling into each of the categories differed from one part of the country to another. Thus there were proportionately more women in New England than in backcountry North Carolina, many more blacks, proportionally, in Virginia than in New Jersey, and a larger proportion of disfranchised adult white males in South Carolina than in Massachusetts.

It is also true that legal limitations on liberty do not necessarily coincide either with a psychological sense of freedom or with social practices. The unfree were rarely, in fact, exploited to the full limit allowed by law. Nor has there been any attempt in this brief essay to present a precise description of legal status based on the myriad of local traditions, statutes, and common law interpretation. The following summaries claim to be correct in outline, not to have exhausted the complexities of the subject, which are vast and largely unstudied. It is clear, however, that for each of the unfree groups the law placed definite theoretical limits on the rights Locke viewed as inalienable.

The black slaves, the most visible of the colonial unfree, comprised approximately 20 percent of the colonial population, a proportion twice as great as that formed by the black population of the United States today. These slaves were legally chattel property. The law saw no self-evident right to liberty attached to the person of the dark-skinned laborer from Africa, and, indeed, the law had little concern for his right to life. The deliberate murder of a slave was not necessarily a felony in Virginia before the Revolution, for the law assumed that no one would intentionally destroy his own estate. Slaves had no right to hold property of their own and enjoyed the use of no more than the master allowed. As for the third right in Jefferson's trinity, pursuing happiness, if that took the form of taking time off from the master's work, it was a punishable offense.

There were a small number of free blacks in Revolutionary America, most of them in the North. Their status was superior to that of the slave, but they were still limited politically, socially, and economically in all of the colonies. For most legal purposes there was no distinction made between free and enslaved Negroes. They might have some time they could call their own for pursuing happiness, but they were forbidden to pursue it in a tavern. In Rhode Island a free black man could not even purchase a quart of cider.

White servants in colonial America comprised a class perhaps half as large as the slave force but unbalanced in age and sex distribution in favor of young adult males. Their status was superior to that of Negroes but still substantially below that of freemen. In many ways the servant was merely a slave with prospects of eventual freedom and whose entry into his lowly station had been more or less voluntary. When, in November 1775, Lord Dunmore attempted to lure blacks into the British army by offering them freedom as a bounty, the same offer was extended to white servants.

The servant's labor belonged to his master twenty-four hours a day, seven days a week. Like the black slave, he was a chattel. He had no property himself but what his master allowed. He could not marry without his master's permission and, like a black man, he could not drink liquor in a tavern. Running away and disobedience were severely punished, and stories of inhuman cruelty to white servants are common. Like a slave, a white servant could be sold against his will away from his wife and family or seized to satisfy his master's debts. There seems little to recommend the legislation governing servants over that governing blacks—with one exception. White servants, unlike slaves, had personal rights to life and contract rights to a minimum standard of living. They could bring suit to enforce these rights and the courts would enforce them even to the extent of freeing the servant outright.

The legal status of colonial women was determined by the tradition of the British common law with certain modifications forced by pioneer American conditions, most of which were made before the end of the seventeenth century. Blackstone's *Commentaries*, which began to circulate as an admired authority among colonial lawyers in the decade before the Revolution, described a theoretical position for English females that varied substantially from that held by free English men. Under common law, Blackstone taught, a woman ceased to exist if she married, for she and her spouse became one flesh and the flesh was his. She was no longer responsible for her debts or even for all of her personal actions. She had no legal control over any property either inherited or earned. And if her husband judged her disobedient or saucy he could chastise her as he did his children and servants. This was considered proper as he might be held responsible for her misbehavior in cases short of murder and high treason. Although divorce laws were relatively liberal for a time in the seventeenth century, a reaction in the Revolutionary era made divorce, regardless of cause, practically impossible for a woman to obtain.

The status of unmarried women, both widows and spinsters, was considerably better. By a law of 1419 known as "couverte de Baron" an unattached woman, the "Feme Sole," was entitled to engage in business enterprises on her own account. A widow was entitled to one-third of the family estate and might be willed even more. So long as she did not remarry she could invest or dispose of this property as she wished. There was, however, great social pressure on women to marry. Although women made up almost half of the total population when all age groups are included, the sex ratio of men to women in the marriageable age group (i.e., between sixteen and sixty) was extremely high—160.8 men to every 100 women. Consequently spinsters were few and they were generally propertyless dependents in the home of a male relative. Widows commonly remarried before their husbands had been buried a year—unless they were remarkably unattractive, elderly, or poor. Those in the last category, who could not support themselves on one-third of their deceased husband's estate, would be subject to the poor laws unless a male relative could be found to take them in. The poor law prescribed compulsory labor for the poor so that impoverished widows might be bound out to serve as domestics. In Wareham, Massachusetts (admittedly an exceptional case) there was an annual auction of indigent widows.

Americans under the age of twenty-one, a clear majority of the population in 1776, were legal infants, and the right to liberty of such persons was far from self-evident to the founding fathers, although they were aware that it seemed to follow, at least for older children, from the Lockean premises. It would be a mistake to confuse the class of legal minors in Revolutionary America with modern adolescents. Blackstone declared a boy of twelve fit to take an oath of allegiance and a girl of seven ready to be given in marriage. The age of discretion for most purposes fell between seven and fourteen and all children above this age group were subject to capital punishment for felonies and bore most of the responsibilities if not the privileges of adults. Children entered the labor force well before they entered their teens, and they developed a degree of maturity and experience in the world that would be considered unhealthily precocious today. The large number of men in their early twenties who served competently as field officers in the Revolutionary armies and sat in the Continental Congresses could only have appeared in a society that considered teenage boys adults even though it deprived them of full legal rights. Male children of the age of sixteen were taxable and liable for militia duty. And since the population of colonial America was generally young, sixteen being the median age, unfree males between sixteen and twenty-one comprised one quarter of the total taxable male population. In an age when the mortality rates among infants and children were high and when a youth of sixteen had less than an even chance of surviving to the age of thirty, the loss of even a few years of liberty was a significant grievance.

Furthermore, theories of child nurture in colonial days were distinctly grim, based on the still formidable patriarchical traditions that had prescribed death for a "rebellious and incorrigible son." Obedience to parents was a duty imposed by divine as well as human law to be enforced by corporal punishment if necessary. Minors were expected to work for their parents as soon as they could walk, but they had no personal property rights before they came of legal age. Authority over children above ten or fourteen was frequently transferred from the natural parents to a master. The institution of apprenticeship was still viable at the time of the Revolution and was the usual path for a young man who did not intend to become a farmer but wished to learn a trade. Girls might also become apprenticed. Apprenticeship articles were drawn to standards set by colonial legislatures and generally required the consent of the child as well as of his parents. But children of poor or otherwise incompetent parents might be sold against their will to masters who promised, sometimes deceitfully, to provide for them adequately and teach them a trade before they came of age.

Once apprenticed, a child's labor belonged to the master as fully as did that of any servant. Even visits to his own parents could be forbidden and the free-time conduct of apprentices was subject to the same sort of restrictions that applied to adult servants or slaves. Disobedience to a master as to a father could be punished with the whip. If a child came to detest the trade his father apprenticed him to, or if the master failed to make him proficient in the craft, his entire future would be warped, for once of age and free it would be too late to begin again to acquire the skills needed to make a living.

These four groups—Negroes, servants, women, and minors—together comprised approximately 80 percent of the two and a half million Americans in the year 1776. The legal doctrine applied to these classes excluded them from the category of persons who should enjoy the "inalienable rights" of which the Declaration speaks. But perhaps the most significant mark of their unfreedom was their usual lack of a right to vote, for the privilege of consenting to the laws was the essential right of a free man in Lockean theory. Indeed, the very word "enfranchise" was defined in the eighteenth century as the equivalent of the word "emancipate"; it meant "to make free."

Interestingly enough, the prohibition on the suffrage does not appear to have been absolute either in law or in fact for any of the unfree groups. Colonial suffrage legislation tended to be vague. Only Virginia, South Carolina, and Georgia specifically confined the franchise to white voters and there are recorded cases of Negroes, mulattoes, and Indians actually casting ballots. When in 1778 a provision excluding blacks from the suffrage was inserted in the proposed Massachusetts constitution, a citizen observed in the *Independent Chronicle* that "a black, tawny or reddish skin is not so unfavorable in hue to the genuine son of liberty, as a tory complection." Rare instances of bond servants casting votes are known and enough servants presumed to exercise the franchise in Albany, New York, to necessitate their specific exclusion from participation in city elections in 1773.

Only Pennsylvania, Delaware, South Carolina, and Georgia specifically disfranchised females who otherwise qualified as property holders. When Hannah Lee Corbin protested to her brother Richard Henry

Lee in 1778 that Virginia women ought not to be taxed if they had not the right to vote, he replied that "women were already possessed of that right," and, apparently, some women did vote for a time in Virginia as well as in New England and the middle colonies. But these cases were rare and it is significant that Mrs. Corbin did not know she had the franchise until her brother so informed her.

Only six states explicitly stated that voters must be twenty-one years of age (Pennsylvania, South Carolina, Virginia, Connecticut, New York, and North Carolina), and there are recorded cases of young men under legal age occasionally registering their votes.

In all likelihood, however, the liberality of colonial suffrage legislation was due to careless draftsmanship rather than to any desire to permit members of the unfree classes to vote. The intention was to limit the franchise to free, adult, white males and others who voted slipped through by accident as a result of laxity among election inspectors. Indeed, we know of such cases chiefly because they served as grounds for complaint in disputed elections.

A fifth group of colonial Americans, adult white males with little or no property, was deprived of the vote in colonial elections and so fell short of full liberty in the Lockean sense. But they were privileged above the other unfree groups since they were legally entitled to acquire property and were protected from physical abuse except such as was administered by public authority after trial as punishment for offenses against the state. Some of these disfranchised males were idiots, invalids, or residents of workhouses. Others were simply too poor to qualify under the arbitrary property requirements of the various electoral laws. Statistically they are the least significant of the unfree, although they have had more than their share of attention from critics of consensus history. They made up between 5 and 10 percent of the total population. If they are added to the 80 percent of the population in the other unfree categories, which were limited not merely in their political rights but in their rights to personal liberty and property as well, then only 10 to 15 percent of the American population remain to qualify as "freemen" in the fullest sense.

It is curious that this startling statistic has somehow escaped comment by historians. While the enslavement of Negroes and disfranchisement of some adult white males may be noted in passing as undemocratic elements in pre-Revolutionary America, the disfranchisement and worse of the other unfree classes is accepted without remark even in our enlightened age. Thus, Elisha P. Douglass defines democracy in his *Rebels and Democrats* as "a political system in which all adult males enjoyed equal political rights." Robert Brown writes in *Middle-Class Democracy and the Revolution in Massachusetts*, "The only valid approach . . . is to find out how many adult men could vote out of the total adult male population," and he concludes that "if anything with the appearance of a man could vote there was little problem of a restricted electorate." And finally, the author of this paper casually observed in *The Eleventh Pillar*, "The important ratio is that of qualified voters to adult white males."

Today almost 65 percent of the total population is enfranchised and in law, at least, virtually all of the people are secured in property rights and protected from physical abuse by private parties. Yet even our age finds it self-evident that women and young people should have been excluded from colonial political life. Since this is the case, we should not find it difficult to understand how the men of two centuries ago could accept the contradiction between their Lockean principles and their discriminatory practice without too much discomfort.

It would be both uncharitable and simplistic to dismiss the founding fathers as hypocrites because they tolerated this inconsistency. Some conflict between ideal principles and social practice is inevitable if the ideals are at all noble and the society composed of human beings rather than angels. Nor is such contradiction undesirable. Quite the opposite, since it induces men, who will always fall short of perfection in their day to day experience, to consider the possibility of alternative social arrangements superior to their own. Thus John Adams was vastly amused when his Abigail presumed to apply the Revolutionary slogans to the condition of married ladies. But after puzzling over her remarks for a month he realized that, indeed, he could discover no moral foundation for government that would justify the exclusion of any class of people from full participation. Of course it was "impossible," he wrote to James Sullivan, that the principle of consent should ever be carried so far. But the logic was undeniable and if it were followed to its conclusion "women will demand a vote; lads from twelve to twenty-one will think their rights not enough attended to; and every man who has not a farthing, will demand an

equal voice with any other, in all acts of state." Adams seems to have
predicted the long range impact of the Revolutionary doctrine accurately enough.

Again, Patrick Henry, facing up to the contrast between his words
and his practice of keeping slaves, wrote, "I will not, I cannot justify
it. However culpable my conduct, I will so far pay my devoir to virtue, as to own the excellence and rectitude of her precepts, and lament my want of conformity to them."

In the final analysis, however, the contradiction was tolerable to
Americans because they compared the extent of liberty in their society not with the Lockean ideal but with the extent of liberty in other
contemporary or historically known societies. From this perspective
there was no doubt that the Americans of 1776 were remarkably free.
Even the slaves, servants, women, and children of America enjoyed
positions superior to those held by similar classes in other lands and
other times. And surely a land in which more than 10 percent of the
population owned property and had a voice in the government was a
wonder in an age when the civilized world was ruled by hereditary
monarchs and property ownership was a prerogative of aristocrats.
Even in England, where the political liberty of the early eighteenth
century had made her people the envy of Europe, no more than 25
percent of "the active male population" had voted in even the freest
parts of the kingdom—and after the first third of the century even this
electorate had dwindled. Yet, to quote J. H. Plumb, "This was England's vast singularity, a unique situation amongst the major powers
of the world."

Surely the gap that separated American society from the Lockean
ideal was no more impressive than that which separated colonial
American society from the societies of Europe. If freedom had a home
anywhere in the world in the year 1776 it was in the new United
States of America. But if "democracy" implies government by consent of the governed or at least by consent of a majority of those governed and not merely of an adult white male elite, then those historians from Bancroft to Brown who have described American society of
the mid-eighteenth century as "democratic" are simply wrong. The
opinion of Carl Becker and many others that colonial governments
"did in a rough and ready way, conform to the kind of government for

which Locke furnished a reasoned foundation" is vastly overstated. And the attempts of the New Left history to view the American Revolution "from the bottom up" will be superficial so long as "the bottom" is conceived in a way that still excludes the majority of the population.

7

From Confederation to Constitution:

The Revolutionary Context

of the Great Convention

LANCE BANNING

• The decade of the 1780s, and especially the years between
the conclusion of the American Revolution and the adoption
of the Constitution of the United States, has long seemed
among the least interesting periods of our national past. Indeed, how could these years compete in excitement and importance with a successful rebellion against the greatest
empire in the world and the ratification of a framework of
government that has been the envy of democratic peoples.
Sandwiched between two events of such transcendent importance, the Articles of Confederation seemed to represent a
resting period, a transition zone from one great event to the
next.

   Lance Banning urges us to look again at the formative period of the American Constitution. The Articles of Confederation, which were proposed to the states on November 17,
1777, and adopted early in 1781, gave the independent nation
a federal form of government and undermined the notion
that the states were sovereign entities. Although reminding
us of the many accomplishments of the Confederation years,
the essay points out that liberty was in peril only a few years
after the victory at Yorktown. How and why the Constitution emerged is the subject of Banning's thoughtful inquiry.

Most Americans recall our Revolution in decidedly selective ways. As
a people, we are not as eager as we used to be to recollect how truly
revolutionary are our roots. Our Bicentennial celebration, for example,

Reprinted from *This Constitution: A Bicentennial Chronicle,* Spring 1985,
published by Project '87 of the American Historical Association and the
American Political Science Association.

focused overwhelmingly on independence and the war with Britain, not on the genuinely revolutionary facets of the struggle. Too often, we commemorated even independence with hoary myths about tyrannical King George and clever minutemen who used the woods and fences to defeat the British regulars. Perhaps, then, it is not so inexcusable as it would first appear for some Americans to think that Thomas Jefferson wrote the Constitution as well as the Declaration of Independence in 1776. If we think of the American Revolution as no more than a sudden, brave attempt to shake off English rule, perverse consistency leads easily to a mistake that lumps together all the documents and incidents connected with the Founding. For a better understanding, as another Bicentennial approaches, we would do well to fit the Constitution back into the revolutionary process from which it emerged.

As John Adams said, the American Revolution was not the war against Great Britain; it should not be confused with independence. The Revolution started in the people's minds at least ten years before the famous shots at Lexington and Concord. It was well advanced before the colonies declared their independence. It continued for perhaps a quarter of a century after the fighting came to an end. It dominated the entire life experience of America's greatest generation of public men. And it was fully revolutionary in many of the strictest definitions of that term. The men who made it wanted not just independence, but a change that would transform their own societies and set a new example for mankind. They wanted to create, as they put it on the Great Seal of the United States, "a new order of the ages" which would become a foundation for the happiness of all of their descendents and a model for the other peoples of the world. To their minds, the federal Constitution was a Revolutionary act, an episode in their experimental quest for such an order.

A REPUBLICAN EXPERIMENT

From a twentieth-century perspective, the American Revolution may appear conservative and relatively tame. There were no mass executions. Social relationships and political arrangements were not turned upside down in an upheaval of shattering violence, as they would be later on in France or Russia or any of a dozen other countries we might name. To people living through it, nonetheless—or watching it from overseas—the American Revolution seemed very radical indeed. It was not self-evident in 1776 that all men are created equal, that governments derive their just authority from popular consent, or that good governments exist in order to protect God-given rights. These concepts are not undeniable in any age. From the point of view of eighteenth-century Europeans, they contradicted common sense. The notions that a sound society could operate without the natural subordination customary where men were either commoners or nobles or that a stable government could be based entirely on elections seemed both frightening and ridiculously at odds with the obvious lessons of the past. A republican experiment had been attempted once before on something like this scale—in England during the 1640s and 1650s—and the ultimate result had been a Cromwellian dictatorship and a quick return to the ancient constitution of King, Lords, and Commons.

Nevertheless, the Americans dreamed revolutionary visions of perfection, comparable in many ways to revolutionary visions of later times. They sought a new beginning, a rebirth, in which hereditary privilege would disappear and all political authority would derive exclusively from talent, public service, and the people's choice. And their commitment to the principles of liberty and equal rights did touch and change most aspects of their common life.

No essay of this length can possibly describe all of the ways in which the Revolution altered American society. To understand the Constitution, though, we have to realize, at minimum, that as they fought the War for Independence, Americans were equally involved in a fundamental transformation of political beliefs and thus of political institutions. The decision to separate from England was also a decision that Americans were a people different from the English, a separate nation with a special mission in the world. This people had no way to understand their new identity except in terms of their historical mission, no way to define or perfect their national character except by building their new order. To be an American, by 1776, was to be a republican, and to become consistently republican required a thorough reconstruction of existing institutions.

A republican experiment, in fact, required rebuilding governments afresh. For in the month between the clash at Lexington and the Declaration of Independence, formal governments dissolved in one American colony after another. The people, who had ordinarily elected only one branch of their local governments, simply transferred their allegiance from their legal governmental institutions to extra-legal revolutionary committees, state conventions, and the Continental Congress. Through the first months of the fighting, the conventions and committees managed very well. Power rested with the people in a wholly literal sense, the people followed the directives of these revolutionary bodies, and those bodies turned the popular determination into armies and materials of war.

Some revolutionaries might have been content to see their states continue indefinitely under governmental bodies of this sort. Many patriots were intensely localistic, and they had learned a fierce distrust of any power much beyond the people's easy reach. Other patriots, however, many more of those who exercised great influence, never saw the revolutionary agencies as anything but temporary. A structure that depended so immediately on the people was good enough for an emergency, but hardly suitable for the longer term. For permanence, most patriots admired a governmental structure that balanced and divided power between different and independent parts, not one that concentrated it in single bodies which performed both legislative and executive functions.

The revolutionaries had been reared as Englishmen, in a tradition that instructed them that liberty was incompatible with the unchecked rule of the majority or with a government composed of only a single branch. Proper constitutions, they believed, depended on consent, but governments existed in order to protect the liberties of all. The revolutionaries had decided that good governments should have no place for aristocrats or kings, but they continued to believe that immediate and undiluted rule by the majority could not provide the wisdom and stability that governments require, nor could it offer proper safeguards for the rights of all. Thus, as they moved toward independence, the revolutionaries started a long search for a governmental structure in which liberty and representative democracy could be combined. This was what they meant by a "republic."

Most of the revolutionary states established written constitutions before the end of 1776. Although they differed greatly in details, these constitutions tended to be similar in broader lines. The colonial experience, together with the quarrel with Great Britain, had taught a

powerful fear of the executive and of the executive's ability to undermine the independence of the other parts of govrnment by use of patronage or "influence." Accordingly, most states created governors too
weak to do such harm. Most stripped the governors of the majority of
their traditional powers of appointment and deprived them of the traditional right to veto legislation. Most provided for election of the governors by the legislative branch. Most confined the chief executives, in
short, to the job of enforcing the legislatures' wills.

According to these constitutions, the legislative power would remain
within the people's hardy grip. The concept of a balance required two
legislative houses, but hostility to privilege was far too sharp to let the
second house become a bastion for any special group, in imitation of
the English House of Lords. Moreover, in societies without hereditary
ranks, it was difficult to reach agreement on a genuinely republican
method for selecting the few men of talent and leisure whose superior
wisdom, lodged in an upper house, was traditionally supposed to check
the passions of the multitude. The revolutionary senates differed relatively little in their makeup from the lower houses of assembly. Democratic Pennsylvania did without an upper house at all and placed executive authority in the hands of a council, rather than a single man,
though this was such a radical departure from general ideas that it
quickly created an anti-constitutional party in that state.

Nearly all the revolutionaries would have failed a modern test of
loyalty to democratic standards. Even the most dedicated patriots were
eighteenth-century men, and eighteenth-century thinking normally excluded many portions of the people from participation in the politics
of a republic: adherents to unpopular religions, women, blacks, and
even very poor white males.

Accordingly, not even Pennsylvania departed so far from tradition
as to give the vote to every male adult. And yet most states moved no-
ticeably in that direction. Most lowered the amount of property one
had to own in order to possess the franchise. Several gave the vote to
every man who paid a tax. All the states provided for annual elections
of the lower house of legislature and, often, for annual elections of the
senate and governor as well. Every part of these new governments
would be chosen by the people or by those the people had elected.
And the legislatures in particular were filled with men whose modest
means and ordinary social rank would have excluded them from higher

office in colonial times. In a variety of ways, these governments were far more responsive to the people than the old colonial governments had been. They were also far more closely watched. The revolutionary air was full of popular awareness of the people's rights.

The revolutionary movement disestablished churches, altered attitudes toward slavery, and partly redefined the role of women in American society. Eventually, of course, revolutionary concepts paved the way for an extension of the rights of citizens to all the groups that eighteenth-century patriots excluded. But whatever else the Revolution was or would become, its essence lay originally in these thirteen problematic experiments in constructing republican regimes. It would succeed or fail, in revolutionary minds, according to the success of these regimes in raising the new order and fulfilling expectations that republicanism would defend and perfect this special people and the democratic social structure that they hoped would become the envy of the world.

A PERMANENT CONFEDERATION

Americans did not intend, at the beginning, to extend the revolutionary experiment in republican government from the states to the nation as a whole. Republics were expected to be small. The Revolution had begun as an attempt to protect the old colonial governments from external interference by a distant Parliament and king. Traditional loyalties and revolutionary ideas were both keyed to the states.

Still, the argument with Britain taught Americans to think that they were a single people, and the War for Independence built a growing sense of nationhood. There was a Continental Congress before there were any independent states. *Congress* declared American independence and recommended that new state governments be formed. *Congress* assumed the direction of the war.

The Continental Congress was an extralegal body. It had simply emerged in the course of the imperial quarrel and continued to exert authority with the approval of the people and the states, all of which sent an unspecified number of delegates to help take care of common concerns. As early as June 12, 1776, these delegates initiated consideration of a plan to place their authority on formal grounds. But the experiences that had led to independence made Americans powerfully

suspicious of any central government, and there were many disagreements in the Congress. Meanwhile, there was also the necessity of
managing a war.

Not until November 17, 1777 did Congress finally present a formal
proposal to the states. This plan, the Articles of Confederation, called
upon the sovereign states to join in a permanent confederation presided over by a Congress whose authority would be confined to matters of interest to all: war and peace; foreign relations; trade with the
Indians; disputes between states; and other common concerns. Each
state would continue to have a single vote in Congress. In matters of
extreme importance, such as war and peace, Congress would act only
when nine of the thirteen states agreed. Since Congress would not directly represent the people, troops or money could be raised only by
requisitioning the states.

The Articles of Confederation did not issue from a systematic, theoretical consideration of the problems of confederation government. For
the most part, they only codified the structure and procedures that had
emerged in practice in the years since 1774. Most of the country
scarcely noticed when they finally went into effect, which was not
until February 1781—three years after they were first proposed. Maryland, which had a definite western border, refused its consent until
Virginia and the other giant states, whose colonial charters gave them
boundaries which might stretch from coast to coast, agreed to cede
their lands beyond the mountains to the Confederation as a whole.
Then, for most of the rest of the 1780s, Americans lived in a confederation of this sort.

Historians have long since given up the old idea that the Confederation years were a period of governmental folly and unmixed disaster.
The Articles established a genuine federal government, not merely a
league of states. The union was to be permanent, and Congress was
granted many of the usual attributes of sovereign authority. Great
things were accomplished. The states secured their independence and
won a generous treaty of peace, which placed their western border at
the Mississippi River. The country weathered a severe post-war depression. Congress organized the area northwest of the Ohio for settlement and eventual statehood. In fact, the Northwest Ordinance of
1787 established the pattern for all the rest of the continental expan-

sion of the United States, providing that new territories would eventually enter the union on terms of full equality with its original members and thus assuring that America would manage to escape most of the problems usually confronted by an expanding empire. It was not an unimpressive record.

THIRTEEN SQUABBLING STATES

Nevertheless, the Articles of Confederation came under increasing criticism from an influential minority even before they formally went into practice. This minority was centered in the Congress itself and around the powerful executive officials created by the Congress, especially Robert Morris, a Philadelphia merchant who was appointed Superintendent of Finance in 1781. Morris and his allies were necessarily concerned with the Confederation as a whole, and they found it almost impossible to meet their responsibilities under this kind of government. By the time the war was over, the Confederation's paper money was entirely worthless—"not worth a Continental," as the phrase still goes. The Confederation owed huge debts to army veterans, to citizens who had lent supplies or money during the war, and to foreign governments and foreign subjects who had purchased American bonds. Dependent on the states for revenues, Congress could not even pay the interest on these obligations. All the states had war debts of their own, and in the midst of a depression, their citizens were seldom willing or even able to pay taxes high enough to make it possible for the republics to handle their own needs and meet their congressional requisitions as well. By 1783, Morris, Alexander Hamilton, James Madison, and many other continental-minded men were insisting on reform. They demanded, at the very least, that Congress be granted the authority to levy a tax on foreign imports, which might provide it with a steady, independent source of revenue.

The need for revenue, however, was only the most urgent of several concerns. Lacking a direct connection with the people, Congress had to work through and depend on the states for nearly everything. Unable to compel cooperation, its members watched in futile anger as the sovereign republics went their separate ways. Some states quarreled over boundaries. Troubled by the depression, others passed competitive duties on foreign imports. The states ignored Confederation treaties, fought separate wars with Indians, and generally neglected congressional pleas for money.

As this happened, American ambassadors in foreign lands—John Adams in England and Thomas Jefferson in France—discovered that the European nations treated the American confederation with contempt. The European powers refused to make commercial treaties that would lower their barriers to freer trade and ease America's commercial problems. England refused to remove her soldiers from forts in the American northwest, insisting that she would abide by the treaty of peace only when the states began to meet their own obligations to cease persecuting returning loyalists and to open their courts to British creditors who wanted to collect their debts.

Nevertheless, the nationalists in Congress were frustrated in their desire for reform. The Articles of Confederation could be amended only by unanimous consent, but when Congress recommended an amendment that would give it the authority to levy a five percent duty on imports, little Rhode Island refused to agree. When Congress asked for power to retaliate against Great Britain's navigation laws, the states again could not concur.

Repeatedly defeated in their efforts at reform, increasingly alarmed by mutual antagonisms between the states, which had grown serious enough by 1786 to threaten an immediate fragmentation of the union into several smaller confederacies, the men of continental vision turned their thoughts to fundamentals. A much more sweeping change, they now suspected, might be necessary to resolve the pressing problems of the current central government. And if the change went far enough, a few of them began to think, it might accomplish something more. It might restore the Revolution to its proper course.

The Revolution, after all, involved a dream of national greatness; and the dream was going wrong. A people who had hoped to be a model for the world was fragmented into thirteen petty, squabbling states. The states would not—or could not—subordinate their separate interests to the good of the Confederation as a whole. Even worse, too many of the states fell short of fulfilling revolutionary expectations within their individual bounds. The early revolutionary constitutions had delivered overwhelming power to the people's immediate representatives in the lower houses of assembly. As these lower houses struggled to protect the people from hard times, they frequently neglected private rights and seldom seemed to give a due consideration to the long-term good. As clashing groups in different states competed to control their house of representatives, nobody could feel certain what the law might be next year, when one majority replaced another. The lower houses of assembly were essentially unchecked by the other parts of government, and to many revolutionaries it appeared that the assemblies proceeded on their ways with slight regard for justice and little thought about tomorrow. The rule of law appeared to be collapsing into a kind of anarchy in which the liberty and property of everyone might depend on the good will of whichever temporary majority happened to control his state. No one could feel secure in the enjoyment of his rights.

LIBERTY IN PERIL

During the 1780s, in other words, the feeling grew that liberty was once again in peril. Alarm was most intense among the men whose duties, education, or experience encouraged them to pin their patriotic feelings on the continent as a whole: certain members of Congress; most of the best-known revolutionary thinkers; most of the former officers of the continental army; many merchants, public creditors, and other men of wealth. Men of social standing were distressed with the way in which the revolutionary principles of liberty and equality seemed to shade into a popular contempt for talent or distinction. Too often, to their minds, the best men lost elections in the states to self-serving, scrambling demagogues, and the revolutionary constitutions made it far too easy for these demagogues to set an ill-considered course or even to oppress the propertied minority in order to secure the people's favor. Continued confiscations of the property of people who had sympathized with Britain and continued use of paper money, which threatened men's investments and their right to hold their property secure, were grievances of particular importance to those who had investments and positions to defend.

And yet the sense of fading hopes and failing visions was not exclusively confined to men of wealth. Anyone whose life had been immersed in revolutionary expectations might share in the concern. Every state seemed full of quarrels. Every individual seemed to be on the scrape for himself. No one seemed to have a real regard for common interests, a willingness to recognize that selfish interests must be limited by some consideration for the good of all. Public virtue, to use the phrase the revolutionaries used, seemed to be in danger of completely disappearing as every man and every social group sought private goods at the expense of harmony and other people's rights. But virtue, revolutionaries thought, was the indispensable foundation for republics, without which they could not survive. If public virtue was collapsing, then the Revolution was about to fail. It would degenerate into a kind of chaos, from which a tyrant might emerge, or else the people, in disgust, might eventually prefer to return to hereditary rule.

So, at least, did many fear. Guided by the same ideas that had impelled them into independence, they saw a second crisis, as dangerous to liberty as the crisis that had led them into Revolution. As they had done in 1776, they blamed their discontents on governments that lacked the character to mold a virtuous people and fit them for their special role. Once more, they turned to constitutional reform. They saw in the problems of the Confederation government not merely difficulties that would have to be corrected, but an opportunity that might be seized for even greater ends, an opportunity to rescue revolutionary hopes from their decay.

The constitutional reformers of the 1780s had several different motives and several different goals. Some had an economic interest in a constitutional reform that would enable the central government to pay its debts and act to spur the economic revival. All wanted to make the government adequate to its tasks and able to command more respect from the rest of the world. Some wanted more: to reconstruct the central government in such a way that its virtues might override the mistakes that had been made in some of the states. They wanted to redeem the reputation of democracy and save the republican experiment from a process of degeneration which threatened to destroy all that they had struggled for.

Shays's Rebellion handed them their chance. Out in western Massachusetts, hard times, large debts, and the high taxes prompted by the state's attempt to handle its revolutionary debt drove many farmers to distress. They first petitioned for relief, but when the legislature refused to issue paper money or to pass the laws required to protect their property from seizure, petitions gave way to rebellion. Farmers forced the courts to close in several counties, and Daniel Shays, a revolutionary captain, organized an armed resistance. The rebels were defeated with surprising ease. The state called out the militia during the winter of 1786, and Shays' forces disintegrated after a minor fight. The incident was nonetheless, for many, the final straw atop a growing load of fears. Armed resistance to a republican government seemed the ultimate warning of a coming collapse.

Earlier in 1786, delegates from five states had met at Annapolis, Maryland, to consider better means of regulating interstate and international trade. Nationalist sentiment was strong among the delegates. Hamilton and Madison were there. The participants quickly agreed that little could be done about commercial problems without a revision of the Articles of Confederation. They said as much in a report to Congress and their states, and Congress endorsed their recommendation for the meeting of a national convention to consider ways to make the central government "adequate to the exigencies of the union." Badly frightened by events in Massachusetts, whose constitution was widely thought to be among the best, every state except Rhode Island answered the call. From this context and in hope that it might save both liberty and union, the Constitutional Convention emerged.

8

Watermelon Armies and Whiskey Boys

GERALD CARSON

• Although Americans hold ambivalent views about alcoholic beverages, it cannot be denied that whiskey has played an important role in our culture from its very inception. The Pilgrims carried liquor with them on the Mayflower, and Congress itself voted to provide supplies of spirits to the American army during Revolutionary times. During the 1700s whiskey was said to be vital to the workers in the Southern states because of the hot climate.

To the Scotch-Irish of Pennsylvania, whiskey was not only an economic commodity but as necessary to their lives as Bibles and plows. Thus, when Alexander Hamilton proposed an internal revenue tax on distilled liquors, rumblings of dissatisfaction arose from the western Pennsylvania frontier. Because they based their livelihood on distilling grain rather than transporting the crop across the mountains, the farmers regarded the tax as discriminatory and leveled their shotguns at the revenue agents who came to collect. Public protests erupted, thousands marched on Pittsburgh, and there was talk of secession from the United States. Ultimately, President George Washington sent in federal troops.

Alexander Hamilton thought that the use of the army would illustrate the power of the newly created government to enforce the law. As you read Carson's witty and colorful account of the Whiskey Rebellion of 1794, consider the question of the use of federal troops to force compliance with a locally unpopular national policy. Does the use of military force, as Hamilton suggested, increase the citizen's respect for and adherence to the national laws? What similarities, if any, do you find between the quelling of the Whiskey Rebellion of 1794 and the use of the military to enforce integrated education in Little Rock, Arkansas, in 1957 and to dispel youth-

ful protesters at the Democratic National Convention in
Chicago in August 1968?

When one recalls that the President of the United States, the Secretary of War, the Secretary of the Treasury and the governors of four
states once mobilized against the farmers of western Pennsylvania
almost as large an army as ever took the field in the Revolutionary
War, the event appears at first glance as one of the more improbable
episodes in the annals of this country. Thirteen thousand grenadiers,
dragoons, foot soldiers and pioneers, a train of artillery with six-
pounders, mortars and several "grasshoppers," equipped with mountains of ammunition, forage, baggage and a bountiful stock of tax-
paid whiskey, paraded over the mountains to Pittsburgh against a
gaggle of homespun rebels who had already dispersed.

Yet the march had a rationale. President George Washington and
his Secretary of the Treasury, Alexander Hamilton, moved to counter
civil commotion with overwhelming force because they well understood that the viability of the United States Constitution was involved.
Soon after he assumed his post at the Treasury, Hamilton had proposed, to the astonishment of the country, that the United States
should meet fully and promptly its financial obligations, including the
assumption of the debts contracted by the states in the struggle for
independence. The money was partly to be raised by laying an excise
tax upon distilled spirits. The tax, which was universally detested in
the West—"odious" was the word most commonly used to describe
it—became law on March 3, 1791.

The news of the passage of the measure was greeted with a roar
of indignation in the back country settlements. The duty was laid
uniformly upon all the states, as the Constitution provided. If the
West had to pay more, Secretary Hamilton explained, it was only
because it used more whiskey. The East could, if it so desired,
forgo beverage spirits and fall back on cider and beer. The South
could not. It had neither orchards nor breweries. To Virginia and
Maryland the excise tax appeared to be as unjust and oppressive as
the well-remembered Molasses Act and the tea duties of George III.
"The time will come," predicted fiery James Jackson of Georgia in
the House of Representatives, "when a shirt shall not be washed
without an excise."

Kentucky, then thinly settled, but already producing its character-istic hand-made, whole-souled liquor from planished copper stills, was of the opinion that the law was unconstitutional. Deputy revenue collectors throughout the Bluegrass region were assaulted, their papers stolen, their horses' ears cropped and their saddles cut to pieces. On one wild night the people of Lexington dragged a stuffed dummy through the streets and hanged in effigy Colonel Thomas Marshall, the chief collector for the district.

Yet in no other place did popular fury rise so high, spread so rapidly, involve a whole population so completely, express so many assorted grievances, as in the Pennsylvania frontier counties of Fayette, Al-legheny, Westmoreland and Washington. In these counties, around 1791, a light plume of wood smoke rose from the chimneys of no less than five thousand log stillhouses. The rates went into effect on July first. The whiskey-maker could choose whether he would pay a yearly levy on his still capacity or a gallonage tax ranging from nine to eleven cents on his actual production.

Before the month was out, "committees of correspondence," in the old Revolutionary phrase, were speeding horsemen over the ridges and through the valleys to arouse the people to arm and assemble. The majority, but not all, of the men who made the whiskey decided to "forbear" from paying the tax. The revenue officers were thoroughly worked over. Robert Johnson, for example, collector for Washington and Allegheny counties, was waylaid near Pigeon Creek by a mob disguised in women's clothing. They cut off his hair, gave him a coat of tar and feathers and stole his horse.

The Pennsylvania troubles were rooted in the economic importance and impregnable social position of mellow old Monongahela rye whiskey. In 1825, for instance, when the Philadelphia Society for Promoting Agriculture offered a gold medal to the person in Pennsyl-vania who carried on large-scale farming operations without providing ardent spirits for his farm workers, the medal could not be awarded. There were no entries for the uncoveted honor.

The frontier people had been reared from childhood on the family jug of farmer whiskey. They found the taste pleasant, the effect agreeable. Whiskey was usually involved when there was kissing or fighting. It beatified the rituals of birth and death. The doctor kept a bottle in his office for his own use under the deceptive label "Arsenic

—Deadly poison." The lawyer produced the bottle when the papers were signed. Whiskey was available in the prothonotary's office when the trial-list was made up. Jurors got their dram, and the constable drew his ration for his services on election day. The hospitable barrel and the tin cup were the mark of the successful political candidate. The United States Army issued a gill to a man every day. Ministers of the gospel were paid in rye whiskey, for they were shepherds of a devout flock, Scotch Presbyterians mostly, who took their Bible straight, especially where it said: "Give strong drink unto him that is ready to perish, and wine unto those that be of heavy hearts."

With grain the most abundant commodity west of the mountains, the farmers could eat it or drink it, but they couldn't sell it in distant markets unless it was reduced in bulk and enhanced in value. A Pennsylvania farmer's "best holt," then, was whiskey. A pack-horse could move only four bushels of grain. But it could carry twenty-four bushels if it was condensed into two kegs of whiskey slung across its back, while the price of the goods would double when they reached the eastern markets. So whiskey became the remittance of the fringe settlements for salt, sugar, nails, bar iron, pewter plates, powder and shot. Along the Western rivers where men saw few shilling pieces, a gallon of good, sound rye whiskey was a stable measure of value.

The bitter resistance of the Western men to the whiskey tax involved both practical considerations and principles. First, the excise payment was due and must be paid in hard money as soon as the water-white distillate flowed from the condensing coil. The principle concerned the whole repulsive idea of an internal revenue levy. The settlers of western Pennsylvania were a bold, hardy, emigrant race who brought with them bitter memories of oppression under the excise laws in Scotland and Ireland, involving invasion of their homes, confiscation of their property and a system of paid informers. Revenue collectors were social outcasts in a society which warmly seconded Doctor Samuel Johnson's definition of excise: "a hateful tax levied upon commodities, and adjudged not by the common judges of property, but wretches hired by those to whom excise is paid."

The whiskey boys of Pennsylvania saw it as simply a matter of sound Whig doctrine to resist the exciseman as he made his rounds with Dicas' hydrometer to measure the proof of the whiskey and his marking iron to brand the casks with his findings. Earlier, Pennsylvania had taxed spirits. But whiskey produced for purely private use was exempt. William Findley of Westmoreland County, a member of Congress at the time and a sympathetic interpreter of the Western point of view, looked into this angle. To his astonishment, he learned that all of the whiskey distilled in the West was for purely personal use. So far as the state's excise tax was concerned, or any other tax, for that matter, the sturdy Celtic peoples of the Monongahela region had cheerfully returned to nature: they just didn't pay. About every sixth man made whiskey. But all were involved in the problem, since the other five took their grain to the stillhouse where the master distiller turned it into liquid form.

The state had been lenient. But now matters had taken a more serious turn. The new federal government in Philadelphia was dividing the whole country up into "districts" for the purpose of collecting the money. And the districts were subdivided into smaller "surveys." The transmontane Pennsylvanians found themselves in the grip of something known as the fourth survey, with General John Neville, hitherto a popular citizen and leader, getting ready to enforce the law, with a reward paid to informers and a percentage to the collectors, who appeared to be a rapacious set.

The first meeting of public protest against the 1791 federal tax was held at Redstone Old Fort, now Brownsville. The proceedings were moderate on that occasion, and scarcely went beyond the right of petition. Another meeting in August, more characteristic of others which were to follow, was radical in tone, disorderly, threatening. It passed resolves to the effect that any person taking office under the revenue law was an enemy of society.

When warrants were issued in the affair of Robert Johnson, the process server was robbed, beaten, tarred and feathered and left tied to a tree in the forest. As the inspectors' offices were established, they were systematically raided. Liberty poles reappeared as whiskey poles. The stills of operators who paid the tax were riddled with bullets in attacks sardonically known as "mending" the still. This led to a popular description of the Whiskey Boys as "Tom the Tinker's Men," an ironical reference to the familiar, itinerant repairer of pots and kettles. Notices proposing measures for thwarting the law, or aimed at coercing the distillers, were posted on trees or published in the *Pitts-*

burgh Gazette over the signature, "Tom the Tinker," nom de plume
of the insurgent John Holcroft and other anti-tax agitators. Findley,
who tried to build a bridge of understanding between the backwoods-
men and the central government, described the outbreak as not the
result of any concerted plan, but rather as a flame, "an infatuation
almost incredible."

An additional grievance grew out of the circumstance that offenders were required to appear in the federal court at Philadelphia,
three hundred miles away. The whiskey-makers saw this distant
government as being no less oppressive than one seated in London,
and often drew the parallel. The Scotch-Irish of western Pennsylvania
were, in sum, anti-federalist, anti-tax, and it may be added, anti-
Indian. West of Pittsburgh lay Indian country. The men of the west
held to a simple concept of how to solve the Indian problem: extermination. The Indians had the same program, in reverse, and were
getting better results. The bungling campaigns which generals Hamar
and St. Clair had conducted in the early 1790's made the people of
the fringe settlements despair of the ability of the Union to protect
them.

Congress amended the excise tax law in 1792 and again in 1794
to lighten the burden on country distillers. A further conciliatory step
was taken. To ease the hardships of the judicial process, Congress
gave to the state courts jurisdiction in excise offenses so that accused
persons might be tried in their own vicinity. But some fifty or sixty
writs already issued and returnable at Philadelphia resulted in men
being carried away from their fields during harvest time. This convinced the insurgents that the federalist East was seeking a pretext
to discipline the democratic West.

One day in July, while the papers were being served, William
Miller, a delinquent farmer-distiller, and political supporter of General Neville, saw the General riding up his lane accompanied by a
stranger who turned out to be a United States marshal from Philadelphia. The marshal unlimbered an official paper and began to read
a summons. It ordered said Miller peremptorily to "set aside all manner of business and excuses" and appear in his "proper person" before
a Philadelphia judge. Miller had been planning to sell his property
and remove to Kentucky. The cost of the trip to Philadelphia and the

fine for which he was liable would eat up the value of his land and betterments. The farm was as good as gone.

"I felt my blood boil at seeing General Neville along to pilot the sheriff to my very door," Miller said afterward. "I felt myself mad with passion."

As Neville and the marshal rode away, a party from the county militia which was mustered at Mingo Creek fired upon them, but there were no casualties. When the General reached Bower Hill, his country home above the Chartiers Valley, another party under the command of John Holcroft awaited him there and demanded his commission and official papers. The demand was refused and both sides began to shoot. As the rebels closed in on the main house, a flanking fire came from the Negro cabins on the plantation. The Whiskey Boys were driven off with one killed and four wounded.

The next day, Major James McFarlane, a veteran of the Revolution, led an attack in force upon Neville's painted and wall-papered mansion, furnished with such marvels as carpets, mirrors, pictures and prints and an eight-day clock. The house was now defended by a dozen soldiers from Fort Fayette at Pittsburgh. A fire-fight followed during which a soldier was shot and McFarlane was killed—by treachery, the rebels said, when a white flag was displayed. The soldiers surrendered and were either released or allowed to escape. Neville was not found, but his cabins, barns, outbuildings and finally the residence were all burned to the ground. Stocks of grain were destroyed, all fences leveled, as the victors broke up the furniture, liberated the mirrors and clock, and distributed Neville's supply of liquor to the mob.

The funeral of McFarlane caused great excitement. Among those present were Hugh Henry Brackenridge, author, lawyer and one of the western moderates, and David Bradford, prosecuting attorney for Washington County. The former wished to find ways to reduce the tension; the latter to increase it. Bradford was a rash, impetuous Marylander, ambitious for power and position. Some thought him a second-rate lawyer. Others disagreed. They said he was third-rate. But he had a gift for rough mob eloquence. Bradford had already robbed the United States mails to find out what information was being sent east against the conspirators. He had already called for the people to make a choice of "submission or opposition . . . with *head, heart, hand* and *voice.*"

At Major McFarlane's funeral service Bradford worked powerfully upon the feelings of his sympathizers as he described "the murder of McFarlane." Brackenridge also spoke, using wit and drollery to let down the pressure and to make palatable his warning to the insurgents that they were flirting with the possibility of being hanged. But the temper of the throng was for Bradford, clearly revealed in the epitaph which was set over McFarlane's grave. It said "He fell . . . by the hands of an unprincipled villain in the support of what he supposed to be the rights of his country."

The high-water mark of the insurrection was the occupation of Pittsburgh. After the fight and the funeral, Bradford called out the militia regiments of the four disaffected counties. They were commanded to rendezvous at Braddock's Field, near Pittsburgh, with arms, full equipment and four days' rations. At the field there was a great beating of drums, much marching and counter-marching, almost a holiday spirit. Men in hunting shirts practiced shooting at the mark until a dense pall of smoke hung over the plain, as there had been thirty-nine years before at the time of General Braddock's disaster. There were between five and seven thousand men on the field, many meditating in an ugly mood upon their enemies holed up in the town, talking of storming Fort Fayette and burning Pittsburgh as "a second Sodom."

Bradford's dream was the establishment of an independent state with himself cast as a sort of Washington of the West. Elected by acclaim as Major General, he dashed about the field on a superb horse in a fancy uniform, his sword flashing, plumes floating out from his hat. As he harangued the multitude, Bradford received applications for commissions in the service of—what? No one quite knew.

Marching in good order, strung out over two and a half miles of road, the rebels advanced on August first toward Pittsburgh in what was hopefully interpreted as a "visit," though the temper of the whiskey soldiers was perhaps nearer to that of one man who twirled his hat on the muzzle of his rifle and shouted, "I have a bad hat now, but I expect to have a better one soon." While the panic-stricken burghers buried the silver and locked up the girls, the mob marched

in on what is now Fourth Avenue to the vicinity of the present Baltimore and Ohio Railroad station. A reception committee extended
nervous hospitality in the form of hams, poultry, dried venison, bear
meat, water and whiskey. They agreed to banish certain citizens ob-
noxious to the insurrectionists. One building on a suburban farm was
burned. Another attempt at arson failed to come off. The day cost
Brackenridge four barrels of prime Monongahela. It was better, he
reflected, "to be employed in extinguishing the fire of their thirst
than of my house." Pittsburgh was fortunate in getting the main body
in and then out again without a battle or a burning.

All through the month of August armed bands continued to patrol
the roads as a "scrub Congress," in the phrase of one scoffer, met at
Parkinson's Ferry, now Monongahela, to debate, pass resolutions
and move somewhat uncertainly toward separation from the United
States. Wild and ignorant rumors won belief. It was said that
Congress was extending the excise levy to plows at a dollar each, that
every wagon entering Philadelphia would be forced to pay a dollar,
that a tax was soon to be established at Pittsburgh of fifteen shillings
for the birth of every boy baby, and ten for each girl.

With the terrorizing of Pittsburgh, it was evident that the crisis
had arrived. The President requisitioned 15,000 militia from Pennsylvania, New Jersey, Virginia and Maryland, of whom about 13,000
actually marched. Would the citizens of one state invade another to
compel obedience to federal law? Here one gets a glimpse of the larger
importance of the affair. Both the national government and the state
of Pennsylvania sent commissioners to the West with offers of pardon
upon satisfactory assurances that the people would obey the laws.
Albert Gallatin, William Findley, Brackenridge and others made a
desperate effort to win the people to compliance, though their motives
were often questioned by both the rebels and the federal authorities.
The response to the offer of amnesty was judged not to be sufficiently
positive. Pressed by Hamilton to have federal power show its teeth,
Washington announced that the troops would march.

The army was aroused. In particular, the New Jersey militia were
ready for lynch law because they had been derided in a western newspaper as a "Water-mellon Army" and an uncomplimentary estimate
was made of their military capabilities. The piece was written as a
take-off on the kind of negotiations which preceded an Indian treaty.

Possibly the idea was suggested by the fact that the Whiskey Boys were often called "White Indians." At any rate, in the satire the Indians admonished the great council in Philadelphia: ". . . Brothers, we have that powerful monarch, Capt. Whiskey, to command us. By the power of his influence, and a love to *his person* we are compelled to every great and heroic act. . . . We, the Six United Nations of White Indians . . . have all imbibed his principles and passions— that is a love of whiskey. . . . Brothers, you must not think to frighten us with . . . infantry, cavalry and artillery, composed of your water-mellon armies from the Jersey shores; they would cut a much better figure in warring with the crabs and oysters about the Capes of Delaware."

Captain Whiskey was answered hotly by "A Jersey Blue." He pointed out that "the water-melon army of New Jersey" was going to march westward shortly with "ten-inch howitzers for throwing a species of mellon very useful for curing a *gravel occasioned by whiskey!*" The expedition was tagged thereafter as the "Watermelon Army."

The troops moved in two columns under the command of General Henry (Light Horse Harry) Lee, Governor of Virginia. Old Dan Morgan was there and young Meriwether Lewis, five nephews of President Washington, the governors of Pennsylvania and New Jersey, too, and many a veteran blooded in Revolutionary fighting, including the extraordinary German, Captain John Fries of the Bucks County militia, and his remarkable dog to which the Captain gave the name of a beverage he occasionally enjoyed—Whiskey.

The left wing marched west during October, 1794, over General Braddock's old route from Virginia and Maryland to Cumberland on the Potomac, then northwest into Pennsylvania, to join forces with the right wing at Union Town. The Pennsylvania and New Jersey corps proceeded via Norristown and Reading to Harrisburg and Carlisle. There, on October 4, President Washington arrived, accompanied by Colonel Hamilton. The representatives of the disaffected counties told the President at Carlisle that the army was not needed but Hamilton convinced him that it was. Washington proceeded with the troops as far as Bedford, then returned to Philadelphia for the meeting of Congress. Hamilton ordered a roundup of many of the rebels and personally interrogated the most important ones. Brackenridge, incidentally, came off well in his encounter with Hamilton, who declared that he was satisfied with Brackenridge's conduct.

By the time the expedition had crossed the mountains, the uprising was already coming apart at the seams. David Bradford, who had been excluded from the offer of amnesty, fled to Spanish Louisiana. About two thousand of the best riflemen in the West also left the country, including many a distiller, who loaded his pot still on a pack horse or a keel boat and sought asylum in Kentucky where, hopefully, a man could make "the creature" without giving the public debt a lift.

The punitive army moved forward in glorious autumn weather, raiding chicken coops, consuming prodigious quantities of the commodity which lay at the heart of the controversy. Richard Howell, governor of New Jersey and commander of the right wing, revived the spirits of the Jersey troops by composing a marching song, "Dash to the Mountains, Jersey Blue":

> To arms once more, our hero cries,
> Sedition lives and order dies;
> To peace and ease then did adieu
> And dash to the mountains, Jersey Blue.

Faded diaries, old letters and orderly books preserve something of the gala atmosphere of the expedition. At Trenton a Miss Forman and a Miss Milnor were most amiable. Newtown, Pennsylvania was ticketed as a poor place for hay. At Potts Grove a captain of the cavalry troop got kicked in the shin by his horse. Among the Virginians, Meriwether Lewis enjoyed the martial excitement, wrote to his mother in high spirits of the "mountains of beef and oceans of Whiskey"; sent regards "to all the girls" and announced that he would bring "an Insergiant Girl to se them next fall bearing the title of Mrs. Lewis." If there was such a girl, he soon forgot her.

Yet where there is an army in being there are bound to be unpleasant occurrences. Men were lashed. Quartermasters stole government property. A soldier was ordered to put a Scotch-Irish rebel under guard. In execution of the order, he ran said insurgent through with his bayonet, of which the prisoner died. At Carlisle a dragoon's pistol went off and hit a countryman in the groin; he too died. On November 13, long remembered in many a cabin and stump-clearing as "the dis-

mal night," the Jersey horse captured various citizens whom they described grimly as "the whiskey pole gentry," dragging them out of bed,
tying them back to back. The troopers held their prisoners in a damp
cellar for twenty-four hours without food or water, before marching
them off at gun point to a collection center at Washington, Pennsylvania.

In late November, finding no one to fight, the army turned east
again, leaving a volunteer force under General Morgan to conciliate
and consolidate the position during the winter. Twenty "Yahoos" were
carried back to Philadelphia and were paraded by the Philadelphia
horse through the streets of the city with placards marked "Insurrection" attached to their hats, in an odd federalist version of a Roman
triumph. The cavalry was composed, as an admirer said, of "young
men of the first property of the city," with beautiful mounts, uniforms
of the finest blue broadcloth. They held their swords elevated in the
right hand while the light flashed from their silver stirrups, martin-
gales and jingling bridles. Stretched over half a mile they came, first
two troopers abreast, then a pair of Yahoos, walking; then two more
mounted men, and so on.

The army, meditating upon their fatigues and hardships, called for
a substantial number of hangings. Samuel Hodgson, Commissary-
general of the army, wrote to a Pittsburgh confidant, "We all lament
that so few of the insurgents fell—such disorders can only be cured
by copious bleedings. . . ." Philip Freneau, friend and literary colleague of Brackenridge, suggested in retrospect—ironically, of course
—the benefits which would have accrued to the country "if Washington had drawn and quartered thirty or forty of the whiskey boys."
Most of the captives escaped any punishment other than that of being
held in jail without a trial for ten or twelve months. One died. Two
were finally tried and sentenced to death. Eventually both were let off.

Gradually the bitterness receded. In August, 1794, General An-
thony Wayne had crushed the Indians at the Battle of Fallen Timbers.
A treaty was concluded with Spain in October, 1795, clearing the
Mississippi for Western trade. The movement of the army into the
Pennsylvania hinterland, meanwhile, brought with it a flood of cash
which furnished the distillers with currency for paying their taxes.
These events served to produce a better feeling toward the Union.

If the rising was a failure, so was the liquor tax. The military adventure alone, without ordinary costs of collection, ran up a bill of $1,500,000, or about one third of all the money that was realized during the life of the revenue act. The excise was quietly repealed during Jefferson's administration. Yet the watermelon armies and the Whiskey Boys made a not inconsiderable contribution to our constitutional history. Through them, the year 1794 completed what 1787 had begun; for it established the reality of a federal union whose law was not a suggestion but a command.

9

The Great Jefferson Taboo

FAWN M. BRODIE

• One of the most talented individuals ever to sit in the White House, Thomas Jefferson is the only American President who may be honestly classified as a Renaissance man. Exceptionally gifted in a wide spectrum of activities, he not only authored the Declaration of Independence and the classic Notes on the State of Virginia but also mastered Greek and Latin, conversed in French and Italian, designed his own estate at Monticello, became an accomplished horticulturist and violinist, founded the University of Virginia, and still made time to participate dramatically in the politics of his era. He distinguished himself as Governor of Virginia, as Ambassador to France, as George Washington's first Secretary of State, as a founder of the Democratic-Republican party, as a spokesman for individual freedom in the Kentucky Resolutions of 1798, and of course as President of the United States. In his inaugural address of 1801, he proclaimed: "We are all Republicans, we are all Federalists." But in his performance as President he displayed a unique talent for mobilizing the members of his party into a cohesive unit.

Jefferson's private life was almost as fascinating as his public career. He was tall and slender with a sunny disposition and excellent health. At the age of thirty-nine, he was widowed by the death of his wife Martha, for whom he felt a deep and lasting affection. The question posed in the following essay by the late professor Fawn Brodie is whether Jefferson then took as a mistress a beautiful slave girl by the name of Sally Hemings. According to Brodie, they did in fact have an affair, and their lovemaking resulted in as many as seven children. Other respected scholars, most notably biog-

Reprinted by permission from *American Heritage* (June 1972). © 1972 American Heritage Publishing Company, Inc.

rapher Dumas Malone, have strongly disputed Brodie's conclusion and insisted that Jefferson was incapable of such immoral behavior. The long and bitter argument on this taboo
subject is likely to continue.

Thomas Jefferson spent his earliest years on a plantation in Tuckahoe,
Virginia, where the blacks outnumbered the whites ten to one. Here
he learned about the hierarchies of power and saw early that a white
child could tyrannize over a black adult. Here his basic sympathy with
emancipation, which we see in him as a young man, had its roots in
what he called, in his *Notes on the State of Virginia*, the "daily exercise in tyranny." But along with a pervasive anger at slavery, there also
developed in Jefferson at some period a conviction he could never
wholly escape, that blacks and whites must be carefully kept separate.
Emancipation of the blacks, he said in his *Notes*, should be accompanied by colonization, whether in Africa, in the West Indies, or in a
separate state in the West.

At age seventy-one he wrote privately, and with some bitterness,
that "amalgamation" of blacks and whites "produces a degradation to
which no lover of his country, no lover of excellence in the human
character can innocently consent." And at seventy-seven, in his unfinished *Autobiography*, he wrote, "Nothing is more certainly written
in the book of fate, than that these people are to be free; nor is it
less certain that the two races, equally free, cannot live in the same
government."

Yet, ironically, one of the stories that clings tenaciously to Jefferson
is that he actually had a family by a slave woman. The so-called Sally
Hemings story broke into the press in great detail in 1802; public
scoldings and bawdy ballads humiliated President Jefferson well into
1805. Throughout the 1830's and 1840's abolitionists elaborated the
story to suggest that Jefferson had had a whole seraglio of black women
and that one of his black mistresses and two of his daughters had been
sold at a slave auction in New Orleans. Jefferson biographers, on the
other hand, have almost unanimously denounced the stories as libellous.

On March 13, 1873, there appeared in an obscure Ohio newspaper,
the *Pike County Republican*, a memoir by one of Sally Hemings' sons,

Madison. The account was lucidly written, suggesting considerable education; when checked with Jefferson's *Farm Book*, the details were remarkably but not totally accurate. Madison Hemings wrote simply, even drily, that his mother had indeed borne Jefferson several children of whom he was one and that she was his only "concubine." This revelation caused a shudder among Jefferson scholars. Since its publication the memoir has been cited often for various details of life at Monticello, but its basic claim of paternity has been totally rejected almost without exception. Curiously, the piece itself has never been reprinted.

Although today's biographers still repudiate the Sally Hemings story, comment on the great Jefferson taboo does not disappear. Instead, we have the spectacle of ever-increasing numbers of pages devoted to its refutation. Merrill Peterson, in *The Jefferson Image in the American Mind*, looked at the documentation with some care, and in his recent biography, *Thomas Jefferson and the New Nation*, he writes:

> The evidence, highly circumstantial, is far from conclusive, however, and unless Jefferson was capable of slipping badly out of character in hidden moments at Monticello, it is difficult to imagine him caught up in a miscegenous relationship. Such a mixture of the races, such as ruthless exploitation of the master-slave relationship, revolted his whole being.

Dumas Malone devotes a whole appendix in his recent volume, *Jefferson the President, First Term* 1801–1805, to a refutation of the charge. He writes:

> It is virtually inconceivable that this fastidious gentleman whose devotion to his dead wife's memory and to the happiness of his daughters and grandchildren bordered on the excessive could have carried on through a period of years a vulgar liaison which his own family could not have failed to detect.

And Professor Malone suggests that Sally Hemings may have told her children that Jefferson was their father out of "vanity."

Certain black historians, on the other hand, including Lerone Bennett, believe that the miscegenation was real and that Jefferson's descendants dot the country from Cambridge, Massachusetts, to San Francisco. Any defense of this thesis causes anguish and outrage among

Jefferson admirers. Why does this story nevertheless persist? Does it touch some chord in fantasy life? Or do people feel that the scholars protest too much? Jefferson, after all, was a widower at thirty-nine. Defenders of Jefferson assure us again and again that miscegenation was out of character for him. But the first duty of a historian is to ask not "Is it out of character?" but "Is it true?"

What one might call "the family's official denial," begun by Jefferson's grandson, Thomas Jefferson Randolph, holds, first, that Jefferson was not at Monticello when Sally Hemings' children were conceived and, second, that they were fathered by Jefferson's nephews, Peter and Samuel Carr. This denial has been gratefully accepted by Jefferson biographers, his admirers, and his heirs. Still, one must note the fact, as Winthrop Jordan has done in his *White Over Black, American Attitudes Toward the Negro, 1550–1812*—and he was the first to say it in print—that Jefferson actually was at Monticello nine months before the births of each of Sally Hemings' children that are recorded in the *Farm Book*. And there is no evidence that she ever conceived a child when he was not there. Moreover, it takes very little research in the enormous file of family letters at the University of Virginia to demonstrate that Peter and Samuel Carr were elsewhere, managing plantations with slaves of their own, during most of the years that Sally Hemings was bearing children at Monticello.

Professor Jordan is the first white historian in our own time to describe dispassionately evidence for the Sally Hemings liaison, as well as the case against it, writing on the one hand that it was unlikely, a "lapse from character unique in his mature life," but noting on the other that it could have been evidence of deep ambivalence and that Jefferson's "repulsion" toward blacks may have hidden a powerful attraction. Jordan finds the story distasteful, however, and regrets that the charge is "dragged after Jefferson like a dead cat through the pages of formal and informal history." Still, he calls for an "unexcited" discussion of the facts.

It is possible to keep such a discussion "unexcited," though the material is dramatic and, at times, tragic. There are many facts that Jefferson scholars have overlooked, and some that have been ignored, apparently because they were too painful to consider. This is not uncommon with biographers, especially those whose sense of identification with their subject is almost total. In all fairness to Sally Hemings, as well as to Jefferson, whether one believes the story or not, phrases like "vulgar liaison," "ruthless exploitation of the master-slave relationship," and even "dragged after Jefferson like a dead cat" simply do not apply.

As everyone knows, Jefferson was a man of very great gifts and special sensibility. Yet we know little about Sally Hemings except that she was a quadroon of considerable beauty and that she was the half sister of his wife. Several of her brothers could read and write, and one may assume that this was true also of Sally. But no letter from her has been preserved, nor any by Jefferson to her.

Still, if it is true that Sally's seven children were also his children, this already illuminates the length and steadiness of their affection for each other and suggests that there may have been much suffering because it could not publicly be honored. A careful marshalling of the facts surely helps to throw light on Jefferson's life and character, and discovering a liaison does not degrade him or her. It may help explain some mysteries, such as why he never married again, and why he lapsed in his later years into ever-increasing apathy toward emancipation of slaves. For it may well be that this special involvement peculiarly incapacitated him for action in helping to change the national pattern of white over black. In any case, the facts may serve to illuminate his general ambivalence—his mixture of love and hate—concerning race.

Jefferson knew and revered two men who had children by slave women. One was his law teacher, George Wythe, whom he called his second father. Wythe, having no children of his own by two white wives, took a black mistress, Lydia Broadnax, whom he had freed. She bore a son, whom he raised with affection, teaching him Greek and Latin and promising him an inheritance in his will. Wythe even named Jefferson in his will as trustee in charge of the boy's education. But this provision was never to be fulfilled. An envious grandnephew of Wythe's named Sweney forged Wythe's name on several checks; seeking to avoid prosecution and also to win the total inheritance, Sweney put arsenic in the coffee and on some strawberries at Wythe's house. The mulatto child died quickly; Wythe lived long enough to disinherit Sweney. Lydia Broadnax, though very ill, survived. But because the only people who could testify against the murderer were blacks, he was acquitted.

Almost as close to Jefferson as George Wythe, at least for a time, was Jefferson's father-in-law, John Wayles. Wayles had had three white wives, who bore him four daughters. When his third wife died, he turned to Elizabeth Hemings, a slave on his plantation and the daughter of an English sea captain and an African slave woman. "Betty" Hemings bore Wayles six children, the youngest a girl named Sally, all of whom came to Monticello with their mother in the inheritance of Jefferson's wife, Martha Wayles. So it can be seen that although Jefferson may have been intellectually opposed to miscegenation, he grew up seeing it close at hand, and in his adult life he had two important models. He could hardly have believed it to be a grave sin.

Jefferson was greatly blessed in his marriage. He loved his wife passionately, and described their union in his *Autobiography* as "ten years of unchecquered happiness." Still, it was full of tragedy. Three of their six children died in infancy. After the birth of their sixth child, on May 8, 1782, Martha Jefferson hovered between life and death for months. When she finally died, on September 6, 1782, Jefferson fainted and, according to his oldest daughter, who was then ten, "remained so long insensible that they feared he never would revive."

> He kept his room for three weeks and I was never a moment from his side. He walked almost incessantly night and day only lying down occasionally when nature was completely exhausted on a pallet that had been brought in during his long fainting fit. My Aunts remained constantly with him for some weeks, I do not remember how many. When at last he left his room he rode out and from that time he was incessantly on horseback rambling about the mountain in the least frequented roads and just as often through the woods; in those melancholy rambles I was his constant companion, a solitary witness to many a violent burst of grief.

Most Jefferson biographers believe that he never again felt any deep or lasting affection for any woman. Gilbert Chinard wrote in 1928 that "there is no indication that he ever fell in love again," and in one fashion or another Jefferson scholars have adhered to the tradition that he became essentially passionless, monastic, and ascetic. Yet this view has had to be reconciled with the fact that Jefferson had a romance in

Paris in the 1780's with an Englishwoman, Maria Cosway. One solution has been to describe it as "superficially frantic," temporary, and playful rather than passionate. But the episode resulted in what are certainly the greatest love letters in the history of the American Presidency—letters whose copies were carefully preserved by Jefferson (and mostly kept hidden by his heirs until 1945), despite the fact that he is thought to have destroyed all his correspondence with both his wife and his mother. Moreover, passion does not usually disappear in a man's life unless his capacity for passion is constricted and warped from the beginning. When at forty-three, four years after his wife's death, he met the enchanting artist-musician and sensed at once the unhappiness of her marriage to the decadent and foppish Richard Cosway, he fell in love in a single afternoon. They saw each other alone many times during five happy weeks in the autumn of 1786, and in August, 1787, she returned to Paris for a second visit, without her husband. She remained four months. The story of this romance, told in *American Heritage* in August, 1971, need not be repeated here, except as it relates in a subtle fashion to the Sally Hemings story.

Jefferson had taken his eldest daughter Martha (Patsy) with him to Paris, leaving Maria (Polly) and baby Lucy with his wife's sister. When Lucy died of whooping cough, Jefferson in a frenzy of anxiety insisted that Polly be sent to Paris. He ordered that a middle-aged slave woman accompany her, one who had had the smallpox. But when Abigail Adams met the ship in London, she saw with some consternation that the maid accompanying the eight-year-old Polly was a young slave girl of striking beauty. It was Sally Hemings. Though Sally was only fourteen, Abigail believed her to be "about 15 or 16" and described her unhappily in a letter to Jefferson as "quite a child . . . wanting even more care" than Polly, and "wholly incapable" of looking after her young charge properly by herself.

It had been a lively voyage, with no other females on the ship, and Captain John Ramsay had quite won Polly's affection. She had become, Abigail reported grimly, "rough as a little sailor." The captain readily agreed with Abigail that Sally Hemings would be of "little Service" to Jefferson and suggested that "he had better carry her back with him." It takes no special imagination to see why, for quite different reasons, Abigail Adams and Captain Ramsay agreed that it

would be better if Sally Hemings did not go on to Paris. But Jefferson
sent his trusted French servant Petit to fetch them, and they arrived
in July, 1787.

Sally Hemings was later described by a Monticello slave as "very
handsome" and "mighty near white" with "long straight hair down
her back." Jefferson's grandson, Thomas Jefferson Randolph, said she
was "light colored and decidedly good looking," and at Monticello she
was described as "Dashing Sally." If she resembled her half sister Martha Wayles Jefferson in any fashion, there is no record of it. But certainly she brought to Paris the fresh, untainted aura of Jefferson's past,
the whole untrammeled childhood with the quantities of slave children, the memory of the easy, apparently guiltless miscegenation of
his father-in-law, the many-faceted reality of black and white in Virginia.

Sally Hemings arrived in Paris shortly before Maria Cosway returned for her second visit, without her husband. There are some in-
dications that Maria was troubled and guilt-ridden, and there were
many reasons why such an affair could not continue. She was a devout
Catholic, and besides, divorce was virtually impossible for an Englishwoman, even a Protestant. Her husband, increasingly restive in London, became nastier in his letters. She went back to England in December, 1787, and Jefferson was again left lonely and bereft. Earlier
he had written to her, "I am born to lose everything I love."

Sally Hemings was now fifteen. She was learning French, as was her
older brother James, who was in Paris as Jefferson's personal servant.
We know from Jefferson's account books that he paid 240 francs to a
Dr. Sutton on November 6, 1787, for Sally's smallpox inoculation, and
that by January, 1788, he had begun for the first time to pay wages to
both James and Sally Hemings, thirty-six francs a month to James and
twenty-four to his sister. The French servants received fifty and sixty
francs. By French law both were free if they chose to make an issue of
it, and they knew it.

The circumstances were propitious for an attachment. Sally Hemings must certainly have been lonely in Paris, as well as supremely
ready for the first great love of her life. She was thrown daily into the
presence of a man who was by nature tender and gallant with women.
He was, moreover, the man whom all the children at Monticello,
whether white or black, had looked upon as a kind of deity. What is
more, if Jefferson had a model in the person of his father-in-law, who

had turned to a slave woman after the death of his third wife, Sally Hemings, too, had a model in her mother, that Betty Hemings who had apparently dominated the private life and passions of John Wayles until his death.

In his *Notes on the State of Virginia* Jefferson had described blacks as more "ardent" than whites, a preconception that could have served only to heighten an interest in Sally at this moment, whatever dilemma it might produce. Moreover, he liked warmly domestic women. Though he took pleasure in intellectual female companions, enjoying the sharp, witty, and inquiring minds of Abigail Adams and several talented Frenchwomen, he did not fall in love with them. In this respect he resembled Goethe and Rousseau, both of whom loved and lived with unlettered women for many years before marrying them. Furthermore, during this Paris sojourn, Jefferson wrote to an American friend, the beautiful Anne Bingham, deploring the new preoccupation of Frenchwomen with politics:

> Society is spoilt by it. . . . You too, have had your political fever. But our good ladies, I trust have been too wise to wrinkle their foreheads with politics. They are contented to soothe and calm the minds of their husbands returning ruffled from political debate. . . . Recollect the women of this capital, some on foot, some on horses, and some in carriages hunting pleasure in the streets, in routs and assemblies, and forgetting that they have left it behind them in their nurseries; compare them with our own countrywomen occupied in the tender and tranquil amusements of domestic life, and confess that it is a comparison of Amazons and Angels.

Maria Cosway was no Amazon. Nor, it can be assumed, was Sally Hemings. Her son Madison tells us nothing of his mother's education or temperament. But he does write of what happened to her in Paris:

> Their stay (my mother and Maria's) was about eighteen months. But during that time my mother became Mr. Jefferson's concubine, and when he was called home she was *enceinte* by him. He desired to bring my mother back to Virginia with him but she demurred. In France she was free, while if she returned to Virginia she would be re-enslaved. So she refused to return with him. To induce her to do so he promised her extraordinary privileges, and made a solemn pledge that her children should be

freed at the age of twenty-one years. In consequence of his promises, on which she implicitlv relied, she returned with him to Virginia. Soon after their arrival, she gave birth to a child, of whom Thomas Jefferson was the father.

Is there any evidence other than Madison Hemings' memoir that a liaison between Jefferson and Sally Hemings began in Paris? If a man is in love, in however clandestine an affair, he must tell someone, if only unconsciously and with inadvertence. This is what happened to Jefferson. In March, 1788, he went to Holland on a diplomatic mission and then continued as a tourist into Germany. Not usually a diary keeper, he did write an almost daily journal of this seven-week trip. It is a matter of great curiosity that in this twenty-five-page document he uses the word *mulatto* eight times:

> The road goes thro' the plains of the Maine, which are mulatto and very fine. . . .
> It has a good Southern aspect, the soil a barren mulatto clay. . . .
> It is of South Western aspect, very poor, sometimes grey, sometimes mulatto. . . .
> These plains are sometimes black, sometimes mulatto, always rich. . . .
> . . . the plains are generally mulatto. . . .
> . . . the valley of the Rhine . . . varies in quality, sometimes a rich mulatto loam, sometimes a poor sand. . . .
> . . . the hills are mulatto but also whitish. . . .
> Meagre mulatto clay mixt with small broken stones. . . .

This appears to be evidence of both a preoccupation and a problem. If, moreover, one contrasts this journal with another he kept when touring southern France in the spring of 1787, before Sally Hemings' disturbing mulatto presence had come to trouble him, one will see that in that account, numbering forty-eight pages, he uses the word *mulatto* only once. The rest of the time he describes the hills, plains, and earth as dark, reddish-brown, gray, dark-brown, and black.

There is another quotation, too, in Jefferson's Holland journal that bears repeating:

> The women here [in Holland], as in Germany, do all sorts of work. While one considers them as useful and rational com-

panions, one cannot forget that they are also objects of our pleasures. Nor can they ever forget it. While employed in dirt and drudgery some tag of ribbon, some ring or bit of bracelet, earbob or necklace, or something of that kind will shew that the desire of pleasing is never suspended in them. . . . They are formed by nature for attentions and not for hard labour.

This is all very tender, and suggests that he was thinking not at all of the splendidly dressed Maria Cosway when he wrote it.

Upon his return to Paris, Jefferson found a letter from Maria Cosway reproaching him for not writing, which he had not done for three months. His reply was affectionate; he described his trip to Germany, and in mentioning the art gallery at Düsseldorf, he made what would seem to be a wholly unconscious confession of his new love:

At Dusseldorpf I wished for you much. I surely never saw so precious a collection of paintings. Above all things those of Van der Werff affected me the most. His picture of Sarah delivering Agar to Abraham is delicious. I would have agreed to have been Abraham though the consequence would have been that I should have been dead five or six thousand years.

Hagar the Egyptian, it will be remembered, was Abraham's concubine, given to him by his wife Sarah when she could not bear a child. Known through legend as mother of the Ishmaelites, she was depicted by artists as having a dark skin.

Jefferson continued in this letter to Maria Cosway: "I am but a son of nature, loving what I see & feel, without being able to give a reason, nor caring much whether there be one." Shortly afterward he formulated what became the most provocative of all his moral directives to society: "The earth belongs to the living and not to the dead." He wrote this in a famous letter to James Madison on September 6, 1789, repeating it in slightly different fashion: "The earth belongs always to the living generation. . . . They are masters too of their own persons, and consequently may govern them as they please."

In another fascinating letter, written to Maria Cosway on January 14, 1789, he described himself as "an animal of a warm climate, a mere Oran-ootan." In 1789 the word *orang-utan* meant for most people not one of the great apes but "wild man of the woods," the literal

translation of the Malay words from which it is derived. There was
much confusion about the relation of the great apes to man; even the
gorilla was as yet unknown in Europe and America. In his *Notes on
the State of Virginia*, published only a few months before Sally Hemings' arrival, Jefferson had indiscreetly written that blacks preferred
white women, just as "the Oran-ootan" preferred "the black woman
over those of his own species." We do not know exactly what Jefferson conceived an "Oran-ootan" to be in 1787, but we do know that in
Paris on October 2, 1788, he sent away to his London bookseller for
a list of books which included E. Tyson's *Oran-outang, or an anatomy
of a pigmy* (1699), a work that tried to clarify the problem of whether
an orang-utan was an ape or a man. All of this would indicate that
Jefferson was suddenly uncomfortable about what he had written in
his book. And well he might be. For when the Federalist press in
America later heard rumors about his slave paramour, it needled Jefferson mercilessly on this very passage. For example, on September
29, 1802, the editor of the Frederick-Town, Virginia, *Herald* quoted
from Jefferson's *Notes*, adding that "by the same criterion he might
be making himself out to be an 'Oranootan.' . . . there is merriment
on the subject."

There is also what one might call "hard," as well as psychological,
evidence that Jefferson was treating Sally Hemings with special consideration. A curious item for April 29, 1789, in Jefferson's Paris account book reads as follows:

> pd Dupré 5 weeks board of Sally   105"
> washing &c   <u>41–9</u>
>   146–9

This suggests the possibility that when Jefferson went to Holland and
Germany he saw to it that Sally was properly chaperoned in a French
home and not left as prey to the French servants in his ministry on
the Champs Elysées. Jefferson's account book shows, too, that in April,
1789, he spent a surprising amount of money on Sally Hemings'
clothes. His figures for that month include ninety-six francs for "clothes
for Sally on April 6," seventy-two more on the sixteenth, and an additional twenty-three francs on the twenty-sixth for "making clothes for
servts," which might also apply to her wardrobe. The total, including

the last, was 191 francs, almost as much as the 215 francs he had spent on his daughter Martha the previous June.

The basic "proof" of the liaison, of course, would be Sally Hemings' pregnancy in Paris at age sixteen. To support this, we have the statement of her son Madison, who could have learned it only from his mother and who, perhaps, learned from her at the same time the French word for pregnant, *enceinte*. But there is additional evidence, for which one must jump ahead almost thirteen years to 1802, when Jefferson was President. Madison Hemings tells us that the child was born "soon after" their arrival back in America, which was in late October, 1789. On September 2, 1802, James T. Callender, co-editor of the Richmond *Recorder*, published the following:

> It is well known that the man, *whom it delighteth the people to honor*, keeps and for many years has kept, as his concubine, one of his slaves. Her name is SALLY. The name of her oldest is Tom. His features are said to bear a striking though sable resemblance to the president himself. The boy is ten or twelve years of age.

Most Jefferson biographers give the impression that Callender was a lying renegade who was determined to destroy Jefferson politically. It is true that he was obsessively a defamer of the great, and that after calling Jefferson a hero for some years he had turned against him venomously. But while Callender repeated and exaggerated scandal, he did not invent it. He had been the first to publish the story of Alexander Hamilton's affair with Mrs. Reynolds, which Hamilton later admitted. He was also the first to publish the ancient rumor that Jefferson before his own marriage had tried to seduce Betsey Walker, the wife of one of his best friends. Poor Jefferson, terribly besieged, and even threatened by Walker with a challenge to a duel in 1803, finally in 1805 admitted privately in a now-famous letter, "When young and single I offered love to a handsome lady; I acknolege its incorrectness."

Callender in 1802 was told by Jefferson's neighbors that Sally Hemings by then had borne Jefferson five children, and he reported this additional scandal in the *Recorder* on September 15. Though Jefferson's *Farm Book* records are scanty up to 1794, we know from scattered entries after that date that Sally Hemings bore four children from 1795 to 1802, and that two of them, both daughters, died in infancy. Once Callender broke the story, other newspapermen felt free to join the attack, and it soon became evident that some of them had been quietly circulating among themselves since 1800 the rumors that Jefferson had a slave mistress. Now those who had not heard of it began checking on their own.

The editor of the Lynchburg, Virginia, *Gazette*, who scolded Jefferson like an indignant parish vicar for not marrying a nice white girl, said that he had waited two months for a Presidential denial of Callender's charges, and then made inquiries and found "nothing but proofs of their authenticity." The Frederick-Town *Herald* editor wrote that he had waited three months before personally checking, and then concluded:

> Other information assures us that Mr. Jefferson's Sally and their children are real persons, and that the woman herself has a room to herself at Monticello in the character of semstress to the family, if not as house-keeper, that she is an industrious and orderly creature in her behaviour, but that her intimacy with her master is well known, and that on this account she is treated by the rest of his house as one much above the level of his other servants. Her son, whom Callender calls president Tom, we are assured, bears a strong likeness to Mr. Jefferson.

This description of Sally's position is very like that given by Madison Hemings:

> We were always permitted to be with our mother, who was well used. It was her duty all her life which I can remember, up to the time of father's death, to take care of his chamber and wardrobe, and look after us children and do such light work as sewing &c.

Jefferson's staunch editor friend, Meriwether Jones, in defending the President in the Richmond *Examiner* on September 25, 1802, made a rare and astonishing public admission that mulatto children were born by the thousands on southern plantations. He admitted also that there was a "mulatto child" at Monticello but denied that Jefferson was the father:

> That this servant woman has a child is very true. But that it is M. Jefferson's, or that the connection exists, which Callender mentions, *is false*—I call upon him for his evidence. . . .

In gentlemen's houses everywhere, we know that the virtue of the unfortunate slaves is assailed with impunity. . . . Is it strange therefore, that a servant of Mr. Jefferson's at a house where so many strangers resort, who is daily engaged in the ordinary vocations of the family, like thousands of others, should have a mulatto child? Certainly not.

John Adams, one of the few statesmen of the time who could testify firsthand about Sally Hemings' beauty, fully believed the Callender story. He said, privately, that it was "a natural and almost unavoidable consequence of that foul contagion in the human character—Negro slavery." But he found circulation of the story saddening. It is said that young John Quincy Adams wrote a ballad about the President and Sally, as did a great many other bad poets at the time.

Jefferson, despite enormous public and private pressure, made no public denial of either the Sally Hemings or the Mrs. Walker story. He insisted that he would not dignify calumny by answering it in the press, though actually he did delegate friends, to whom he supplied material, quietly, to write defenses on his behalf. We know he wrote at least one article during the crisis of these scandals and published it under the pseudonym Timoleon, but curiously it answered only one charge, both obscure and false, namely, that he had paid one Gabriel Jones a debt of £50 in depreciated currency.

There were other defenses made, however, that touched on Sally Hemings. William Burwell, Jefferson's private secretary in 1805, in an unpublished memoir now in the Library of Congress, tells us that at Jefferson's request he wrote a series of articles for the Richmond *Enquirer* in 1805 in reply to accusations of a Virginia plantation owner, Tom Turner, in the Boston *Repertory*. Turner had accused Jefferson of a whole list of misdemeanors, including the favorite Federalist canard that he had acted as a coward when, during the Revolution, the British invaded Virginia while he was governor of the state. Turner had also insisted that the Sally Hemings story was "unquestionably true." The Burwell articles, called "Vindication to Mr. Jefferson," appeared serially in the Richmond *Enquirer* in August and September of 1805. They consisted chiefly of a vigorous defense of Jefferson's wartime governorship. But of the slave-paramour charge Burwell, on September 27, 1805, said only that it was "below the dignity of a man of understanding."

Finally, in 1805, apparently under great pressure, Jefferson wrote a private letter, now missing, to his Attorney General, Levi Lincoln. In it, presumably, he answered more, possibly all, of the many charges being heaped upon him in the venomous Federalist press. He sent a copy to Robert Smith, Secretary of the Navy, on July 1, 1805, with a covering letter, part of which we have already quoted, in which he acknowledged offering love to Betsey Walker. But he then added that this story was "the only one founded in truth among all their allegations against me." Because of that statement, some Jefferson scholars believe that this covering letter is "a categorical denial" by Jefferson of the Sally Hemings story.

And yet the original letter to Levi Lincoln, the copy to Robert Smith, and presumably the letterpress copy Jefferson almost always made of his letters have all inexplicably disappeared. One wonders why. If this letter contained the denial Jefferson's friends had been hoping to see for almost three years, what became of it and the copies? The covering letter to Robert Smith is very ambiguous. Who knows exactly which "allegations against me" Jefferson had chosen to list in the missing letter? It is conceivable that this letter and its copies disappeared because there was something essentially and inadvertently damaging to Jefferson in them.

The story of the abuse heaped upon Jefferson during his Presidency in regard to his intimate life has never been told in full detail. Nor have the evidences of his anguished reaction to this abuse ever been pieced together in such a fashion that one can see the extent of his humiliation and his suffering. Nevertheless, despite the savagery of the attacks, despite the dozen or so published pornographic ballads, Jefferson kept Sally Hemings and her children at Monticello. In 1805 and 1808 she bore two more sons.

Years later Thomas Jefferson Randolph, Jefferson's favorite grandson, who was born in 1792 and spent many summers at Monticello, in effect growing up with Sally Hemings' children, talked to biographer Henry Randall confidentially about the controversy. Randall reported privately that Randolph described one of the children as looking so much like Jefferson that "at some distance or in the dusk the slave, dressed in the same way, might have been mistaken for Mr. Jefferson." Since he was a house servant, Randall noted, "the likeness between master and slave was blazoned to all the multitudes who visited this political mecca." When Randall asked Randolph why Jefferson did not send this family away from Monticello to another of his plantations, the grandson replied that though "he had no doubt his mother would have been very glad to have them thus removed," still "all venerated Mr. Jefferson too deeply to broach such a topic to him," and "he never betrayed the least consciousness of the resemblance."

One is reminded here of Tolstoi, also a great egalitarian, who had an illegitimate son by a serf on his estate before marrying the Countess Sophia. This son became Tolstoi's coachman—similarly visible for everyone to see. But he was never educated like Tolstoi's numerous legitimate children nor made part of the inner family.

Both Thomas Jefferson Randolph and his sister, Ellen Randolph Coolidge, blamed their uncles, Peter and Samuel Carr, instead of their grandfather, for the paternity of Sally Hemings' children. Randolph told Randall in all seriousness that he himself had "slept within sound of his [Jefferson's] breathing at night," and "had never seen a motion, or a look, or a circumstance" that was suspicious. Still, in an article about his grandfather, he wrote that Jefferson's bedroom-study was his sanctum sanctorum, and that even his own daughters never sat in it.

In the end, much evidence is contained in the history of Sally Hemings' seven children. Despite the strenuous "family denial" and the secrecy Jefferson himself, not surprisingly, seems to have encouraged, a considerable amount of information is available about them. Ellen Randolph Coolidge, in discussing the "yellow children" at Monticello in an unpublished letter, wrote that she knew of her "own knowledge" that Jefferson permitted "each of his slaves as were sufficiently white to pass for white to withdraw quietly from the plantation; it was called running away, but they were never reclaimed." "I remember," she wrote, "four instances of this, three young men and a girl, who walked away and staid away—their whereabouts was perfectly known but they were left to themselves—for they were white enough to pass for white."

TOM

There are three runaways listed in Jefferson's *Farm Book*. Jamy, son of Critta Hemings, born in 1787 when Jefferson was still in Paris, ran away in April, 1804. Beverly and Harriet, two children of Sally Hem-

ings, ran away in 1822. It is possible that the fourth runaway referred
to by Ellen Coolidge was the oldest son of Sally Hemings, the one
Callender derisively called "president Tom." Though he is described
in the newspapers of 1802 as resembling Jefferson, in one respect he
remains the most mysterious of all Sally Hemings' children because he
is not listed in the *Farm Book* under the name of his mother, as are
the others. Since there are at least six different slaves named Tom recorded at various times in the *Farm Book,* only one listed with a birth
year, absolute identification of "Tom Hemings" in this old record is
not possible.

Jefferson listed his slaves first in 1774, again in 1783, but not again
till 1794. During his Presidency, 1801 through March, 1809, he neglected his *Farm Book* altogether. Almost all his slaves are listed by first
name only except Betty, Peter, and John Hemings and two or three
others, including an old slave, Tom Shackleford. Sally Hemings is
easily identified, both by her birth year, 1773, and by the names of
her children, listed and indented under her own, at least when they
were small. Of the several slaves in the *Farm Book* named Tom, one
appears frequently among the Hemings family slaves, which are usually listed together. He does not appear on the official inventories of
1794, 1798, and 1810, but shows up consistently on the food and
clothing distribution lists from 1794 to 1801. It can be argued that
this "Tom" represents Tom Shackleford without his last name. If
true, then it would seem that Jefferson did not choose to list Sally
Hemings' oldest son regularly among his slaves and may have considered him free from birth.

Martha Jefferson Randolph mentions a "Tom" in a letter to her father on January 22, 1798, describing an epidemic of sickness in the
neighborhood:

> Our intercourse with Monticello has been almost *daily*. They
> have generally been well there except Tom and Goliah who are
> both *about* again and poor little Harriot who died a few days
> after you left us.

This "Harriot," we know from *Farm Book* entries, was Sally Hemings'
daughter, and the "Tom" may have been her son. There were two
slaves named Goliah at Monticello, one an old man and the other a
child of seven.

There are no listings in the *Farm Book* between 1801 and 1810. By this time Tom Shackleford had died, but there are several listings of a "hired" Tom in 1810 and 1811. One can speculate that this was "Tom Hemings," and that he was by then old enough for regular wages. Since no slave named Tom appears after 1811 in the *Farm Book*, it is possible that Sally Hemings' son left Monticello in that year, when he was twenty-one. This would have been a fulfillment of Jefferson's promise to Sally, as described by her son Madison.

Madison Hemings, who was born in 1805, makes no mention of an older brother Tom. It is possible that the "president Tom" who was the subject of all the ribald publicity from 1802 through 1805 was persuaded to leave the shelter of Monticello after he became old enough to make the transition into white society on his own. Even in 1805 he would have been fifteen, old enough to leave. He could have returned for the summers of 1810 and 1811, long enough to appear in various distribution lists. Madison Hemings wrote that the child his mother conceived in France "lived but a short time." Here he is obviously confusing him with the two small daughters who died in 1796 and 1797. It is conceivable that Sally Hemings, burned by the scandal-mongering publicity of 1802–1805, chose not to discuss this son with anyone after his departure and made every effort to protect his identity in the white society by a mantle of silence. Such behavior is common even today among relatives of a black who "passes."

HARRIET AND EDY

Jefferson was in political semiretirement at Monticello from January 16, 1794, to February 20, 1797. He wrote to Edward Rutledge on November 30, 1795, "Your son . . . found me in a retirement I doat on, living like an Antediluvian patriarch among my children & grandchildren, and tilling my soil." The celebrated French rationalist, Comte de Volney, a fugitive from the French Revolution, visited Jefferson in Monticello in 1796. He noted in his journal some astonishment at seeing slave children as white as himself: "Mais je fus étonné de voir appeler noirs et traiter comme tels des enfants aussi blancs que moi." They resulted, he said, from miscegenation between mulatto slave women and the white workmen Jefferson hired. But were some of these children in fact Jefferson's?

Two daughters were born to Sally Hemings during this temporary retirement: Harriet, on October 5, 1795, and Edy, whose name is listed twice in 1796 in the *Farm Book* under Sally's name and then disappears. Edy, it can be assumed, died in 1796, since she appears in no slave listings under her mother's name thereafter. We know that Harriet died in 1797, not only because she disappears from *Farm Book* listings after that year, but also by Martha Jefferson's report in January, 1798, already quoted. If Jefferson wrote a letter of sympathy to Sally Hemings, there is no record of it. What has been preserved is his reply to Martha, a letter of such melancholy that it suggests something more than peripheral involvement. He said in part:

> Indeed I feel myself detaching very fast, perhaps too fast, from every thing but yourself, your sister, and those who are identified with you. These form the last hold the world will have on me, the cords which will be cut only when I am loosened from this state of being. I am looking forward to the spring with all the fondness of desire to meet you all once more.

BEVERLY

Beverly, a son, was born to Sally Hemings on April 1, 1798, eight months and twenty days after Jefferson's arrival in Monticello from Philadelphia on July 11, 1797. We know nothing of Beverly's youth except a tantalizing reference in the reminiscences of the Monticello slave named Isaac, who referred to "the balloon that Beverly sent off," and the fact that he is listed as a runaway at age twenty-four. Madison Hemings wrote that "Beverly left Monticello and went to Washington as a white man. He married a white woman in Maryland, and their only child, a daughter, was not known by the white folks to have any colored blood coursing in her veins. Beverly's wife's family were people in good circumstances." All of this suggests that Beverly had some schooling at Monticello and could have had some financial assistance from Jefferson, as did his sister Harriet.

HARRIET (No. 2)

A second Harriet, named after the child that died in 1797, was born in May, 1801, and it must be noted that Jefferson was in Monticello from May 29 to November 24, 1800. Harriet was listed as a runaway in the *Farm Book* in 1822. Edmund Bacon, an overseer at Monticello, said later of this slave girl:

> He [Jefferson] freed one girl some years before he died, and there was a great deal of talk about it. She was nearly as white as anybody and very beautiful. People said he freed her because she was his own daughter. She was not his daughter: she was _____'s daughter. I know that. I have seen him come out of her mother's room many a morning when I went up to Monticello very early. When she was nearly grown, by Mr. Jefferson's direction I paid her stage fare to Philadelphia and gave her fifty dollars. I have never seen her since and don't know what became of her. From the time she was large enough, she always worked in the cotton factory. She never did any hard work.

Bacon, however, did not come to Monticello as overseer till 1806, after six of Sally's seven children were born, and he never lived in the big house.

Madison Hemings wrote of his sister Harriet with a touch of irony:

> Harriet married a white man in good standing in Washington City, whose name I could give, but will not, for prudential reasons. She raised a family of children, and so far as I know they were never suspected of being tainted with African blood in the community where she lived or lives. I have not heard from her for ten years, and do not know whether she is dead or alive.

MADISON

Madison Hemings, named after James Madison, was born January 19, 1805. Jefferson was not in Monticello at his birth, but had been there from April 4 to May 11, 1804. Madison's reminiscences, on the whole remarkable for their accuracy of detail concerning Monticello, show evidence of considerable education, though he insists he learned to read "by inducing the white children to teach me." Of his relations with Jefferson he writes in his memoir:

> He was uniformly kind to all about him. He was not in the habit of showing partiality or fatherly affection to us children. We were the only children of his by a slave woman. He was affec-

tionate toward his white grandchildren, of whom he had fourteen, twelve of whom lived to manhood and womanhood.

The slave Isaac in his reminiscences reported that "Sally had a son
named Madison, who learned to be a great fiddler," but we do not
know whether it was Jefferson, himself an able violinist, who taught
the young slave who claimed to be his son. Freed by Jefferson in his
will, Madison lived for a time with his mother (by then also free) in
Albermarle County, Virginia, married a free black woman in 1834,
and after his mother's death in 1835 went west to Ohio, where he
made his living as a carpenter.

ESTON

Jefferson was in Monticello from August 4 to October 1, 1807. Eston
Hemings was born May 21, 1808. As with Beverly, Harriet, and Madison, his name appears many times in the *Farm Book* under the name
of Sally Hemings. He was one of the five slaves freed in Jefferson's
will, all of whom were members of the Hemings family. Madison
Hemings wrote that Eston married a free black woman, immigrated
to Ohio, and then went on to Wisconsin.

Jefferson's will contained the request that the Virginia legislature be
petitioned to permit Madison and Eston Hemings to stay in the state
if they so chose. Otherwise, by Virginia law, which barred free Negroes, they would automatically have been banished. Still, it must be
noted, by Jefferson's own reckoning, based on Virginia's legal definitions of the time, these youths were white. When a friend wrote to
him in 1815 asking at what point a black man officially changes into
a white man, Jefferson replied explicitly, "Our canon considers two
crosses with the pure white, and a third with any degree of mixture,
however small, as clearing the issue of negro blood."

And what, in the end, was "the condition" of Sally Hemings? Jefferson did not free her in his will, but left this service for his daughter
Martha to perform, which she did two years after Jefferson's death in
1826. Had Jefferson freed her during his lifetime and made the necessary request from the Virginia legislature that she be allowed to remain in the state, the news would have been trumpeted over the na-

tion. This publicity he was probably unwilling to subject himself to, and it is conceivable that Sally Hemings never requested it. Still, it is a melancholy discovery to find her listed on the official inventory of Jefferson's estate, made after his death, as an "old woman" worth thirty dollars. She was then fifty-three.

Madison Hemings wrote that his mother lived with him and Eston Hemings in a rented house until her death in 1835. The U.S. Census of Albermarle County in 1830 listed Eston Hemings as head of a family, and as a white man. The other members of this family are listed under his name by age and sex only, as was traditional at the time. There is a listing of a woman—fifty to sixty years of age—described as white. This is Sally Hemings. So the census taker, in making this small descriptive decision, underlined the irony and tragedy of her life.

As for Jefferson, he had watched with increasing despair over the years as Virginia permitted slavery to expand and as the laws controlling slaves became ever more repressive. He had seen the social degradation imposed upon Sally Hemings' five living children by the taboos and rituals of the slave society in which he was inextricably enmeshed. So rigid were these taboos that he could not admit these children to be his own, even when they passed into white society, without social ostracism and political annihilation. Whether one believes they were his children or not, one cannot deny that he paid dearly for their presence on that enchanted hill. He could not abandon the slave society in Virginia if he would, and he would not if he could. Overwhelmed at the end with a crushing burden of debt—$107,000—he could not find his way to free in his will more than five of his hundred-odd slaves. He had lived almost half of his life, in the phrase he used to describe himself to Maria Cosway at age seventy-seven, "like a patriarch of old." And so his ambivalence—which may well have served to lessen for him the sense of the tragedy of it all—was continually compounded.

II THE YOUNG REPUBLIC

10

Public Versus Private Education: The Neglected Meaning of the Dartmouth College Case

ELDON L. JOHNSON

• Almost alone among the great nations of the world, the United States has two distinct systems of higher education—one public and the other private. The reasons for such a dichotomy are many and varied, but if we look for the origins of the American pattern no issue will loom larger than the Dartmouth College case. Indeed, the United States Supreme Court's judgement on this litigation in 1819 is often regarded as the single most important judicial decision in all of American history.

"It is a small college," noted Daniel Webster (class of 1801) in his eloquent defense, "and yet there are those who love it." He referred to the attempt of New Hampshire to change the college into a state university, to be called Dartmouth University. The charter of the institution, which was established in 1769 under Congregationalist auspices, was the issue in dispute. The state argued that Dartmouth was essentially a public corporation whose powers were exercised for public purposes and were subject to public control. The Dartmouth trustees countered with the claim that the college was a private eleemosynary institution.

Chief Justice John Marshall, in giving the opinion of the high court in 1819, ruled that Dartmouth's charter was a contract within the meaning of the United States Constitution and that as a contract it could not be repealed or altered by legislation. The Dartmouth College decision was a stunning defeat for those in every state who wanted to transform the colonial colleges into state universities under public control. In essence, the Supreme Court ruling meant that Harvard, Yale, Princeton, Columbia, Pennsylvania, and similarly

Reprinted by permission of the *Journal of the Early Republic*.

chartered institutions were and could remain independent. Henceforth, individual states would have to start from scratch to create their own institutions of higher learning.

Dartmouth, meanwhile, went on to great distinction as a center of academic excellence and established medical, business, engineering, and graduate schools of high quality. Although the institution became a university in fact, its trustees have always clung to the name which they fought so hard to keep in 1819—Dartmouth College.

The Dartmouth College case, its climactic decision coming amidst intellectual and institutional churnings in the formative years of American higher education, has been examined and reexamined far more for its constitutional than its educational meaning. The U.S. Supreme Court decision of 1819 is famous in constitutional law for its statements on private rights and corporation privileges. It is, perhaps, the most quoted decision of all, but for reasons that have nothing to do with education. Two great questions remain. What were the educational ideology and goals in the attempted reform of the Dartmouth charter? And what was the effect on the development of the supposed alternative of public higher education? Almost no attention has been given the first question, fundamental though it would seem; and the little attention given the second, with one notable exception, has been based on questionable inference. A return to these educational questions seems overdue since a college was the centerpiece, the state was trying to change it, the court said what could not be done and intimated what could, and both the educational ideas espoused and the educational prohibitions imposed must have reverberated down through history for alert ears to hear. One's curiosity is also piqued by that little explained sentence in which one historian suggested that public higher education was thus held back fifty years—an idea since echoed by others without much examination. The effect on private higher education, bolstered by the court's vigorous defense of private philanthropy, is much less in doubt and will be treated here only indirectly.

All know about Daniel Webster and his pleading for the small college that some still loved (although actually, in number of graduates produced, it was second only to Harvard). All know too about John Marshall, who, as chief justice, wrote what could not be done to the college. But who knows about William Plumer, governor of New Hampshire, and what this Yankee Jeffersonian was trying to do? And who knows of the overall significance of the Dartmouth College case in the evolution of public higher education? History is a plaster which is hard to change once applied.

It all began in a church quarrel. The relation of Dartmouth's professor of divinity to the local church triggered a larger controversy about who would run the college. Trustees were soon galvanized into factions in their long festering relations with President John Wheelock. Losing his grip after more than thirty years, he invoked the royal charter which the colonial governor had issued in 1769 to Wheelock's father, Eleazar, and went to the New Hampshire legislature for relief. Thus began, in the words of a Dartmouth historian, "a quarrel which was to end in the Supreme Court of the United States, with all the nation looking on." The president, abetted by the minority trustees, memorialized the legislature for public remedy; the opposing trustees took sufficient umbrage to dismiss Wheelock before the resulting legislative investigating committee could report; and the charter (private or public?) became a burning public issue. Newspapers took sides. Pamphlets appeared for and against. Indignation ran against both Wheelock's dismissal and the "dynasty" he tried to perpetuate through the charter.

In time, the issue was politicized. Federalists tended to support the status quo and Republicans favored change; so the New Hampshire election of 1816 was waged on the issue. Afterwards, the new governor, William Plumer, made charter reform one of the two critical issues on which he called for legislative remedy. Following a bitter, protracted struggle of parliamentary maneuver, attempted delay, investigations, and embarrassing divisions (all along political lines), the legislature narrowly voted to "improve" the royal charter carried over into republican times—to make the governance of the college more public and less self-perpetuating, and to conceive the new embodiment as "Dartmouth University." The state injected itself dramatically into college affairs by increasing the number of trustees; giving veto power to a large new board of overseers to be named by the governor and council, who were obligated to inspect the doings of all officers; requiring president and professors to take an oath to support the United States and New Hampshire constitutions; calling for an annual presidential report to the governor on enrollment and the "state of funds"; and guaranteeing "perfect freedom of religious opinion."

But it was not to be so simple. The opposing trustees who were carried over and their college allies dug in their heels, frustrated a quorum, drove governor and legislature to try again with amendments, took the great majority of students off campus for continued instruction, hired the most distinguished lawyers, and carried the matter to the courts. Eventually, the highest state court upheld the act and an appeal was taken to the Supreme Court solely on the grounds that the college charter was a contract inviolate under the Constitution. With Daniel Webster pleading and with other distinguished lawyers participating, Chief Justice Marshall and fellow justices (with one dissent), held for the college in *Trustees of Dartmouth College* v. *Woodward* in 1819. The state legislative act was void because the college was a charitable institution, not a public corporation; hence the charter was a contract and could not be impaired under the Constitution.

What did this mean, at the time and for the future? In looking back, it is now clear that the case originated in differing conceptions of the college mission and of institutional responsibility. It is also clear that it helped shape American higher education in its formative years. Yet the educational significance of the Dartmouth case has been neglected, particularly in understanding what Governor Plumer and his allies were attempting, in ideas as well as in action.

It may be noted at the outset that William Plumer was a public man in the best tradition of the Enlightenment in early America. He was an independently minded, self-educated lawyer who made significant political and intellectual contributions, both locally and nationally. At twenty-six years of age, he entered the state legislature, where he served eight terms and rose to speaker of the house and president of the senate. The revised state constitution of 1792 was so much of his shaping that opponents called it "Plumer's Constitution." Despite his professed indifference when out of public office, politics kept calling him back from law, farm, and books—once to the United States Senate, 1802–1807, and repeatedly to the governorship of New Hampshire, in 1812, and for three yearly terms from 1816 to 1819. Plumer began as a Federalist but deplored blind party loyalty and, despite his initial dislike and suspicion of Jefferson, eventually shifted to the Republican party.

While not so consistently liberal as Jefferson, Plumer pressed religious liberty with such fervor that he provoked violent recriminations. He embraced reform and thought well ahead of his time: in treatment of prisoners and debtors, in legal codification, in educational philosophy, and in advocacy of an income tax. Beyond that, he had ideas about virtually everything, as shown in the 186 essays he wrote and published between 1820 and 1829. He was widely read, often quoting Bacon, Montaigne, Locke, Rousseau, Pope, Gibbon, and Adam Smith. His private library was almost half the size of Dartmouth College. From his exposure to the nation's capital in the formative years, he resolved to write the definitive history of North America and was encouraged to do so by Jefferson, John Quincy Adams, and others. What he left, instead, were many useful biographical remnants and significant aid to new regional historical societies. All in all, he was a fiercely independent man of intellectual substance, "a man of conviction, of stubborn courage, and of devotion to principles wider than his own horizons and nobler than his own character." Paying tribute to the local bar which so helped shape the young Daniel Webster in Portsmouth, New Hampshire, biographer Henry Cabot Lodge named Plumer as "the most eminent" and "a man of cool and excellent judgment," who "was one of Mr. Webster's early antagonists, and defeated him in their first encounter."

This was the man whose position as governor of New Hampshire brought him into the midst of the Dartmouth College controversy. Given his qualities and values, however, it is quite likely that he would have spoken out on the issues of the case in any event. Partisan politics was indeed present. With plenty of initiative from both sides, it sprang both from current interest and past history. It reflected the intense public controversy engendered and testified that a "public interest" was perceived by many common citizens and their leaders. Moreover, as John S. Whitehead pointed out in *The Separation of College and State*, Dartmouth had long followed the collegiate pattern of the time, sought uneasy alliances with the state, asked state favors, and thus incurred political risks from the fierce battle between Federalists and Republicans for state supremacy. Indeed, one line of legal defense held that "our Legislature has often interfered and had thus gained a kind of prescriptive right of interference." Isaac Hill, partisan Republican editor of the *New Hampshire Patriot and State Gazette*, thought that "the future governance of D. College," if "judiciously managed, will be a means of perpetuating the republican majority in the State." When the Federalists attempted to thwart the two great legislative changes of 1816—both judicial reform and charter reform—the college reformers gladly joined the issues for the fall election, and prepared to deal with the unconvinced Dartmouth trustees in the "common interest of our party." The governor was dragged in further than expected because another "long and unpleasant session" was required for patch-up amendments to produce a workable quorum of trustees, with fines for holdouts. In this political climate, the aggrieved and irascible President Wheelock easily precipitated a nasty battle over his reinstatement, which became hopelessly confused with broader governance considerations. However, as a later president of the college said, "It would be unjust . . . to recall this ancient controversy from the side of the College without making the frank acknowledgement that the College invited the interference of the State."

On the charter and governance issues, Plumer clearly acted with competent legal knowledge and legitimate interest in sound public policy. He knew what other states had tried to do, recognized the unsettled legal implications, and had already taken the position that legislatures were incautiously passing acts of incorporation, often "in the nature of grants," without reserving legislative power of repeal or modification "when they cease to answer the end for which they were made, or prove injurious to the public interest." This plea for charters of public responsibility was expressed in Plumer's first gubernatorial message to the legislature four years before the Dartmouth crisis. On vindicating President Wheelock, Plumer's own letters are singularly free of political motivation, although he received commendation for "defense of our venerable friend" and never flinched from battle with the old Federalists. While he once equated Republican victory with "justice to the injured [President] Wheelock," he later wrote that "it has long been a subject of great regret to me that the name of Dartmouth University has been considered as a political party question." Looking beyond presidential restoration, Plumer asked his partisan allies to join in devising "a system . . . to prevent the college being again exposed to similar evils." His subsequent naming of the board members from both parties gave some credibility to his florid hope "that when the sod shall be green on my grave those who survive me will say I have preferred men of merit to political partisans." His concern was for a certain type of institution, more broadly representative, that would reflect his strong views about education with public relevance and responsibility; hence, he fervently urged a trustee to public duty lest "the University remain unorganized . . . and perhaps the current of public opinion [be] turned against the Institution."

Fortunately, we also have a clear picture of Plumer's educational philosophy in a remarkable series of newspaper essays written under the name of "Cincinnatus" two years after the Supreme Court rebuff. He was critical of existing collegiate education and thought it called for radical reform. Such reform would have three major thrusts. It would come from institutions under public control and support, state oriented rather than church oriented. It would emphasize educational application to daily life—the useful, the scientific, the ordinary vocations. It would be open to the poor as well as the rich.

American institutions had become slightly more liberal than the English, but the same "mistaken policy" prevailed, wherein *the great object of colleges was to educate young men for priesthood*, rather than to qualify them for the duties of civil life." Harvard and Dartmouth were both church-ridden, too subject to "principles unfavorable to the progress of education in the higher branches of literature and science." Hence the usual inquiry was "not whether the public need other colleges, but whether *particular sects* want them." Instead, colleges should be "formed and governed" without regard to religion or party. "The commonwealth of letters is free—men of erudition of all countries, sects, and parties are its members—and no scholar can be alien from it." Existing colleges were good for the education of the clergy (they needed it, he said) but they should be more—"of a different character . . . suited to the pursuits and business of *this life*." This conviction that contemporary collegiate education was too "monkish" appeared again and again in Plumer's writings; in fact, he thought the ecclesiastical rather than civil emphasis might be "hostile to our republican system."

What was wrong with the colleges was typified by the retention of, and emphasis on, ancient languages and the mode of their teaching. He objected when his children and grandchildren were subjected to Greek, Latin, or Hebrew and rejoiced when French or German was taken. He did not want the prime of life wasted on useless learning and, worse yet, on the form rather than the substance: on the language of the ancients instead of the opinions, ideas, and knowledge possessed by the ancients.

For remedy, Plumer would first put an end to the private-public ambiguity being played upon, as he learned to his sorrow in the Dartmouth case. "When the government of our colleges apply to the people or to the legislature for aid," he wrote, "they represent the college as a *public institution*."

> But when the legislature of the State enact [*sic*] laws for their better regulation and improvement, then the college is to be considered as a *private corporation* exempt from all legislative acts. . . . Let the legislature establish *a public Academy* in each county in the State, subject to the control . . . of civil government. . . . After such academies are established, and the people experience their salutary effects, the legislature will have an easy task to establish a public college or university upon similar principles. Society owes too much to education to justify legislators who neglect the means for its support.

He did not believe that institutions like Dartmouth, many of which received partial public support, were private in the public-hands-off sense held by the Supreme Court; but, if so, then alternative public institutions should be established. Such institutions, moreover, should and would be responsive to the need for new kind of education—useful education.

The academies Plumer conceived would start with "nothing but what is useful and subservient to the business of human life," and the new college or university would correct the mistake of not adopting "effectual measures for instructing youth in the useful arts [and] in science." As "now constituted and governed," however, no college can give "useful and complete education." Plumer underscored the point: "In what school, academy or college are the principles and sciences of agriculture, of commerce, of manufactures, or of mechanics taught? These are important subjects in which we have a direct and deep interest: for it is from them we derive all the means of substance." Similar sentiments came from Jonathan Baldwin Turner and Justin Morrill forty years later, at the inception of the national system of land grant colleges. It is fitting that in closing his twenty-fifth article on education in the Cincinnatus series, Plumer wrote, *"utility* has been my sole object."

Nor were these educational constructions mere post-Supreme Court rationalizations. While the then new "Dartmouth University" should have given him encouragement, he wrote his friend Salma Hale: "I have long wished to see a fundamental change in these institutions; to have more of the time of students devoted to the acquisition of *useful* rather than ornamental knowledge—the knowledge of *things* rather than that of *words*—and to make proficiency in the *living* rather than the *dead* languages." Then he added plaintively, "I hope for these changes in our university, but I have no reason to expect them." The things/words, living/dead, useful/ornamental dichotomies were a constant refrain.

Utility led to another reform objective. Since life is short, time should be best used; but the great time needed for college preparation and for learning the dead languages "necessarily excludes a vast proportion of our youth from those institutions." So long as this condition continued, public tax support was not justified. Let the "rich and idle" enjoy such, "but free the common people from the support of establishments in the enjoyment of which they cannot participate." This man who later thought Andrew Jackson's election and "the mad spirit of Jacksonism" the greatest misfortune to befall the nation, nevertheless wrote about education in the context of the "common people," the "common affairs of life," the dangers of "the privileged orders," and the need for more responsive institutions befitting the new republicanism.

What Plumer wanted is best summarized in the positive portion of an essay that criticized the existing colleges with unusual severity. Yes, "even in their present state," they could be of some good:

> But to render them extensively useful to the public, they require a radical reform. They should no longer be schools of theology but civil institutions—instead of being private they should be public establishments, not governed by sectarian priests but by men of literature and science without regard to their professions—instead of *dead* languages, the *living* languages should be

taught—the modern discoveries in philosophy and the useful arts
should be promptly adopted; and youth instructed in the arts
and sciences that are applicable to the business of human life.

These were the educational ideas of the man who led the attempt
to amend the Dartmouth charter. They had the immediate potency
of his political influence and, on a more enduring basis, they were
representative of something larger than himself. During the three or
four decades before the ardent advocacy of the 1850s, sentiment for
a more responsive kind of higher education was not lacking. It was
muted both inside and outside the colleges by dormant enrollments
and the flood tide of denominationalism—yet Thomas Jefferson did not
stand alone. There were political leaders and opinion-makers who
made possible all the early state universities. There were others who
promoted particular educational reforms that produced the ingredients
later to be clustered together in institutions controlled and supported
by state governments. When these unsung authors and actors are
brought from obscurity, William Plumer will be prominent among
them. If his word was not wholly original nor his deed wholly enduring, he the better reflected his time and the ferment that would later
transform American higher education, with an alternative closely allied
with the state. He reflected the transitional period in which, according
to one historian, family, church, and community influence over education had waned and the "whole range of education had become an
instrument of deliberate social purpose."

The first question can now be answered—what educational change
was attempted at Dartmouth? As in most political crises, strange bed-
fellows thought differently but acted together. Some wanted merely
to restore President John Wheelock and some merely to defeat political opponents, but what mattered and endured was more substan-
tive. The central attempt was to make Dartmouth more accountable
to public authority and needs, in greater harmony with the ideals of
a democratic secular state and a society of equals. Significantly, that
reform effort was the deliberate expression of a sovereign state (the
organized New Hampshire public) through all its branches: the executive recommendation, the legislative enactment, and the judicial
approval. As the articulate spokesman for many Jeffersonian values of
the time, Plumer spelled out the supporting philosophy and the educational results hoped for, once the form was adopted. He gave the

rationale from which immediate action proceeded and the goals toward which growth was to be directed. These new desiderata were then put at the mercy of quite inadequate means: transforming an existing institution through state "control" that relied on the presence of state officers without the presence of state taxes. But however rebuffed and delayed, the central idea would persist and later flower in institutions that Plumer and his allies countrywide would have found congenial.

The second question about the effect on the development of public higher education can best be approached by examining what happened in New Hampshire first and then elsewhere. The effect upon Dartmouth itself is important because the strategy of the 1816 legislation was to reform an *existing* institution by launching something public and something called a "university." Deposed President John Wheelock's nephew strongly lobbied for a university divided into colleges, as the law contemplated; and when the new Dartmouth University trustees met without a quorum in 1816, they received a committee report that proposed both some curricular broadening and institutional reorganization, with Colleges of Theology, Medicine, and Law. The curious fact is that Dartmouth unofficially had called itself a "university" as early as 1782 and through the catalogs of the entire 1801–1814 period. That was rather the academic fashion of the time and was abandoned, ironically at Dartmouth, only when the legislature sought to impose precisely that name. Were Webster and colleagues influenced by the fact that in English law "university" meant a public corporation, whereas "college" meant a private charity? Before the Supreme Court, Webster derided "the swelling and empty authority" in the "mock elevation to . . . a university." Even Governor Plumer once conceded that "University" and "College" conveyed no real difference. The profound difference was the existence, nevertheless, of two institutions, competing both legally and often ludicrously for students, keys, books, possession of buildings, commencement dates, and public favor. The incongruity climaxed when both institutions held commencements and both conferred honorary degrees on President James Monroe when he visited New England in 1817. The new state-originated institution was a disaster by any standard, with its unhappy status never better shown than in the accountability report that the new legislation required to be filed with the governor. "University" President William Allen labored valiantly but could report accurately only on the number of students—sixteen. The state of funds, official board actions, and everything else was unknown, ambiguous, or speculative. With remarkable understatement, the president confessed to the governor after the Supreme Court decision that "some officers were discouraged." The short-run effect on the existing college was disastrous, too; but how it recovered and later rose to its present esteemed position is not central to our present purposes.

It was unclear whether Dartmouth was a single college temporarily ruptured by fuzziness about the public-private balance or two institutions already set on contrasting courses. The situation was confounded by the insufficient solution the state attempted, as best shown by the conclusion of two New Hampshire legislative committees that state "control" was necessary but that reform of the charter of the existing college would yield that desired result. Relying on the sufficiency of this remote and indirect public patronage for "the cause of literature and science" (not uncommonly proposed elsewhere in New England at the time), one committee took the view that "the surest and most effectual means . . . are to be found in extending to our highest seminary of learning a *controlling* as well as fostering protection— thereby uniting its interests and destinies more firmly with the government of the State." Events were soon to demonstrate that Dartmouth was not the proper subject and a "fostering protection" was not a sufficient method. Furthermore, there is no evidence that Plumer, either as governor or Dartmouth University board member, was determined to force his personal ideas on the new Dartmouth, or that he could have done so through trustees or overseers sometimes as unreliable as executive-appointed judges. He had already failed to wring from the legislature a governing body as publicly representative and responsive (that is, not self-perpetuating) as he wanted. He more than once lamented that his ideas had little hope of acceptance, either under state reform or after the judicial reprieve. He again wrote: "Those institutions are in the hands of men who appear little inclined to change their present course, and still less to acknowledge a right in the people or the legislature to effect a reformation." Whether because of ennui, disillusionment, or decision not to run for gubernatorial reelection, he in 1818 began to excuse himself from university duties and from commencement, with pleas of ill health and hopes for a more useful successor. He apparently did nothing later to foster a public university or to identify with such feeble university-starting efforts as the literary fund gambit of Governor Samuel Bell. Even in logical openings in correspondence with public figures, Plumer withheld comment on university reform, apparently looking back somewhat bitterly on the Dartmouth case as a lost, if not last, opportunity.

Contrary to common assumption, however, this aborted state plan for Dartmouth did not summarily end agitation for state-controlled higher education in New Hampshire. Two great ironies are worthy of mention. In the heat of battle, none other than Daniel Webster suggested the instigation of a plan to create a state-officered "University of New Hampshire" as a means of finding peace; and a loyal Dartmouth trustee group offered a face-saving compromise which would have assured the essential public oversight Plumer sought but could not then gracefully accept. Neither he nor they then knew that trustee acceptance of the compromise would have, because of trustee consent, removed the hinge on which *Dartmouth* v. *Woodward* was to turn. These ambivalent gestures merely recognized, however grudgingly, the durability of the public dimension of the issue; and it remained for Plumer's political successor, Governor Samuel Bell, to make two other valiant attempts to found a separate new university. First, he worked with the 1819 legislature in setting up a committee to devise complete plans for a "public literary institution in this State." But the astutely chosen chairman, President William Allen of the short-lived university, declined the honor because he thought that one college in New Hampshire was enough and he continued to believe that Dartmouth reform of the attempted kind, but with trustee consent, could and should appropriately monopolize legislative patronage. Second, in 1821 the governor and the legislature set up a "literary fund" from a stamp tax on bank circulation. The annual receipts were to support education in the higher branches of literature and science, provided significantly that support should never go to any institution *not* under the direction and control of the state. The muddling of the public-private dichotomy was never better illustrated than when Dartmouth came forward aggressively to seek the money, with willingness to create a Board of Overseers as the "public" price. As the money accumulated, debate ensued on whether to divert it for general state expenses, "for the establishment of a College in some central place," or for schools in the towns. But the public university forces could never muster enough strength to prevail. Their proposed use of the literary fund for a "New Hampshire University" in 1827 passed in the senate, but lost in the house by a two-to-one majority.

That was the high point of public university advocacy in New Hampshire in the half century following the attempted Dartmouth changes. The following year, the new governor began claiming that enough colleges existed in New England, Dartmouth sufficed with its private support, and therefore the towns should receive the literary fund for common schools. As last, that recommendation prevailed. But the seeds of something distinctive, destined eventually to yield fruit, were planted at the same time; that is, the need for agricultural research and training began to be articulated. In the same message that turned off the public university thrust, Governor John Bell lucidly spelled out what he thought, in contrast, was needed—"an experimental farm and agricultural school." It was a remarkable prevision of the later land grant college, with emphasis upon practical as well as scientific education, broader student access, student labor, and even an embryonic extension system. This was all too advanced for the lower house, which resolved neither to purchase an experimental farm nor to "adopt any measures in relation to the same."

This history of muddlement and parsimony detracts from the surmise that if the Dartmouth College case had gone the other way, New Hampshire might have had a flourishing state university at once. Other evidence magnifies the doubt. First of all, the legislature was not the slightest disposed to provide financial support. To make the reformed Dartmouth "a well-endowed institution" with "a liberal patronage" might have been William Plumer's intention, as his son later contended; but the legislature showed no concurrence. In fact, Plumer was himself a zealot of governmental economy. The state even treated shabbily the university trustees and officers who, after the Supreme Court foreclosure, had to appeal for help on the grounds that they had acted in good faith with the legislature's desire "to improve what was thought to be a public institution." Such help as had been given already to the new "public university" amounted to a four thousand dollar *loan*; and its eventual cancellation (because of no alternative for a defunct institution) was a measure of the legislature's largess.

Things were no better across the river in Vermont, where the incubus of the Dartmouth case did not exist. The spirit of the times, in other words, was well reflected in the studied ambiguity of Governor Jonas Golusha, who said to the Vermont legislature in 1816: "If any further aid to education should be deemed necessary, I doubt not that it will receive all the encouragement that present circumstances of the state will admit." That translated into no aid in 1816, 1817, and 1818. The evidence is that intellectual, political, and budgetary forces stripped Governor Samuel Bell and his enthusiastic senate committee of their confidence in 1820 that a public institution "will sooner or later go into operation under the high auspices of the people of New Hampshire." It was much later, rather than sooner. The New Hampshire College of Agriculture and Mechanical Arts was established in 1866, and the name changed to University of New Hampshire in 1923.

Therefore, the consequences within the involved state would seem superficially to be precisely what Tewksbury said: a fifty-year retardation of the state university movement. The fact is one thing, the causes another, as outlined above. In one sense, quite ironically, New Hampshire had been judicially prompted to do what it presumably wanted to do, only to do it in a more direct way. Certainly, it could have founded an institution beneficially dedicated to that specific place—New Hampshire—since the reasoning of both Chief Justice Marshall and Justice Story had gone to some lengths to show that Dartmouth had no ties to geography or service-to-place. But when it came to the doing, the need for a public alternative was not clearly established. Education dominated by religion was more rather than less popular, despite Governor Plumer's hostility, and the good thoughts about education were drowned out by the bad thoughts about taxes. How slowly the "public" concept had evolved, even in fifty years, is shown by New Hampshire's attempt to piggyback its new land grant college on Dartmouth College once more in 1866. It was a tribute to Dartmouth, which made generous concessions, and it was a vote for governmental frugality; but, foredoomed as an unhappy marriage, it was also an indication that little heed was given either the lesson learned by Plumer or the government's remedy stated by Marshall.

The Dartmouth case had repercussions outside New Hampshire also, both on and beyond the state versus college issue. The interest was greater and the information more widespread than some historians have implied. Even before the case was resolved, the New-York Historical Society was asking Plumer for all relevant documents. The issue of state intrusion was a half-century old and the *North American Review* promptly and approvingly presented the Supreme Court's state-restraining decision in January 1820, because none other "excited deeper interest in the public mind" and all colleges "stood on no surer foundation than Dartmouth College." Likewise thinking Dartmouth's fate "perhaps of equal importance to every other literary and charitable corporation of our country," Timothy Farrar, Webster's former partner, immediately rushed the decision (with its history and pleadings) into print in 1819 to reach the public in addition to the professional audience of the official Wheaton report. The case itself had attracted the nation's best legal talent on both sides, and Governor Plumer had sent his 1816 charter reform message to Thomas Jefferson, prompting approval and the famous reply that "our lawyers and priests generally inculcate this doctrine . . . that the earth belongs to the dead, and not to the living." With still closer interest, the colleges of the Northeast were clearly aroused. When a College Congress was held in Boston in 1818 with representatives from Yale, Harvard, Bowdoin, the University of Vermont, Williams, and Andover Theological Seminary present, Dartmouth College President Brown was invited but Dartmouth University President Allen was not. The Dartmouth appellants had already asked other colleges to help defer court costs, but President Kirkland of Harvard declined because the highest court might uphold the state decision, increasing its authority a hundredfold and making its application nationwide. Such were then the dubious odds in the public-private battle, with weighty authority on each side. Out of interest among other colleges, a Yale professor did go to Washington to hear the evidence presented. State and college officials, donors, and their legal counsel could hardly have been uninformed, unimpressed, or unaffected after the exhaustive treatment and rounded reasoning, on both sides, in the state court in 1817 and the federal court in 1818–1819.

It is important to remember, however, that the public overlay on Dartmouth was only the first to be tested, not the first to be attempted. Long ago, Lester W. Bartlett summarized the history of post-Revolution attempts at state control in Massachusetts, Connecticut, Pennsylvania, and New York, showing that New Hampshire's later attempt was by no means the most "oppressive" or "threatening," if judged by the percentage of state officials on the college boards. Dartmouth history differed, however, in the complete polarization of forces, the duality of institutions, the legal deadlock, and the firm resolve to derive a guiding precedent from a local example. As Harvard's history before and after showed, legislative tampering (state officers on boards, vetoing powers, visitations) did not keep the institution from being private, yet did not make it public. Nor was the Dartmouth case to be the last. In 1831, for example, the Maine legislature intruded into Bowdoin College to squeeze out President William Allen. Having come there from the headship of the short-lived "public" version of Dartmouth, Allen paradoxically had to switch roles and resort to the federal courts for the same kind of victory that his opponents had enjoyed in 1819.

It was on the public-private distinction that *Dartmouth* v. *Woodward* had the greatest effect nationwide. While the decision meant that the states could no longer reform private colleges without the consent of the trustees involved, unless such power had been reserved, it also called attention quite specifically to how the public *could* do what William Plumer attempted. Chief Justice Marshall wrote: "That education is . . . a proper subject of legislation, all admit. That there may be an institution founded by government, and placed entirely under its immediate controul, the officers of which would be public officers, amenable exclusively to government, none will deny." Therefore, after 1819, every state legislature with collegiate reform ambitions had new limitations upon it and clarified opportunities before it, even if this dictum merely advertised the obvious. As a result, there was increased potential for affecting the establishment and growth of state universities—either hastening or retarding them.

It would be folly to attribute all that later happened to the Dartmouth case, without awareness of many other factors. Some state universities existed before 1819 and those which came after had other initiatives quite apart from Dartmouth, such as the First Amendment impetus to a secular state university; the public land grants, first for new states and later for all states through the Morrill Act; and the changing conception of what was "public" enough to call for governmental response. But the Dartmouth decision thrust in the opposite direction also and became entwined with the great antebellum proliferation of "Christian" colleges, both denominational and non-denominational. In the church-state confrontation born of revolutionary fervor, religion

rose to clear dominance in collegiate education. Francis Wayland
wrote in 1842: "Almost every college in this country is either originally, or by sliding from its primitive foundation, under the control of
some religious sect." In fact, the dominance was so great that the sliding extended even to established state universities, often submerging
the public parts and dominating the self-perpetuating boards, as ex-
hibited in all six of the state universities then existing in the original
states. That this was a drag on the evolution of "godless universities"
cannot be doubted.

A reexamination of the Dartmouth case is a vivid reminder that institutions of higher education have evolved from myriad forces much
too complex and attenuated to be explained by sudden events and decisive single cases. It is also a reminder that we, like Plumer and the
Dartmouth trustees, are captives of our time and that we are prone to
transfer from present to past that which was never there. When we
apply "public" to collegiate institutions, we connote the concept of
tax-supported, government-owned, and state-run schools, none of which
would have been intelligible in 1816. "Private" higher education—
untouchable and untouched by the state—had not yet arrived, if yet
conceived. Dictionaries and encyclopedias of that time make clear that
"public" meant merely what was "done by many," or for the common good, or open to common use—which obviously could have meant
a group of "private" individuals. That explains why Governor Plumer
thought Dartmouth was already a public institution, why the New
Hampshire court unanimously agreed, and why both sides could accept the "guardian care" and "visitorial power" of the state. Two decades later, in his critique of colleges (then virtually all church-
controlled), Francis Wayland carefully described them as "public
institutions." This confusion between the object of existence and the
finality of control also explains why everyone on the "public" side at
that time had unwarranted confidence in the sufficiency of state control by the mere laying on of hands via governing boards. Later experience was to show that state support, not a vacuous state presence or
concern, was the real key to public higher education. That meant taxation and annual appropriations——again concepts quite foreign to the
public-private blurring of 1816, when all kinds of education still relied
on unassured annual combinations in which the public and tax parts,

if they existed at all, were merely folded into the endowment and current donations parts.

Making a distinction that was to have a profound effect on the relations between state and college, Chief Justice Marshall's language drove a giant wedge into a small fissure. The twin nuclei of private and public could now be separated. They had been conceptually and, in time, would be operationally. But Marshall did not say the poles he identified were the only options. He did not rule out the continuation of some mix between college and state. Not surprisingly, practical men in both college and public life chose for a long time to strive for a balance or an accommodation, rather than an exclusionary extreme. This point is made with convincing documentation by John S. Whitehead, in *The Separation of College and State*. He challenges the conventional wisdom that the Dartmouth College case immediately severed the college-state alliance and clearly set apart public and private higher education. He shows that the Dartmouth trustees accepted their victory as leaving them in the ascendancy in running the college, but they saw no reason to break off the long-standing (if sometimes uneasy) state-college accommodation of mutual gain. As time went on, both at Dartmouth and at other institutions in other states, it was the state rather than the college that opted out of the alliance. With this foreclosure of public support, which went increasingly to public schools and to the public colleges and universities, and with the rise of private philanthropy in American life, the alliance was severed and the public-private distinction became clearly discernible—with President Charles Eliot of Harvard as the chief articulator. That, however, was after 1870. It had taken fifty years to sort out the public-private interest, to pull state and college fully apart, and to find the will as well as the way to separate and maintain "public" and "private" institutions. Interestingly enough, the case followed roughly the same time pattern in gaining its fame on constitutional grounds in "defense of vested rights" against the state, as Webster himself put it.

These were forces which prolonged the reliance on institutions of the familiar type (with a public-private blurring) and resisted the creation of an alternative (with complete separation). Such forces *included* the Dartmouth controversy and its intellectual options but were much larger and, in the aggregate, more conclusive. Gradualism, over a long continuum of interacting forces, was the key. Therefore, to say that the public-private split did not fully materialize until the 1870s is not to deny that forces generated as far back as 1816 and 1819 played a contributing or even determining role. Surely after the Marshall decision cutting off one approach for the state and pointing out another, and after all the intellectual and philosophical debate, "public" had to imply a more activist, initiating, supporting role—thus challenging and gradually replacing the mere authorizing, exhorting, and supervising posture of the state. Plumer's solution did not work. Something more would be required.

At the other pole, the chartered colleges with self-perpetuating boards were given new impetus and governmental immunity that flowered in the "denominational era," and remain as a rich heritage in that great segment of higher education now called "private." Chancellor Kent wrote in his *Commentaries* that the Dartmouth case did more than any other single governmental act "to give solidity and inviolability to the literary, charitable, religious, and commercial institutions of our country." Noting this growth under the new legitimacy, the *Encyclopedia Americana* of 1830 feared that colleges would proliferate on a faulty analogy to the common schools, where "there can hardly be too many of them," little realizing the full potency of that analogy as burgeoning new public institutions were added to the private profligacy.

Rivalry between emerging types of institutions was inevitable. Indeed, it ran to debilitating extremes before the rediscovery that, with creative accommodation, public and private can be complementary. Fortunately, the "public" part was rarely carried to the extreme contemplated in some of the judicial pleadings and opinions—that is, to operation as a wholly undifferentiated and unbuffered part of civil government. Nevertheless, the Supreme Court's separation of public and private went too far in higher education, as it did also in constitutional law. A federal judge recently said that Marshall made it too easy for himself, by "drawing so bright a line between 'a civil institution to be employed in the administration of the government' and 'a private eleemosynary institution,'" and that the court itself no longer feels bound to follow the formulation of 160 years ago. The line was originally blurred; separation was carried too far; blurring is with us again.

Meanwhile, much educational history has rolled by, partly shaped by the Dartmouth case.

For those who want to reduce complex historical questions to simplicity, the Dartmouth experience will be frustrating. In fact, to attempt to keep the strains unsnarled and to unfurl a neat answer is to abuse the evidence. The Dartmouth episode in its entirety, not merely the court case, helps us identify the contributing ingredients of significant change but does not nicely measure their relative weight in the total balance. Beyond doubt, however, it was an event in the formative years of American higher education which helped shape the future. Intellectually, it elicited rough educational ideas and honed them in debate; it strengthened the philosophy of some kind of a higher education alternative, increasingly called "public"; and it hastened the Darwinian effect among educational modes increasingly at odds. Operationally, it defined the options for both state and college; it clarified the inadequacy of state control without state support; and it assured a richer variety of institutional embodiments for the nation. Negatively, the state would thereafter have to respect existing institutional charters or gain the consent of the trustees. There was a chilling effect on state intrusion into higher education governance anywhere anytime. Positively, the state could achieve its purposes via new charters by reserving the appropriate power for later reform, or it could found wholly public institutions committed to the service of a particular place. Conceptually, this great attention to a public alternative could have been a hastening factor in the rise of state colleges and universities—the reverse of the common Dartmouth attribution. But, pragmatically, other factors, chiefly political readiness, were determining. The state had to perceive a need and overcome both opposition from existing church-related institutions and from reluctant taxpayers. It was effective political will that was tardy, and far more the cause of delay among state universities than the Dartmouth impact.

No one can read the learned decisions by Chief Justice William M. Richardson of New Hampshire and by Justices Marshall, Washington, and Story of the Supreme Court without being reminded that the options all emerged in the context of education, not of commerce—of the small college, not, as later, the big corporation. In restoring that awareness, we are also reminded that with its clashing ideas (including the neglected ones of William Plumer), its national attention and significance, and its effect on the state in relation to both private and public higher education, the Dartmouth controversy was a significant peak, perhaps still inadequately explored, on an important watershed of American educational history.

II

The Canal That Built a Nation

RAYMOND SCHUESSLER

• In 1783, after the United States had won its independence from England, the redcoats finally left New York City. Most were anxious to leave the crummy little town that had twice burned during the seven years of British occupation. Fewer than 25,000 miserable persons lived there, and there was little to indicate that Manhattan Island would soon become the metropolis of the Western world.

By 1860 New York and its adjacent suburbs in Brooklyn counted more than one million residents, as the Hudson River city had far outdistanced the former leaders, Philadelphia and Boston. Many factors influenced Gotham's phenomenal growth, but none was more important than the Erie Canal. The most successful and important public works project in American history before the interstate highway system was begun in 1956, the "Canal That Built a Nation" required a staggering bond program when it was begun in 1817. Opening for its full length in 1825, the Erie Canal was so incredibly successful that it paid for itself within a few years, and it spawned dozens of immitators in the half century which followed. Its impact was as dramatic as it was immediate. Transportation costs between the Old Northwest and America's busiest port fell by 90 percent, and the canal became a major route for immigrants moving inland from the Atlantic seaports.

The following essay by Raymond Schuessler recounts the history and route of this most influential of America's internal improvements and shows how Syracuse, Rochester, and Buffalo, as well as the Empire City itself, grew to prominence along the waterway to the West.

Reprinted (with permission) from New York Alive magazine, 152 Washington Ave., Albany, NY 12210.

Back in the early 1800s, when America was expanding and settlers were pushing west, people knew that poor transportation was hampering the development of New York State and perhaps the entire Northeast. The central part of the state, with its rich valleys, was isolated; people living farther to the west were shipping and receiving their products from the seaport of Quebec, a practice it was feared that could lead many settlers back to the sympathies of Britain.

It was frustrating for residents of central New York to take in bumper crops and develop waterpower for factories, and be unable to ship their goods anywhere at a reasonable price. Businessmen in those days found that a consignment of goods transported by wagon and intermittent boats would cost as much money to carry as they would fetch on the market at Albany. In 1814 Robert Fulton wrote that it cost $2.00 to send a barrel of flour one hundred and thirty miles overland, yet the same barrel could go one hundred and sixty miles by water for 25 cents. If you had goods that could walk, like cattle, fine; but you couldn't make much profit from goods that had to be transported. Some traders on the Great Lakes would sooner ship down the Mississippi River and up around the seacoast, some three thousand miles to New York City, than ship overland on a wagon train.

If, as many people hoped, a canal could be built to expedite the movement of people and goods westward from the Hudson River to the Great Lakes, America's commerce and wealth would grow by leaps and bounds. There was little doubt in a businessman's mind that if the country was to grow, its waterways, the main avenues of transportation, had to grow too.

Many people had suggested that the Hudson River should be connected by a canal to the Great Lakes. But others thought it was sheer madness, an impossible engineering feat since the difference in elevation was between five hundred to six hundred feet, a great deal was forested wilderness and swamps, scores of rivers would have to be crossed and much private land would be cut in half, necessitating countless bridges.

When the subject was first broached in the New York State Legislature, it was received with "such expressions of surprise and ridicule as are due to a very wild or foolish project." First of all, the legislators objected, there were no engineers or equipment in the country to build it, and second, the canal would have to be fourteen times longer than any yet built in the country. (Up to that time the longest canal in America was the Middlesex Canal between Boston and Merrimack, some twenty-seven miles long.)

One of the moving powers behind the canal was Dewitt Clinton, who, once convinced of its merit, spent much time and energy in promoting the idea (and during his term as Governor of New York saw it completed).

In 1808 the state Senate authorized a survey. The surveyor, James Geddes, tramped through the wilderness, sleeping on beds of leaves and clubbing small animals for food before he succeeded in mapping a favorable route from Lake Erie to the Seneca River, the most difficult part of the route. This survey was taken by Senator Joshua Forman to President Jefferson in Washington. But Jefferson, with all his genius, though agreeing it was a fine project, suggested that it be taken up again in about a hundred years.

Yet, if there ever was a canal that had to be built, it was the Erie. Finally, in 1817, the state Legislature passed the Canal Law. And on July 4th of that year, Governor Dewitt Clinton plowed the first furrow in the canal, two miles south of Rome, and the digging was on. This was the biggest job yet attempted in America.

Since the toughest sections were at either end, work was begun in the middle. To start with insoluble problems and frustrations would have been disastrous not only to the workers but to the public. By working at the easier part, the canal's builders hoped to gain enough experience to handle the tougher problems later.

Actually no one in America knew much about digging or constructing a canal. Planners sent one man, Canvass White, to England, in 1817, to learn something about the art; and he brought back notes and a few instruments. But the Erie Canal itself became a school of engineering where the engineers practically learned on the job, reading books and discussing new theories during lunch. But with American ingenuity and creativeness, they fumbled through perfectly.

The canal followed the water level route most of the way along the Mohawk River grade, but it still had to battle obstacles.

Before construction could be started, engineers had to figure out where all the water would come from to keep the canal flowing. So the route was carefully laid out by streams and lakes to afford a constant supply of water at all times to replace leakage and evaporation. Many gates and sluices had to be devised to feed this water to the canal and prepare drainage areas to let off excess water during floodtime. A level surface had to be provided along the edges of the canal for the tow-path on which mules and horses would tow the ships. These towpaths were crisscrossed with branches thrown over with dirt.

The canal was to be forty feet wide on the surface, four feet deep and twenty-eight feet on the bottom. Stakes were driven sixty feet apart to mark the course and holes bored to twelve feet to test the na-ture of the soil. By January of 1818, some fifty-eight miles were under construction between Ithaca and the Seneca River by twenty-five hun-dred men and seven hundred horses.

Work was leased out to small farmers along the way—at one section fifty contractors worked on the first sixty miles. The competition fos-tered by such a system generated a furious rush of building, as con-tractors hoped to get additional contracts at other areas. Each contrac-tor was expected to repair his stretch at his own expense. Workers got about 50 cents a day. The contractors got 10 to 14 cents per cubic yard of earth and up to $2.00 for hard work. The engineers received about $2000 per year.

Equipment was primitive. There was no huge earth-moving machin-ery in those days, but only horse-drawn scrapers, plows, and wagons. As the canal progressed, crude machinery was devised. A dumping wheelbarrow was put together to carry off the mud quicker. A stump puller was invented since much of the course was through wooded area: a huge sixteen-foot-high wheel that wound a chain around an axle and popped out stumps at the rate of forty per day.

In some spots, such as the swamps below Syracuse, the men had to fight malaria and typhus such as the men did in Panama years later. But the work went on.

Residents would crowd the banks along the route and watch all day as the labor progressed, cheering the men on. The entire country was, in fact, watching the progress of the "Big Ditch." Soon ninety-six miles of the canal had been dug, and some areas were already in use.

This was an engineering feat of no small measure. The canal had to ascend through the Mohawk Valley, nearly five hundred feet above the Hudson River (the distance varies in almost every book on the sub-ject), and it had to employ a combined ascent and descent of six hun-dred and seventy-five feet, which required eighty-three locks and lifts, ranging from six to twelve feet. One of the toughest sections was an area alongside the Mohawk River between Schenectady and Albany, where twenty-seven locks had to be used to descend the mountains. And you just couldn't run a canal into a river and come out the other side. So aqueducts had to be built that allowed the canal to flow over the river in its own sluice box, so to speak.

These aqueducts were marvels of engineering genius. They were supported by sturdy stone arches supporting water-filled flumes of timber and wide enough to contain a stone towpath for the mules and horses. In one spot, at Crescent, twelve miles from Albany, the canal had to cross the Mohawk River on an aqueduct close to twelve hundred feet long. In all, eighteen aqueducts had to be built on the route.

To save time and money, some small streams were bridged only with a raised towpath for the horses while the creek was dammed below the crossing with guard locks that when closed formed a quiet pool for the boats to be towed across. In addition, three hundred bridges had to be built over the canal where it cut the farmer's land in two.

Many emergencies arose along the way, but miraculously the solution popped up just as often. When water seepage became serious, a blue clay was found nearby that was perfect for sealing the banks. When it looked like expensive cement would have to be imported, engineers found a native lode of limestone in Madison County, which when made into cement hardened even more under water.

In 1820 the waterway was just south of Syracuse, and great celebrations were held that Fourth of July that included seventy-five boats on the canal waters. By 1822 the canal was open for two hundred and twenty miles and allowed some eighteen hundred boats over its stretch. So heavy was the traffic that a speed limit of four miles an hour was instituted.

One newspaper wrote in the summer of 1823: "A boat leaves this place (Utica) for Rochester every day for a trip down to the Genesee River. The boats are well built and fitted in the style of magnificence that could hardly be anticipated in the infancy of canal navigation in America."

Another critic wrote: "To behold a vessel committed to the water four hundred miles inland and in a place which ten years ago was wilderness, excites emotions of great exhilaration."

Work began at the Buffalo end in August of 1823. Oxen pulled crude plows to begin the digging. The toughest job of all, however, was the three-mile cut through solid rock twenty miles from Buffalo; the rock had to be pulverized with dynamite.

But more burdensome yet was designing and building a double set of five locks palced side by side to carry the canal up an elevation of seventy-six feet on the rock ridge at Lockport. It was the engineering marvel of its time.

The celebration at Buffalo in 1825 to mark the completion of the canal was a gay one attended by Governor Clinton and many other dignitaries. Then a string of cannons about eight to twelve miles apart were fired in relay along the route until the noise traveled all the way from Buffalo to Albany and down to New York City in fifty-five minutes. It was probably the longest salute in history.

A fleet of ships carrying the Governor and others traveled the entire route from Buffalo eastward and was saluted by bands playing along the route and cheering crowds at every village. At Albany there was a great celebration, and in New York City the entire city plus thousands of visitors gathered to cheer the boat parade. Water from Lake Erie was poured into the Atlantic—truly a wedding of the lakes and the sea. One writer said: "The completion of the Erie Canal has been celebrated with greater eclat, pompous show and parade, not unlike those triumphal games and processions that were given to some of the Roman Emperors."

Another writer exclaimed in awe: "After Alexander of Macedon had carried his arms into India he did not descend the Indus with greater triumph or make a prouder display."

The printers' guild had a float in which it printed and distributed poetic cards that prompted many mothers to tear them out of their daughter's blushing hands. One read:

> The monarch of the briny tide
> Whose giant arm encircles earth
> To virgin Erie is allied
> A bright-eyed nymph of mountain birth . . .
> She meets the sceptred father of the main
> And in his heaving bosom hides her virgin face.

The Erie Canal might not have been much when compared with the gigantic Panama Canal, but it was something in its day. Financially, it was a complete success. Even before it had been completed it began to make money. In fact, its tolls were more than the interest charges before it was completed, and in twelve years, its capital costs, which included improvement and the construction of branch canals, had been paid off. Albany had increased its business four times in two years—freight rates between New York and Buffalo dropped from $100.00 per ton by land to $10.00 a ton through the canal.

In 1835 business was so good that the Ditch was ordered enlarged for bigger boats. It was then widened to seventy feet and deepened to seven feet, and the locks doubled to handle two-way traffic.

Probably no one has really assessed the tremendous influence of the canal. Cities boomed on its arteries. Buffalo now became the greatest grain holding center in the nation. New England shipped its lumber West, and manufactured goods flowed back and forth. Towns like Lockport, Middleport and Shelby Basin and others grew into existence. Everywhere the canal turned or had branches civilization came to life. It contributed not only to the growth of the region through which it passed but to the growth of states such as Ohio, Illinois, Michigan and Indiana. Lake freighters now hauled supplies for settlers, machinery and other goods for European markets. For everyone it meant better, more comfortable living.

People moving west spurred industry and farming and opened the heart of America clear to the Mississippi and even California when the gold fever struck. Many New England towns were nearly emptied by this easy access route to the West. Moreover, it spurred other communities to build canals and increase their capacity to work and produce and improve the land.

But it wasn't long before the railroads intruded and slowly took away some of the canal's cargo, until by 1869, the railroad carried as much as the canal. In 1882 the canal was made a free canal, but even so trains usurped more and more cargo.

By 1898 traffic on the canal was so lean and the railroad's political power so great in opposing any improvement to the canal that the waterway became rundown from disuse and neglect.

In 1903, New York State decided to get some use out of it by turning it into a "barge canal." It was widened to seventy-five feet and deepened to twelve feet, so that tugs could replace the mule and push the huge barges through. Many parts of the old canal were relocated.

Historians and canal enthusiasts have tired to preserve and restore relics of the old canal and have succeeded at times in turning some old locks into recreational and study areas. But mostly the relics—a broken aqueduct, a grass-covered ravine—are being bulldozed and run over with highways and shopping centers. Yet you can still find remnants of the old Erie Canal if you drive the backroads of Central New York. Many are visible in corn fields, meadows and orchards or abandoned near the edges of small towns. So sturdily was the old ditch built that many locks and inlets still stand solid and straight after more than one hundred and fifty years—a monument of another era.

12

The Old Northwest

JAMES E. DAVIS

• An ongoing theme in American history has revolved around
what is believed to have been the real participatory democracy
that existed on the frontier. It was a democracy, so it is said,
that eroded with the industrialization and urbanization of the
landscape. From the romantic French settler J. Hector St.
Jean de Crèvecoeur to Thomas Jefferson to Alexis de Toque-
ville this idea of an idyllic rural ideal was handed down. No
one, however, elaborated it more fully than Frederick Jackson
Turner, who gave the Presidential address at the 1893 convention of the American Historical Association in Chicago. It
was the West, he said, which focused American energies; and
it was the West—wild, isolated, and infinitely challenging—
which formed that peculiarly adventurous democrat, the
American. "Stand at the Cumberland Gap," Turner asserted,
"and watch the procession of civilization marching single
file." A century later one could have watched the same parade
at the South Pass in the Rockies.

Much of the rhetoric and style of political life in the
United States can be traced to the persistent appeal of the
frontier concept. President Jimmy Carter's visits to Midwestern farms and to town meetings in New England were clearly
attempts to appeal to the sentiment and/or the belief that the
heart of American democracy is and always has been in the
hamlets and rural areas.

This idealized portrait of early American life has been challenged by many historians since the end of World War II.
Richard C. Wade has argued that it was the cities, not the
farms, that were the spearheads of the frontier; others have
questioned whether the entire vision of Jeffersonian democ-

From James E. Davis, "New Aspects of Men and New Forms of Society: The
Old Northwest, 1790–1820," *Journal of the Illinois State Historical Society*
69 (1976): 164–72. Reprinted without footnotes by permission of the author
and publisher.

182

JAMES E. DAVIS

racy was a myth from the start. But the view that the frontier fostered a special kind of egalitarianism and democratic spirit is one that will not die. In the essay which follows, Professor James E. Davis brings out evidence that grass-roots democracy was more than just a dream for early settlers. Whether Davis's view of Old Northwest society as being characterized by "creativity and egalitarianism" is accurate or just Jeffersonian mythology in a new form is up to the reader to decide.

They came to the lands north of the Ohio River from many places: the valleys and highlands of the Upper South, the coastal plains and inland regions of the Middle Atlantic states, and the boulder-strewn hills of New England. Between the end of the American Revolution and the admission of Illinois to the Union in 1818, settlers hacked their way through dense forests, established farms and communities along waterways, and pushed on to the broad expanses of prairie country. Their reasons for migrating were as numerous as their origins. Perhaps the majority were enticed westward by hopes of economic gain. Some were motivated by curiosity and a sense of adventure; others by misfortune—economic disaster, death in the family, a brush with the law, or persecutions accompanying the French Revolution and Napoleonic upheavals.

The lands were not empty when the newcomers arrived. The Indian population, although decreasing, was still powerful enough in the 1790s to inflict stinging defeats on federal forces in Ohio, and as late as the War of 1812 the Indians and their British sponsors lashed into the region with surprising strength. After the war the influence of Great Britain diminished, and the Indians—their offensive power curtailed—grudgingly yielded vast tracts of land to the Americans. The newcomers also encountered French and French-Indian residents, whose way of life was in eclipse. In short, those whose livelihood was dependent upon furs, Indians, and isolated outposts yielded to those who cleared the land, broke the prairie, and sank the taproot of rural family life.

Usually disdainful of the French and the Indians, the American settlers sought to subdue the wilderness and re-create the best aspects of their own cultures. In that attempt they were only partially successful.

The society that did evolve was a curious hybrid of outside ideas, aspirations, customs, and institutions, altered somewhat by elements of the French and Indian cultures and tempered by the sometimes harsh realities of the wilderness.

Two traits of the new settlers seem to have predominated: creativity and egalitarianism or republicanism. The purpose of this paper is to examine those traits and their likely causes, and to suggest, in turn, how life in the Old Northwest was influenced by them.

Republicanism in the late 1700s and early 1800s assumed several forms. One was a high, perhaps inflated, self-confidence that was reflected everywhere, particularly in the independent, even haughty and surly, attitudes of hired workers. Elias Pym Fordham, who came to the region in 1817, observed: "No white man or woman will bear being called a servant. . . . Hirelings must be spoken to with Civility and cheerfulness." Observing the republican West shortly after the War of 1812, Isaac Holmes warned, "Male and female servants, or, as they are there called 'helps,' must eat and drink with the family." From early Princeton, Indiana, it was reported that even servants brought from England to America were soon "on a happy equality, rising up last and lying down first, and eating freely at the same time and table. None here permit themselves to have a master, but negroes." A friend of Henry Bradshaw Fearon's, having the temerity to ask a pioneer woman for her master, received this bristling republican response, "In this country there is no mistresses nor masters; I guess I am a woman citizen." If it is true that republican spirit and democratic institutions have as their basis a self-confident population, then the opening years of the nineteenth century in the lands north of the Ohio augured well for an egalitarian society.

The accessibility of public officials further illustrates the prevalence of republicanism. Unlike the East, where magistrates, military officers, and politicians were held in awe, the Old Northwest was characterized by an easy familiarity between the public and authorities. One observer, perhaps somewhat carried away, wrote: "I wish I could give you a correct idea of the perfect equality that exists among these republicans. A Judge leaves the Court house, shakes hands with his fellow citizens and retires to his loghouse. The next day you will find him holding his own plough. The Lawyer has the title of Captain, and serves in his Military capacity under his neighbour, who is a farmer

and a Colonel." Richard Flower wrote from his farm near Albion, Illinois: "I went into my field the other day, and began a conversation
with my ploughman: his address and manner of speech, as well as his
conversation surprised me. I found he was a colonel of militia, and a
member of the legislature." The unpretentiousness of public officials
was also observed by John Palmer, traveling near Cincinnati in 1817.
After meeting a certain Judge Lowe, who was also a tavern-keeper,
Palmer commented, "It no doubt seems singular to the English
reader, to hear of judges and captains keeping taverns . . . but it is
very common in this republican country." The accessibility of public
officials and the familiarity with which they were treated appears to
have bred, among their constituents, a healthy suspicion of government and politicians.

Yet the spirit of republicanism was liveliest when ordinary citizens
plunged headlong into politics. It was widely believed that eligible
voters should participate, or be willing to participate, in public affairs.
In the early settlements, according to one historian: "Candidates were
perpetually scouring the country . . . defending and accusing, de-
faming and clearing up, making licentious speeches, treating to corn
whiskey, violating the Sabbath, and cursing the existing administration. . . . And every body expected at some time to be a candidate
for something." Newcomers to the Old Northwest cast off habits of
social deference, and for the first time in their lives scrambled after
the numerous public positions that had to be filled if society was to
function. In every village and courthouse, inexperienced people were
thrust into roles of leadership. More important, the problems with
which those political novices grappled were fundamental, dealing as
they did with transportation, education, defense, and administration.
Furthermore, the solutions arrived at in the early days of settlement
established the tone of the community for decades to come.

The resolution of problems of frontier life illustrates the creativity
of the pioneers in the Old Northwest. The Western waterways, filled
with snags and subject to seasonal fluctuations, called for particularly
creative solutions. By the 1820s, strange-looking, shallow-draft boats,
powered by high-pressure, lightweight engines, were successfully navi-
gating the Western waters.

Other problems generated equally creative, if not always completely
effective, solutions. The difficulties encountered in breaking the un-

yielding prairie grass and constructing adequate fencing elicited from nimble minds a host of solutions. When settlement outstripped the effective reach of territorial or state government, popular *ad hoc* committees sprang into existence. New sicknesses, as well as old ones, prompted strange cures from quack and doctor alike. Richard Lee Mason, traveling through Indiana in 1819, commented on the strange food substitutions: "Yolk of egg, flour and water mixed is a good substitute for milk and is often used in coffee in this country. Rye is frequently substituted for coffee and sage tea in place of the Imperial." Such commonplace solutions to daily problems were only part of the unending experimentation that occurred at all levels of society and in all aspects of life. The numerous difficulties accompanying settlement produced an impressive amount of inventiveness and adaptability.

The economy of the Old Northwest, unlike that of the East, was not specialized. Few settlers were *full-time* judges, teachers, clergymen, legislators, or even farmers. Professional men performed manual tasks and suffered no loss of esteem as a result. One traveler in early Ohio noted: "The doctor returns from his rounds . . . feeds his pigs; and yet his skill as a physician is not doubted on that account. Nor is the sentence of the magistrate . . . esteemed less wise or impartial, even by the losing party of his wrangling disputants, because Cincinnatus-like, he is called from the plough tail to the bench of justice." Other settlers turned from one job to another and still another; such jacks-of-all-trades could be found in the Northwest long after Illinois achieved statehood. A Swedish traveler, Gustaf Unonious, wrote of that kind of mobility: "The speed with which people here change their life calling and the slight preparation generally needed to leave one calling for another are really surprising, especially to one that has been accustomed to our Swedish guild-ordinances. . . . A man who today is a mason may tomorrow be a doctor, the next day a cobbler, and still another day a sailor, druggist, waiter, or school master." Unonious may have exaggerated somewhat, but it is undeniably true that many early Illinoisans sampled a dozen occupations over the course of a lifetime—learning from each and transferring knowledge and skills from one activity to the next.

There are several reasons for the growth of republicanism and creativity in the Old Northwest. One was the diverse nature of those who settled the land. Each migratory group and each household arrived with its own ideas concerning the future of the new society. The resulting suspicions and disputes between Protestant and Catholic, Southerner and Northerner, and native and immigrant insured that there would be no deferential society in the Old Northwest. Family name, religious affiliation, and political influence probably counted for less in the unfolding society of the Old Northwest than in the more highly ordered and structured society of the East. The pluralism of the new society guaranteed that common problems would be attacked from a number of directions. And solutions were probably found more quickly than would have been the case if only one cultural group had settled the region.

The very act of migration also fostered republicanism and creativity. Migration was selective, beckoning to the fresh lands a disproportionately large number of young adult males and generally discouraging the old and females. Selective migration, it appears, also discouraged the very wealthy, the very poor, and the timid and trouble-laden. It is clear that society in the Old Northwest from 1790 to 1820 was no mere reproduction of Eastern society, efforts to the contrary notwithstanding. Rather, the selective nature of migration created vacuums, and those vacuums generated a republican rush for the political and social positions formerly held by those who stayed behind.

Those who even considered migrating were precisely those who were able, and perhaps eager, to see new possibilities and new ways of doing things. Timothy Flint, for example, asked, "What mind ever contemplated the project of moving from the old settlements over the Alleghany mountains . . . without forming pictures of new woods and streams, new animals and vegetables, new configurations of scenery, *new aspects of men and new forms of society?*" For many, the promise of the Old Northwest began not with actual arrival in the region but with creative and liberating dreams of "new aspects of men and new forms of society."

The trek westward removed the immigrants from scenes of defeat and frustration and gave them an exhilarating and immediate success, which encouraged them to seize further opportunities for advancement. A variety of people were thrown together and enriched each other by swapping bits of news, methods of travel, and farming techniques.

In short, the act of migration performed several functions: it selectively eliminated certain kinds of settlers, raised expectations, heightened confidence, and generated a creative mix of diverse people. As we have seen, settlers in the new lands scrambled for new positions, moved from occupation to occupation, and refused to have masters. Habitual deference collapsed, at least temporarily, and a number of years passed—perhaps a decade or two—before the fabric of society was tightly drawn. In the early days, it was virtually impossible for a settler to awe his fellows with his name, past social standing, or connections. Rather, people exerted themselves—they *willed* themselves—into new roles and thereby transformed themselves and their society.

The abundance and availability of good land were crucial to that transformation. That fact was not lost on Francis Hall, who traveled in the Old Northwest shortly after the War of 1812. Of the pioneer, he wrote, "With his axe on his shoulder, his family and stock in a light waggon, he plunges into forests, which have never heard the woodman's stroke, clears a space sufficient for his dwelling, and first year's consumption, and gradually converts the lonely wilderness into a flourishing farm." Farmers were relatively self-sufficient—making much of what they needed from materials at hand, and selling only

Physicians' advertisements from a Kaskaskia (Illinois) newspaper

DR. W. L. REYNOLDS,

Has removed to his new shop, on Charter street, where he can always be found. He has fresh and genuine *Cow Pock Matter*, and those who wish to avail themselves of its salutary effects, had better make early application. He continues to practice *Physic, Surgery and Midwifery* with the most unremitted attention. Those who have accounts of more than six months standing with him will please to call and settle, as his shop cannot be supplied without money.   Aug. 22

DOCTOR JOEL C. FRASER

Determining on a permanent residence at St. Charles, solicits the patronage of a general and liberal public as a practitioner of *Medicine* and *Surgery*—All calls in the line of his profession will be attended to with cheerfulness, and promptitude.

He has on hand some genuine *Vaccine or Cow-Pock Matter*, a safe and effectual preventive of the Small Pox. Those who wish to enjoy the advantage of the vaccine discovery, will please to call immediately. The poor will be inoculated GRATIS.   Sept. 17, 1817.

rarely to distant markets. (It appears that almost every farmer supplemented his income by providing overnight shelter for travelers.) That many settlers were self-sufficient farmers was regarded with favor by such agrarian critics as Johann David Schoepf: "These incessant emigrations, of which there will be no end so long as land is to be had for little or nothing, hinder the taking up of manufactures. . . . It is more befitting the *spirit* of this population, and that of all America, to support themselves on their own land . . . than to live better continually employed for wages."

Writing of immigrants from England who settled near Olive-green Creek in Ohio, William Tell Harris noted, "Though they have not been here more than fourteen months, they have grown corn, potatoes, pumpkins, cucumbers, greens, melons, and tobacco, sufficient to render them *independent* of their neighbours for support." Traveling in Ohio in 1819, Richard Lee Mason wrote of "*Independent* people in log cabins. They make their own clothes, sugar and salt, and paint their own signs." Land was within the reach of the average citizen in the Old Northwest and even the average alien. To a considerable degree the availability of land created, however briefly, something approaching an *economic* democracy in the Old Northwest; and that condition in turn provided the security necessary for people to express their republican tendencies and engage enthusiastically in political democracy.

Although land was plentiful and cheap, labor was not. According to William Faux, "Nothing is reckoned for land; land is nothing; labour every thing. In England it was almost vice versa." Artisans, craftsmen, and ordinary laborers were at a premium in the Old Northwest, and they knew it. Their economic independence was greater than it had been elsewhere and so, too, was their self-confidence. Until there were large pools of surplus farm labor—which were not available before perhaps the late 1830s—laborers strutted about in good republican style, confident in the knowledge that their services commanded premium wages.

Business and professional success in the Old Northwest required fewer skills, less capital, and less experience than were needed in the East or the Sweden of Gustaf Unonious. The cobbler who grew weary of mending boots and shoes could associate with a man practicing medicine, observe him as he concocted and dispensed cures, pay him a fee for a kit of pills and instruments, and then himself begin to practice medicine. Ease of changing jobs undoubtedly promoted republicanism and, according to Unonious, creativity as well. After noting, "A man who today is a mason may tomorrow be a doctor, the next day a cobbler," Unonious admitted that "distinct inconveniences arise from this situation; yet undeniably this unlimited freedom is exactly one of the important reasons why America has advanced with such tremendous speed. It has indeed given opportunity for many humbugs to flourish, but at the same time it has called forth many able men and has spurred them on to greater efforts." The virtual absence of restraining professional societies encouraged people to go from occupation to occupation, learning from each and transferring knowledge to each.

Republicanism and creativity were also fostered by generally inactive or ineffective state and federal governments. Government, it is true, did help to pave the way for settlement through diplomacy, warfare, purchase, and survey. But even with the consolidation of national power during the 1790s, the federal government was unable to enforce treaty provisions, subdue Indians north of the Ohio, or remove illegal squatters on public lands. More important, what we now consider the basic responsibilities of government—local defense, transportation, education, and protection from criminals—often rested primarily with *ad hoc* committees of local settlers. Just as diversity prevented one strain of culture from dominating all of the other strains, the absence of a strong and pervasive government insured that republican assertiveness and creativity would not be crushed or inhibited by exclusionary tests of religion, political correctness, or ideological purity. Francis Hall was well aware of that fact. Of the nation's expansion, he said, "Such is the growth, and such the projects of this transatlantic republic, great in extent of territory, in an active and well-informed population; but above all, in a *free government*, which not only leaves individual talent unfettered, but calls it into life by all the incitements of ambition most grateful to the human mind."

One observer, witnessing the influx of settlers into the region, was moved to write: "A sense of relative consequence is fostered by their growing possessions, and by perceiving towns, counties, offices and candidates springing up around them. One becomes a justice of the peace, another a county judge and another a member of the legislative assembly. Each one assumes some municipal function, pertaining to schools, the settlement of a minister, the making of roads, bridges, and public works. A sense of responsibility to public opinion, self respect, and a due estimation of character and correct deportment are the consequence."

Those arriving late in the settlement process often found that the best land—the town sites, bridge sites, mill sites, and simply the best soil—was either occupied or prohibitively expensive. They also found that entrenched interests controlled county and state political offices and social positions. Some of the late arrivals stayed on as hired help or tenant farmers; others, realizing that opportunity lay farther to the west, pushed on. In short, whether or not a settler in the Old Northwest became a creative republican depended, at least in part, upon the date of his arrival.

It is impossible to make a characterization that would apply to all the settlers who came to the Old Northwest. Yet today's historian would almost certainly agree with an 1818 visitor to the Old Northwest, who wrote, "The thinking man who wants to witness the expansion and development of a new people in a new land will here find a sweeping and an interesting field for his studies."

13

Indian Policy in the Jacksonian Era

RONALD N. SATZ

• As Frederick Jackson Turner, Bernard De Voto, Richard A. Bartlett, William H. Goetzmann, and dozens of other historians have noted, the expansion of the United States from its narrow base along the Eastern Seaboard to almost continental size has been a central fact of American development. The story of the confrontation and eventual domination of the vast and empty spaces by successive waves of pioneer Americans has become our national epic.

Much less attention has been focused on the fact that the settlement of the West ranks among the many examples of naked aggression offered by history. In simple terms, an entire people was removed, a people whose claims to the land often dated back hundreds of years before it was even seen by the first white man. Those Indians that did not die in battle, or from hunger, or from diseases introduced by the new "Americans" were pressed onto reservations that kept getting smaller and smaller, despite treaties and guarantees from the federal government.

That this history was largely ignored for a century and more is hardly surprising given the treachery and the shameful methods used to separate the Indians from what was once theirs. Scholars who did write on the subject were usually so convinced of their own racial and cultural superiority over the native people that their accounts are properly suspect.

The essay by Ronald N. Satz is part of a reappraisal by younger historians of the assumptions held by nineteenth-century policymakers concerning the removal of Indian tribes. Were the claims of these relatively nomadic Indians greater than those of the pioneers who wanted to cultivate the land

Michigan History, Bureau of History, Michigan Department of State.

and create a cornucopia of plenty in the midst of a wilderness?
Or would you agree with twentieth-century historian Satz
(and nineteenth-century English traveler Frances Trollope)
that, as Satz puts it, "Indian removal epitomized everything
despicable in American character"?

There has long been a tendency among scholars to view the Indian removal policy of the Jacksonian era in dualistic terms—the forces of evil
supported removal while the forces of humanity opposed it. Recently,
Francis Paul Prucha, George A. Schultz, and Herman J. Viola have
attempted to show that enlightened thought supported Indian removal
as a means of rescuing the eastern Indians from the evil effects of close
contact with the advancing white frontier. Yet even these historians
admit that the actual removal process entailed numerous hardships for
the Indians.

This paper is an attempt to assess the goals, execution, and results
of the Indian removal policy in the 1830s and 1840s by focusing on
the application of that policy in the Old Northwest. The events surrounding the removal of the Five Civilized Tribes from the South
have long been, to use the words of Grant Foreman, "a chapter un-
surpassed in pathos and absorbing interest in American history." This
dramatic episode has, to some extent, obscured similar events taking
place farther north during the same period of time. The Old Northwest provides an interesting test case for an examination of the differences between the rhetoric and the reality of the removal policy. The
Indians in this region were not the beneficiaries of anything approaching the tremendous outpouring of public sympathy for the Cherokees
and their neighbors in the Southeast. If the Cherokees faced a "Trail
of Tears" in spite of the great volume of petitions, letters, and resolutions presented to Congress in their behalf, what happened to the Indians in the Old Northwest who lacked such enthusiastic public
support?

An essential ingredient to an understanding of the Indian policy in
this period is the recognition that President Jackson and his successors
in the White House, the War Department, the Office of Indian Affairs, and Indian agents maintained that the removal policy would
bring at least four major benefits to the Indians. These included:

1. fixed and permanent boundaries outside of the jurisdiction of American states or territories;
2. isolation from corrupt white elements such as gamblers, prostitutes, whiskey vendors, and the like;
3. self-government unfettered by state or territorial laws; and
4. opportunities for acquiring the essentials of "civilized" society—Christianity, private property, and knowledge of agriculture and the mechanical arts.

Such were the benefits that government officials claimed the removal policy would bring the Indians. As a test case of the application of this policy, let us focus our attention on events in the Old Northwest.

President Jackson asked Congress on December 8, 1829, to provide him with authority to negotiate treaties to transfer Indians living east of the Mississippi River to a western location. Jackson and his congressional supporters, in their great rush to push through such legislation, seemed unconcerned about the technical aspects of any great migration of eastern Indians to the trans-Mississippi West. Opponents of the scheme, however, raised several important questions: Would emigration be purely voluntary? Would treaty commissioners negotiate only with acknowledged tribal leaders or would land be purchased from individuals? How many Indians would go? What kind of preparations and resources would be necessary for them? What would be the specific boundaries between emigrant tribes? How would the indigenous tribes in the West react to the intrusion of new people? During the debates on the Removal Bill, Tennessean David Crockett warned that it was a dangerous precedent to appropriate money for the executive branch without specifically knowing how the president intended to use it. Crockett warned that if Congress turned a deaf ear to the rights of the Indians then "misery must be their fate."

Unfortunately for the Indians, Congress passed the Removal Act in May 1830, and, despite the opposition of the nascent Whig party, Indian removal became a generally accepted policy in the ensuing decades. Throughout this period, congressional interest focused on patronage, partisan politics, and retrenchment to the detriment of the administration of Indian affairs. While the Whigs found it expedient to condemn aspects of the removal policy when they were struggling to capture the White House, they found it desirable to continue the policy once in office. Henry R. Schoolcraft, an Indian agent in Michigan Territory, poignantly described a serious defect of American Indian policy when he noted that "the whole Indian race is not, in the political scales, worth one white man's vote." The result of this situation, as David Crockett had warned, was misery for the Indians.

Among those who witnessed the actual dispossession of the eastern tribes in the Jacksonian era were two foreign travelers who, while not being authorities on the American Indians, nevertheless clearly recognized the deceptions involved in the treaty-making process. French traveler Alexis de Tocqueville poignantly observed that American officials, "inspired by the most chaste affection for legal formalities," obtained Indian title "in a regular and, so to say, quite legal manner." Although bribery and threats often accompanied treaty making and the formal purchases of Indian land, the United States had legal confirmation of its acquisitions. Indeed treaty negotiators were able to "cheaply acquire whole provinces which the richest sovereigns in Europe could not afford to buy" by employing such tactics as bribery or intimidation. Another European visitor, English Captain Frederick Marryat, accurately reported that "the Indians . . . are *compelled* to sell—the purchase money being a mere subterfuge, by which it may *appear* as if the lands were not being wrested from them, although, in fact, it [*sic*] is."

President Jackson had early indicated that his primary interest was the removal of the southeastern tribes. Although congressmen from the Old Northwest advised him following the passage of the Removal Act that the time for securing removal treaties in their region was "auspicious," Old Hickory informed them that his immediate concern was to set into motion a great tide of southern Indian emigration. Events in Illinois in the spring of 1832, however, played into the hands of the supporters of Indian removal in the Old Northwest.

In the spring of 1832, a hungry band of a thousand Sac and Fox Indians and their allies left their new home in Iowa Territory and crossed the Mississippi River en route to their old capital on the Rock River. Under the leadership of the proud warrior Black Hawk, this band, which included women and children, entered Illinois in search of food and as a means of protesting against their treatment by white frontiersmen. Mass hysteria swept the Illinois frontier with the news that the Indians had crossed the river. Governor John Reynolds called up the state militia to repel the "invasion" despite the fact that Black

Hawk's band was clearly not a war party. The result was a short, bloody conflict brought on largely as a consequence of the actions of drunken state militia. The ruthless suppression of the so-called "Indian hostilities" in Illinois and neighboring Wisconsin in 1832, and the seizure of a large part of the trans-Mississippi domain of the Sac and Fox Indians as "indemnity" for the war, broke the spirit of other tribes in the Old Northwest. Under pressure from the War Department, the Winnebagos in Wisconsin soon signed a removal treaty ceding their land south of the Wisconsin River. One by one, other tribes succumbed to similar pressure.

As critics of the Removal Act of 1830 had feared, the War Department obtained many of these land cessions by bribery. Agents courted influential tribal leaders by offering them special rewards including money, merchandise, land reserves, and medals, among other things. Sometimes treaty commissioners selected chiefs to represent an entire tribe or group of bands. The Jackson administration, for example, secured the title to the land of the United Nation of Chippewa, Ottawa, and Potawatomi Indians in northeastern Illinois, southeastern Wisconsin, and southern Michigan by "playing Indian politics." Indeed, the very existence of the United Nation was the result of the government's insistence on dealing with these Indians as if they were a single unit. Yet neither the great majority of the Chippewas and Ottawas nor all of the Potawatomi bands recognized the authority of the so-called United Nation. The government's policy of dealing with the entity as the representative of all Chippewas, Ottawas and Potawatomis was a clever maneuver to oust these Indians from their lands. By working closely with mixed-blood leaders and by withholding Indian annuities, the War Department secured the desired land cessions from the United Nation in the early 1830s.

During the Jacksonian era, the War Department frequently used economic coercion as a means of securing Indian title in the Old Northwest. Since the 1790s, the department had invested funds appropriated by Congress for purchasing Indian land in state banks or stocks and had paid the Indians only the annual interest on the amount owed them under treaty stipulations. This annuity or trust fund system gave government bureaucrats virtual control over funds legally belonging to the Indians. Although Thomas Jefferson played an important role in establishing the precedent of withholding Indian annuities as a means of social control, this procedure became a standard policy after 1829.

Treaty commissioners, Indian agents, and other field officers of the War Department found that withholding annuities was a convenient means of inducing recalcitrant Indians to sign treaties and to emigrate. Commissary General of Subsistence George Gibson advised the Jackson administration, "Let the annuities be paid west of the Mississippi [River], and there is no reason to doubt that the scheme of emigration would meet with little future opposition." American officials maintained considerable influence over tribal politics by determining who would receive the annuities.

Another measure used to encourage Indians to make land cessions was the inclusion of provisions in removal treaties for the granting of land reserves to chiefs, mixed-bloods, or other influential members of the tribes. The motivation behind this practice was twofold. First, it allowed government officials to combat Indian and American opposition to the removal policy based on the fact that some Indians had demonstrated a willingness and capability of accepting the white man's "civilization." When Andrew Jackson encountered strong opposition to his efforts to remove the Cherokees and the other so-called Civilized Tribes from their Southern domain, he conceded that Indians willing to accept the concept of private property should be allowed to remain in the East on individual reserves and become citizens of the states in which they resided. Secondly and more importantly for the Old Northwest, the practice of providing reserves of land to certain Indians was an ingenious device for bribing chiefs or influential tribesmen into accepting land cession treaties and for appeasing white traders into whose hands their reserves were certain to fall.

Treaty commissioners in Indiana found it impossible to secure land cessions from the Miami and Potawatomi Indians without the approval of the Wabash Valley traders to whom they were heavily in debt. Land speculators and settlers regarded the Miami and Potawatomi reserved sections adjacent to the Wabash River and the route of the Wabash and Erie Canal as choice lands. Wabash Valley traders, Indian agents, and even United States Senator John Tipton ultimately secured most of these lands from the Indians and rented them to white settlers for high profits after the Panic of 1837. By 1840 treaties with the Miamis and Potawatomis of Indiana had provided for nearly two hundred thousand acres of individual reserves. The largest holders of these reserves were not Indians but Wabash Valley traders W. G. and G. W. Ewing and Senator Tipton. Thousands of acres of Indian land elsewhere in the Old Northwest also fell into the hands of speculators.

In spite of the fact that speculators and traders often pressured the Indians into relinquishing their reserves before the government even surveyed the ceded tribal land, little was done to protect the Indians from such swindlers. Indiana Whig Jonathan McCarty, a bitter political adversary of Senator Tipton, introduced a resolution in Congress in 1835 calling for an investigation of the handling of Indian reserves, but no action resulted. Jackson, and his successors in the White House, were anxious to tone down investigations of alleged frauds in Indian affairs in order to avoid possible political embarrassments. Even some of the staunchest opponents of the removal policy benefited directly from the sale of Indian lands. Daniel Webster, Edward Everett, Caleb Cushing and Ralph Waldo Emerson were among those who speculated in Indian lands in the Old Northwest.

In addition to granting land reserves to Indians, the War Department followed the practice of including provisions in removal treaties for the payment of Indian debts to traders as a means of promoting removal. Since the Indians relied heavily on traders for subsistence and advice in the Old Northwest, the inclusion of traders' debts was often crucial to successful treaty negotiations. Although the recognition of these debts helped to promote the signing of land cession treaties, the practice also meant that the Indians lost huge sums of money to men who frequently inflated the prices of the goods they sold or falsified their ledgers. Transactions at treaty negotiations relative to the sale of Indian land, the adjustment of traders' claims, and the like were a complex business, yet many Indians, especially the full bloods, did not know the difference between one numerical figure and another.

The administration of Indian affairs in the mid-1830s was particularly vulnerable to criticism. The Panic of 1837 led many traders to exert political influence on treaty commissioners to have phoney Indian debts included in removal treaties. Commissioners Simon Cameron and James Murray awarded the politically influential American Fur Company over one hundred thousand dollars in alleged debt claims against the Winnebagos in Wisconsin in 1838 in return, according to rumor, for a large kickback. Only the military disbursing agent's refusal to pay the traders ultimately led to the exposure of the fraud. One eyewitness to this episode subsequently claimed that it was worse than the Crédit Mobilier scandal. An English visitor to Wisconsin several years after the incident reported that the acknowledgment of traders' claims during annuity payments was still a "potwallopping affair" in which the Indians left as empty-handed as when they had arrived. Both the Tyler and Polk administrations, in response to complaints from some congressmen, honest Indian agents, and concerned frontier residents, denounced the practice of acknowledging traders' debts in treaties. But the tremendous political influence of the traders, together with the War Department's emphasis on the speedy removal of Indians from areas desired by whites, led the government to follow the path of expediency. Traders continued to receive payments for their claims throughout the Jacksonian era.

If the techniques already mentioned failed to entice the Indians to emigrate, there was always brute force. The state of Indiana probably had one of the worst records in this respect. The Potawatomis ceded their last holdings in Indiana in 1836, but the treaty provisions allowed them two years to emigrate. Whites quickly began moving onto their land in order to establish preemption rights. As tension between the Indians and the whites grew, the Indiana militia rounded up the Potawatomis in 1838. When Chief Menominee, who had refused to sign the removal treaty, objected to the proceedings, the soldiers lassoed him, bound him hand and foot, and threw him into a wagon. The militia then hastily set into motion the Potawatomi exodus to the West—the "Trail of Death" along which about one hundred and fifty men, women, and children died as a result of exposure and the physical hardships of the journey. Several years later the Indiana militia also rounded up the Miami Indians in similar fashion to expedite their removal to the West.

By the end of Jackson's second term, the United States had ratified nearly seventy treaties under the provisions of the Removal Act and had acquired about one hundred million acres of Indian land for approximately sixty-eight million dollars and thirty-two million acres of land in the trans-Mississippi West. While the government had relocated forty-six thousand Indians by 1837, a little more than that number were still in the East under obligation to remove. According to the Office of Indian Affairs, only about nine thousand Indians, mostly in the Old Northwest and New York, were without treaty stipulations requiring their relocation, but there is evidence to indicate that the number of such Indians east of the Mississippi River at this time was much larger than the Indian Office reported. Indeed, there were probably more than nine thousand in Wisconsin Territory alone! The dearth of reliable population statistics for Indians during the Jacksonian era is a perplexing problem. By 1842, however, the United States had acquired the last area of any significant size still owned by the Indians in the Old Northwest. Only scattered remnants of the great tribes that had once controlled the region remained behind on reservations or individual holdings, chiefly in Michigan and Wisconsin.

The removal treaties of the Jacksonian era contained liberal provisions for emigrants and those remaining behind on reserves. They offered emigrants rations and transportation, protection en route to their new homes, medicine and physicians, reimbursement for abandoned property, funds for the erection of new buildings, mills, schools, teachers, farmers and mechanics, and maintenance for poor and orphaned children. The treaties read as if they were enlightened agreements. Yet there were several inherent defects in the treaty-making process. One of these was the assumption that the Indian leaders dealing with the government commissioners represented the entire tribe. Another was the assumption that the Indians clearly understood the provisions of the agreements. Still another was the fact that the Senate often amended or deleted treaty provisions without prior consultation with tribal leaders. Although treaty stipulations were provisional until ratified by the Senate, settlers rarely waited for formal action before they inundated Indian land. While Alexis de Tocqueville noted that "the most chaste affection for legal formalities" characterized American treaty making with the Indians, he also argued that "it is impossible to destroy men with more respect to the laws of humanity."

In spite of the favorable terms promised in removal treaties, most emigrants faced numerous hardships on their journeys to their new homes. A major reason for their misery was the system of providing them food and transportation by accepting the lowest bid from contractors. Many unscrupulous expectant capitalists furnished the Indians with scanty or cheap rations in order to make a sizeable profit from their contracts. The contractors were businessmen out to make money, and they were quite successful. Thomas Dowling, who received a contract in 1844 to remove six hundred Miami Indians from Indiana for nearly sixty thousand dollars, boasted to his brother that he would make enough profit to "rear the superstructure of an independence for myself, family, and relations."

In addition to the evils of the contract system, Indian emigrants also suffered from the government's perpetual concern for retrenchment. Although removal treaties provided for the medical care of emigrants, the War Department prohibited agents from purchasing medicine or surgical instruments until "actually required" during the economic hard times after 1837. Such instructions greatly hampered the effectiveness of the physicians accompanying migrating parties. To make matters worse, emigrants from the Old Northwest, many of them weakened by their constant battle with the elements of nature en route to the trans-Mississippi West, found themselves plagued with serious afflictions. Efforts to economize in removal expenditures by speeding up the movement of emigrants also led to much suffering. The War Department ordered in 1837 that only the sick or very young could travel west on horseback or by wagon at government expense. Even before this ruling, efforts to speed up the movement of migrating parties under orders from Washington officials proved detrimental to the Indians. An agent in charge of the removal of the Senecas from Ohio earlier in the 1830s, for example, wrote his superior that "I charge myself with cruelty in forcing these unfortunate people on at a time when a few days' delay might have prevented some deaths, and rendered the sickness of others more light, and have to regret this part of my duty."

Now let us examine the success of the removal policy in terms of the so-called benefits that government officials had argued it would bring to the Indians after their relocation. The first benefit was fixed and permanent boundaries outside the jurisdiction of American states and territories. Even before the Black Hawk War, the French travelers Alexis de Tocqueville and Gustave de Beaumont had voiced concern over the government's failure to establish a permanent Indian country for the northern Indians comparable to the one it was setting off west of Arkansas for the southern tribes. Sam Houston, a good Jacksonian Democrat, assured the travelers that Indian-white relations in the Old

Northwest were not as critical as in the South. He pointed out that permanent boundaries were unnecessary for the northern tribes since they would eventually be "pushed back" by the tide of white settlement. Following the Black Hawk War, Houston's contention proved correct.

The history of the relocation of the Winnebago Indians from Wisconsin illustrates the government's failure to systematically plan fixed boundaries for emigrants from the Old Northwest. When the War Department pressured the Winnebagos into signing a removal treaty at the cessation of the Black Hawk War, it left them with two alternative locations. One was the so-called "neutral ground" in Iowa between the Sac and Fox Indians and their Sioux enemies to the north. This location proved too precarious for the Winnebagos, who quickly made their way back to the second designated area that was within the territorial limits of Wisconsin, north of the Wisconsin River. When the Winnebagos moved into this area, they found themselves too tightly crowded together to live according to their old life styles. As a result, they frequently returned to the sites of their old villages south of the Wisconsin River.

In returning to their old homesites, the Winnebagos encountered other Indians as well as white settlers. While the War Department had induced the Winnebagos to leave southern Wisconsin in order to free them from white contact in that area, it had relocated tribes from New York there in order to free them from white contact in New York. Both the Winnebagos and the New York Indians relocated in Wisconsin soon became the victims of the great land boom that swept the territory in the 1830s as whites eagerly sought Indian land for settlement and timber.

By 1838 the Winnebagos had ceded all of their land in Wisconsin and had promised to move to the neutral ground in Iowa, but the "final" removal of the last band of these Indians in 1840 required the use of troops. For several years after their relocation, the Indian Office attempted to transfer them from Iowa to the Indian country west of Missouri. In 1841 the Tyler administration planned to have them join other northern tribes in a new Indian territory north of the present Iowa-Minnesota border and south of, roughly, the 46th parallel. This new location would appease residents of Iowa who were clamoring for the removal of the Winnebagos and settlers in Wisconsin who were anxious to expel the Winnebago stragglers and the New York Indians who had settled there. Such a northern location would also placate the citizens of Arkansas and Missouri who opposed any additional influx of Indians on their western borders. The War Department favored this plan because it would provide a safe corridor for white expansion to the Pacific through Iowa and would place the Indians of the Old Northwest far south of the Canadian border thus luring them away from British-Canadian influence.

In spite of the War Department's plans, large numbers of Winnebagos drifted back to Wisconsin during the 1840s. Efforts to relocate them in present-day Minnesota between the Sioux and their Chippewa enemies led again to Winnebago defiance. Despite the use of military force to compel them to go to their "proper homes," the Winnebagos were greatly dispersed in Wisconsin, Iowa, and Minnesota at the end of the decade, to the annoyance of white settlers in those areas. The condition of these Indians clearly indicates that the War Department was lax in undertaking long-range planning for a permanent home for the tribes of the Old Northwest. The government continually reshuffled these Indians in order to make room for northeastern tribes and the growing pressures of white settlement. Whenever the white population pattern warranted it, the War Department merely redesignated new locations for the Indians. Nor did the government pay much attention to the needs of emigrants. Menominee Chief Oshkosh, in complaining about Winnebago intrusions on Menominee land in Wisconsin in 1850, cited several reasons why the Winnebagos continually left their new locations and returned to Wisconsin; these included the poor soil in their new country, the scarcity of game there, and, most importantly, their dread of their fierce Sioux neighbors.

The agony of the Winnebagos was not unique. Many other tribes faced the prospect of removing to an allegedly permanent location more than once. Continued white hostility following the Black Hawk War led the United Nation of Chippewas, Ottawas, and Potawatomis, for example, to give up their claims to northern Illinois, southeastern Wisconsin and several scattered reserves in southern Michigan in 1833 for a tract of land bordering the Missouri River in southwestern Iowa and northwestern Missouri. The new Potawatomi lands included the Platte Country, the region in present-day northwest Missouri watered by the Little Platte and Nodaway rivers. This area was not included in the original boundaries of Missouri in 1820. The inclusion of the Platte Country in the land designated for the Potawatomis demonstrates once again the poor planning of the War Department. In 1832 Missouri Governor John Miller had called for the annexation of this region and Missouri Senators Lewis F. Linn and Thomas Hart Benton joined him in arguing that the area was necessary for the political and economic growth of their state. Although over one hundred Potawatomis had signed the original treaty, the War Department, in its effort to appease Missourians, secured an amended treaty, signed by only seven Indians, that substituted a similar amount of land in Iowa for the Platte Country.

While the government was seeking to modify the original treaty to placate Missouri, Potawatomis who had signed that document moved to the Platte Country. The number of tribesmen there grew as small bands from Indiana continued to travel West in accordance with the provisions of the original treaty. Many Potawatomis came to view the government's new proposed location for them in Iowa as being too close to the Sioux. The Jackson administration reluctantly permitted them to settle temporarily in the Platte Country until they could find suitable sites for new villages in southeastern Iowa. There were still approximately sixteen hundred Potawatomis in the Platte Country in March 1837 when President Martin Van Buren proclaimed the area part of the state of Missouri. The War Department soon ejected them from there and resettled them in southwestern Iowa and Kansas. Government officials consolidated the Potawatomis into one reservation in northcentral Kansas in 1846 and subsequently relocated them in Oklahoma during the 1860s.

The experiences of the Winnebago and Potawatomi Indians clearly indicate that the new boundaries for emigrants from the Old Northwest were far from permanent. Treaty commissioners merely reshuffled the tribes around as frontiersmen, speculators, and state officials pressured the War Department to open more Indian land to white settlement. Federal officials failed to undertake long-range planning for the establishment of permanent boundaries for the emigrant tribes from this region. The sole effort in this direction before 1848, the Tyler administration's attempt to create a northern Indian territory, failed because the War Department had neglected the needs and the desires of the Indians.

At the end of the Jacksonian era, Indian Commissioner William Medill reported that the Polk administration had begun to mark off a northern Indian "colony" on the headwaters of the Mississippi River for "the Chippewas of Lake Superior and the upper Mississippi, the Winnebagoes, the Menomonies, such of the Sioux, if any, as may choose to remain in that region, and all other northern Indians east of the Mississippi (except those in the State of New York), who have yet to be removed west of that river." Together with the removal of Indians from the "very desirable" land north of the Kansas River to a southern "colony" west of Arkansas and Missouri, Medill hoped that the concentration of the northern Indians on the headwaters of the Mississippi River would provide "a wide and safe passage" for American emigrants to the Far West. Medill's report of November 30, 1848, was a tacit admission of the government's failure to provide Indian emigrants from the Old Northwest with fixed and permanent boundaries as guaranteed by the Removal Act of 1830. Throughout this period, the exigencies of the moment determined the boundaries that American officials provided for the Indians.

The second alleged benefit of removal was isolation from corrupt white elements such as gamblers, prostitutes, whiskey peddlers, and the like. The government's lack of planning for the permanent relocation of the tribes of the Old Northwest meant that these Indians were continually in the path of the westward tide of white settlement. Although Congress passed a Trade and Intercourse Act in 1834 to protect the Indians from land hungry whites, as well as whiskey peddlers and similar groups, nothing, including Indian treaty rights, stopped the advance of white settlement. Liquor was readily available to most tribes. In 1844 Thomas McKenney, an expert on Indian affairs, reported that the Menominees in Wisconsin, who had undergone several relocations, were "utterly abandoned to the vice of intoxication." Efforts to strengthen the Trade and Intercourse Laws in 1847 failed once again to halt the liquor traffic. Frontier citizens, especially the traders and their powerful political allies, blatantly refused to cooperate in enforcing the laws.

Tribal self-government unfettered by state or territorial laws was the third benefit that removal was supposed to bring the Indians. Yet the Trade and Intercourse Acts of 1834 and 1847 placed the Indians at the mercy of the white man's conception of justice. The legislation clearly provided that American laws would take precedence over Indian laws and customs in all cases involving both groups. Since the local judicial officers in the white communities adjoining Indian settlements reflected the dominant attitudes of their respective communities and often had ties with local businessmen and traders, they were not always effective administrators of the federal laws designed to protect the Indians from whiskey peddlers or other avaricious whites. The presence of federal Indian agents and military detachments near Indian settlements, moreover, meant that the Indians were not completely sovereign. Indian agents and the commanding officers of frontier posts often played "Indian politics." They found it much easier to deal with a central tribal authority rather than a series of chiefs or headmen and encouraged the recognition of one individual as the principal tribal leader. One vehicle used to accomplish this purpose was the allocation of Indian annuities. By determining who would receive the annuities, the War Department manipulated tribal politics. The result of such efforts was the emasculation of tribal self-government.

The fourth alleged benefit of removal was "civilization." American officials involved in the formulation and execution of Indian policy argued that the Indians lacked the essentials of civilized society—Christianity, private property, and knowledge of agriculture and the mechanical arts. Indian removal, they maintained, would provide ample opportunities for the uplifting of the Indians. Yet the removal policy did not bring great benefits, in terms of the white man's "civilization," to a significant number of Indians.

The constant reshuffling of tribes to new "permanent" locations failed to promote Indian interest in the white man's "civilization." How could the Winnebagos who had suffered tremendous social and psychological strains as a result of their continuous uprooting and relocation be expected to have interest in, or make significant advances in, the adoption of Christianity or any of the other so-called prerequisites of "civilized" society? Other Indians had similar reactions.

The events surrounding the acquisition of Chippewa and Ottawa lands in Michigan demonstrate some of the reasons for the failure of government efforts to promote its "civilization" program among the Indians of the Old Northwest. In 1836 the Chippewas and Ottawas had ceded their lands with the understanding that the government would allot them permanent reservations in northern Michigan and provide blacksmiths, farmers, and teachers to help them learn white trades and farming techniques. The land cession treaty provided federal funds to accomplish the "civilization" of these Indians, but the entire project was doomed before it began.

When the Senate considered the ratification of the treaty, it amended the document so that the reserves in northern Michigan would only be temporary residences. The Indians were understandably disturbed by this unilateral alteration of the treaty, and they were reluctant to move to temporary reserves in order to clear the land and to take up farming. Commissioner of Indian Affairs Carey Allen Harris, moreover, urged that government funds for these Indians be kept to a minimum until they settled at a permanent location.

Because their "permanent" boundaries always seemed to be temporary ones, the Indians of the Old Northwest found it more convenient to live off their annuities than to labor in their fields. As Chippewa Indian George Copway lamented, "no sooner have the Indians gone on and made improvements, and our children began to like to go to the school houses which have been erected, than we hear the cry of the United States government, 'We want your lands'; and, in going from one place to another, the Indian looses [sic] all that he had previously learned." As a result of this situation, the Indians paid more attention to the fur traders than to the school teachers. The tribes in this region relied heavily on the traders for food and goods. Government officials tended to see this dependence on the traders as a sign of idleness or weakness of character. Their ethnocentricism blinded them to the fact that farming had long been women's work among these tribes. The fur trade, wild grain, and fish were traditionally much more important to the livelihood of these Indians than American agricultural products.

Other problems inherent in the "civilization program" included the personnel employed to "civilize" the Indians. Such appointments offered patronage-hungry politicians a means of rewarding their supporters. Consequently, the teachers hired to work with the Indians did not always bring altruistic motives to their jobs. Some of them were even "indolent and shif[t]less." The employment of missionaries as civilizing agents caused special problems. Interdenominational rivalries greatly impeded their work. Some Indians demonstrated open hostility to missionaries because they associated them with efforts to remove their people from their ancient homes. Presbyterian minister Peter

Dougherty found that his preaching of the Gospel to the Chippewa Indians in Michigan was greatly impeded by the belief of "heathen" Chippewas that the acceptance of Christianity would lead to their removal. For several reasons, therefore, the "civilization" program actually suffered because of the removal policy.

Regardless of the intentions of federal officials, the Indian removal policy in the Jacksonian era did not bring the tribesmen the benefits that they had predicted. Scholars such as Prucha, Schultz, and Viola have argued that the architects of the removal policy had thought that it was in the best interests of the Indians. If the formulators and executors of the policy actually believed this, their assumption proved erroneous for the Indians of the Old Northwest. While there was no policy of racial extermination or genocide perpetrated against the Indians of this region, there can be no doubt that the removal policy led to tribal demoralization. Whether noble intentions or nefarious ones lay behind the removal policy, the results were disastrous for the Indians. As one scholar recently asserted, "it is sometimes difficult to tell whether the Indian has suffered more at the hands of his 'friends' or at the hands of his 'enemies.'"

Frances Trollope, an English visitor to the United States, wrote in 1832 that Indian removal epitomized everything despicable in American character, especially the "contradictions in their principles and practice." "You will see them one hour lecturing their mob on the indefeasible rights of man," she wrote, "and the next driving from their homes the children of the soil, whom they have bound themselves to protect by the most solemn treaties." American Indian policy in the Old Northwest during the Jacksonian era serves as a grim reminder of what can happen to a politically powerless minority in a democratic society. It also demonstrates that scholars must be careful not to confuse the rhetoric of government policies with the realities involved in executing these policies.

14

Women, Work, and Protest
in the Early Lowell Mills

THOMAS DUBLIN

• The United States underwent a profound industrial transformation in the years between 1820 and 1860. At the earlier
date, agriculture and foreign trade dominated the economy,
and more than three-fourths of the labor force worked on
farms. Such manufacturing as there was typically took place
in houses or in very small establishments serving a local market. By the outbreak of the Civil War, the proportion of the
work force employed outside agriculture had jumped to 41
percent, and the cotton textile and boot and shoe industries
were well developed.

No section of the nation was more affected by the impact
of early industrialization than the Northeast. In 1790, Samuel
Slater set up the first permanent spinning mill in Pawtucket,
Rhode Island; in 1793, Alexander Hamilton established the
Society for Useful Manufacturers in Paterson, New Jersey;
and in 1813, the first fully integrated textile factory began op-
erating in Waltham, Massachusetts. Soon thereafter, the factory system began to dominate the economies of the growing
urban centers throughout the region.

As Thomas Dublin indicates in the following essay, women
had an important place in this emerging industrial economy.
The new mills tempted farmers' daughters to leave their rural
homes—at least temporarily—to accumulate savings for marriage. By 1860, more than 60,000 women were employed in
the cotton textile industry in New England alone. The pattern for such work was set in Massachusetts at the junction of
the Merrimack and Concord rivers just below the Pawtucket
Falls. In 1821, a group of Boston businessmen began to buy

Reprinted by permission from Thomas Dublin, "Women, Work, and Protest
in the early Lowell Mills," *Labor History*, 16 (Winter 1975), 99–116. Copyright ©1975 by *Labor History*.

land secretly in the area, and the following year they began to build the Merrimack Manufacturing Company. The town which grew up there was incorporated as Lowell in 1826, and by 1850 it was the leading textile center in the United States. More importantly, it was seen as an experiment, as a vindication of American methods that would prove superior to those of the Old World. As Dublin indicates, however, the experiment was not as idyllic as its proponents wanted to believe, and the dream of a new United States industrial order soon gave way to the grim realities of debilitating factory work and labor strife.

In the years before 1850 the textile mills of Lowell, Massachusetts, were a celebrated economic and cultural attraction. Foreign visitors invariably included them on their American tours. Interest was prompted by the massive scale of these mills, the astonishing productivity of the power-driven machinery, and the fact that women comprised most of the workforce. Visitors were struck by the newness of both mills and city as well as by the culture of the female operatives. The scene stood in sharp contrast to the gloomy mill towns of the English industrial revolution.

Lowell was, in fact, an impressive accomplishment. In 1820, there had been no city at all—only a dozen family farms along the Merrimack River in East Chelmsford. In 1821, however, a group of Boston capitalists purchased land and water rights along the river and a nearby canal, and began to build a major textile manufacturing center. Opening two years later, the first factory employed Yankee women recruited from the nearby countryside. Additional mills were constructed until, by 1840, ten textile corporations with thirty-two mills valued at more than ten million dollars lined the banks of the river and nearby canals. Adjacent to the mills were rows of company boarding houses and tenements which accommodated most of the eight thousand factory operatives.

As Lowell expanded, and became the nation's largest textile manufacturing center, the experiences of women operatives changed as well. The increasing number of firms in Lowell and in the other mill towns brought the pressure of competition. Overproduction became a problem and the prices of finished cloth decreased. The high profits of the early years declined and so, too, did conditions for the mill operatives. Wages were reduced and the pace of work within the mills was stepped up. Women operatives did not accept these changes without protest. In 1834 and 1836 they went on strike to protest wage cuts, and between 1843 and 1848 they mounted petition campaigns aimed at reducing the hours of labor in the mills.

These labor protests in early Lowell contribute to our understanding of the response of workers to the growth of industrial capitalism in the first half of the nineteenth century. They indicate the importance of values and attitudes dating back to an earlier period and also the transformation of these values in a new setting.

The major factor in the rise of a new consciousness among operatives in Lowell was the development of a close-knit community among women working in the mills. The structure of work and the nature of housing contributed to the growth of this community. The existence of community among women, in turn, was an important element in the repeated labor protests of the period.

The organization of this paper derives from the logic of the above argument. It will examine the basis of community in the experiences of women operatives and then the contribution that the community of women made to the labor protests in these years as well as the nature of the new consciousness expressed by these protests.

The pre-conditions for the labor unrest in Lowell before 1850 may be found in the study of the daily worklife of its operatives. In their everyday, relatively conflict-free lives, mill women created the mutual bonds which made possible united action in times of crisis. The existence of a tight-knit community among them was the most important element in determining the collective, as opposed to individual, nature of this response.

Before examining the basis of community among women operatives in early Lowell, it may be helpful to indicate in what sense "community" is being used. The women are considered a "community" because of the development of bonds of mutual dependence among them. In this period they came to depend upon one another and upon the larger group of operatives in very important ways. Their experiences were not simply similar or parallel to one another, but were inextricably intertwined. Furthermore, they were conscious of the existence of community, expressing it very clearly in their writings and in labor protests. "Community" for them had objective and subjective dimensions and both were important in their experience of women in the mills.

The mutual dependence among women in early Lowell was rooted in the structure of mill work itself. Newcomers to the mills were particularly dependent on their fellow operatives, but even experienced hands relied on one another for considerable support.

New operatives generally found their first experiences difficult, even harrowing, though they may have already done considerable hand-spinning and weaving in their own homes. The initiation of one of them is described in fiction in the *Lowell Offering*:

> The next morning she went into the Mill; and at first the sight of so many bands, and wheels, and springs in constant motion, was very frightful. She felt afraid to touch the loom, and she was almost sure she could never learn to weave . . . the shuttle flew out, and made a new bump on her head; and the first time she tried to spring the lathe, she broke out a quarter of the treads.

While other accounts present a somewhat less difficult picture, most indicate that women only became proficient and felt satisfaction in their work after several months in the mills.

The textile corporations made provisions to ease the adjustment of new operatives. Newcomers were not immediately expected to fit into the mill's regular work routine. They were at first assigned work as sparehands and were paid a daily wage independent of the quantity of work they turned out. As a sparehand, the newcomer worked with an experienced hand who instructed her in the intricacies of the job. The sparehand spelled her partner for short stretches of time, and occasionally took the place of an absentee. One woman described the learning process in a letter reprinted in the *Offering*:

> Well, I went into the mill, and was put to learn with a very patient girl. . . . You cannot think how odd everything seems. . . . They set me to threading shuttles, and tying weaver's knots, and such things, and now I have improved so that I can take care of one loom. I could take care of two if only I had eyes in the back part of my head.

After the passage of some weeks or months, when she could handle the normal complement of machinery—two looms for weavers during the 1830s—and when a regular operative departed, leaving an opening, the sparehand moved into a regular job.

Through this system of job training, the textile corporations contributed to the development of community among female operatives. During the most difficult period in an operative's career, the first months in the mill, she relied upon other women workers for training and support. And for every sparehand whose adjustment to mill work was aided in this process, there was an experienced operative whose work was also affected. Women were relating to one another during the work process and not simply tending their machinery. Given the high rate of turnover in the mill workforce, a large proportion of women operatives worked in pairs. At the Hamilton Company in July 1836, for example, more than a fifth of all females on the Company payroll were sparehands. Consequently, over forty percent of the females employed there in this month worked with one another. Nor was this interaction surreptitious, carried out only when the overseer looked elsewhere; rather it was formally organized and sanctioned by the textile corporations themselves.

In addition to the integration of sparehands, informal sharing of work often went on among regular operatives. A woman would occasionally take off a half or full day from work either to enjoy a brief vacation or to recover from illness, and fellow operatives would each take an extra loom or side of spindles so that she might continue to earn wages during her absence. Women were generally paid on a piece rate basis, their wages being determined by the total output of the machinery they tended during the payroll period. With friends helping out during her absence, making sure that her looms kept running, an operative could earn almost a full wage even though she was not physically present. Such informal work-sharing was another way in which mutual dependence developed among women operatives during their working hours.

Living conditions also contributed to the development of community among female operatives. Most women working in the Lowell mills of these years were housed in company boarding houses. In July 1836, for example, more than 73 percent of females employed by the Hamilton Company resided in company housing adjacent to the mills. Almost three-fourths of them, therefore, lived and worked with each other. Furthermore, the work schedule was such that women had little opportunity to interact with those not living in company dwellings. They worked, in these years, an average of 73 hours a week. Their work day ended at 7:00 or 7:30 P.M., and in the hours between supper and the 10:00 curfew imposed by management on residents of company boarding houses there was little time to spend with friends living "off the corporation."

Women in the boarding houses lived in close quarters, a factor that also played a role in the growth of community. A typical boarding house accommodated twenty-five young women, generally crowded four to eight in a bedroom. There was little possibility of privacy within the dwelling, and pressure to conform to group standards was very strong (as will be discussed below). The community of operatives which developed in the mills it follows, carried over into life at home as well.

The boarding house became a central institution in the lives of Lowell's female operatives in these years, but it was particularly important in the initial integration of newcomers into urban industrial life. Upon first leaving her rural home for work in Lowell, a woman entered a setting very different from anything she had previously known. One operative, writing in the *Offering*, described the feelings of a fictional character: "The first entrance into a factory boarding house seemed something dreadful. The room looked strange and comfortless, and the women cold and heartless; and when she sat down to the supper table, where among more than twenty girls, all but one were strangers, she could not eat a mouthful."

In the boarding house, the newcomer took the first steps in the process which transformed her from an "outsider" into an accepted member of the community of women operatives.

Recruitment of newcomers into the mills and their initial hiring was mediated through the boarding house system. Women generally did not travel to Lowell for the first time entirely on their own. They usually came because they knew someone—an older sister, cousin, or friend—who had already worked in Lowell. The scene described above was a lonely one—but the newcomer did know at least one boarder among the twenty seated around the supper table. The Hamilton Company Register Books indicate that numerous pairs of operatives, having the same surname and coming from the same town in northern New England, lived in the same boarding houses.

If the newcomer was not accompanied by a friend or relative, she was usually directed to "Number 20, Hamilton Company," or to a similar address of one of the other corporations where her acquaintance lived. Her first contact with fellow operatives generally came in the boarding houses and not in the mills. Given the personal nature of recruitment in this period, therefore, newcomers usually had the company and support of a friend or relative in their first adjustment to Lowell.

Like recruitment, the initial hiring was a personal process. Once settled in the boarding house a newcomer had to find a job. She would generally go to the mills with her friend or with the boarding house keeper who would introduce her to an overseer in one of the rooms. If he had an opening, she might start work immediately. More likely, the overseer would know of an opening elsewhere in the mill, or would suggest that something would probably develop within a few days. In one story in the *Offering*, a newcomer worked on some quilts for her house keeper, thereby earning her board while she waited for a job opening.

Upon entering the boarding house, the newcomer came under pressure to conform with the standards of the community of operatives. Stories in the *Offering* indicate that newcomers at first stood out from the group in terms of their speech and dress. Over time, they dropped the peculiar "twang" in their speech which so amused experienced hands. Similarly, they purchased clothing more in keeping with urban than rural styles. It was an unusual and strongwilled individual who could work and live among her fellow operatives and not conform, at least outwardly, to the customs and values of this larger community.

The boarding houses were the centers of social life for women operatives after their long days in the mills. There they ate their meals, rested, talked, sewed, wrote letters, read books and magazines. From among fellow workers and boarders they found friends who accompanied them to shops, to Lyceum lectures, to church and church-sponsored events. On Sundays or holidays, they often took walks along the canals or out into the nearby countryside. The community of women operatives, in sum, developed in a setting where women worked and lived together, twenty-four hours a day.

Given the all-pervasiveness of this community, one would expect it to exert strong pressures on those who did not conform to group standards. Such appears to have been the case. The community influenced newcomers to adopt its patterns of speech and dress as described above. In addition, it enforced an unwritten code of moral conduct. Henry Miles, a minister in Lowell, described the way in which the community pressured those who deviated from accepted moral conduct:

> A girl, suspected of immoralities, or serious improprieties, at once loses caste. Her fellow boarders will at once leave the house, if the keeper does not dismiss the offender. In self-protection, therefore, the patron is obliged to put the offender away. Nor will her former companions walk with her, or work with her; till at length, finding herself everywhere talked about, and pointed at, and shunned, she is obliged to relieve her fellow-operatives of a presence which they feel brings disgrace.

The power of the peer group described by Miles may seem extreme, but there is evidence in the writing of women operatives to corroborate his account. Such group pressure is illustrated by a story (in the *Offering*)—in which operatives in a company boarding house begin to harbor suspicions about a fellow boarder, Hannah, who received repeated evening visits from a man whom she does not introduce to the other residents. Two boarders declare that they will leave if she is allowed to remain in the household. The house keeper finally informed Hannah that she must either depart or not see the man again. She does not accept the ultimatum, but is promptly discharged after the overseer is informed, by one of the boarders, about her conduct. And, only one of Hannah's former friends continues to remain on cordial terms.

One should not conclude, however, that women always enforced a moral code agreeable to Lowell's clergy, or to the mill agents and overseers for that matter. After all, the kind of peer pressure imposed on Hannah could be brought to bear on women in 1834 and 1836 who on their own would not have protested wage cuts. It was much harder to go to work when one's roommates were marching about town, attending rallies, circulating strike petitions. Similarly, the ten-hour petitions of the 1840s were certainly aided by the fact of a tight-knit community of operatives living in a dense neighborhood of boarding houses. To the extent that women could not have completely private lives in the boarding houses, they probably had to conform to group norms, whether these involved speech, clothing, relations with men, or attitudes toward the ten-hour day. Group pressure to conform, so important to the community of women in early Lowell, played a significant role in the collective response of women to changing conditions in the mills.

In addition to the structure of work and housing in Lowell, a third factor, the homogeneity of the mill workforce, contributed to the development of community among female operatives. In this period the mill workforce was homogeneous in terms of sex, nativity, and age. Payroll and other records of the Hamilton Company reveal that more than 85 percent of those employed in July 1836 were women and that over 96 percent were native-born. Furthermore, over 80 percent of the female workforce was between the ages of 15 and 30 years old; and only ten percent was under 15 or over 40.

Workforce homogeneity takes on particular significance in the context of work structure and the nature of worker housing. These three factors combined meant that women operatives had little interaction with men during their daily lives. Men and women did not perform the same work in the mills, and generally did not even labor in the same rooms. Men worked in the picking and initial carding processes, in the repair shop and on the watchforce, and filled all supervisory positions in the mills. Women held all sparehand and regular operative jobs in drawing, speeding, spinning, weaving and dressing. A typical room in the mill employed eighty women tending machinery, with two men overseeing the work and two boys assisting them. Women had little contact with men other than their supervisors in the course of the working day. After work, women returned to their boarding houses, where once again there were few men. Women, then, worked and lived in a predominantly female setting.

Ethnically the workforce was also homogeneous. Immigrants formed only 3.4 percent of those employed at Hamilton in July 1836. In addition, they comprised only 3 percent of residents in Hamilton company housing. The community of women operatives was composed of women of New England stock drawn from the hill-country farms surrounding Lowell. Consequently, when experienced hands made fun of the speech and dress of newcomers, it was understood that they, too, had been "rusty" or "rustic" upon first coming to Lowell. This common background was another element shared by women workers in early Lowell.

The work structure, the workers' housing, and workforce homogeneity were the major elements which contributed to the growth of community among Lowell's women operatives. To best understand the larger implications of community it is necessary to examine the labor protests of this period. For in these struggles, the new values and attitudes which developed in the community of women operatives are most visible.

II

In February 1834, 800 of Lowell's women operatives "turned-out"— went on strike—to protest a proposed reduction in their wages. They marched to numerous mills in an effort to induce others to join them; and, at an outdoor rally, they petitioned others to "discontinue their labors until terms of reconciliation are made." Their petition concluded:

> Resolved, That we will not go back into the mills to work unless our wages are continued . . . as they have been.
> Resolved, That none of us will go back, unless they receive us all as one.
> Resolved, That if any have not money enough to carry them home, they shall be supplied.

The strike proved to be brief and failed to reverse the proposed wage reductions. Turning-out on a Friday, the striking women were paid their back wages on Saturday, and by the middle of the next week had returned to work or left town. Within a week of the turn-out, the mills were running near capacity.

This first strike in Lowell is important not because it failed or succeeded, but simply because it took place. In an era in which women had to overcome opposition simply to work in the mills, it is remarkable that they would further overstep the accepted middle-class bounds of female propriety by participating in a public protest. The agents of the textile mills certainly considered the turn-out unfeminine. William Austin, agent of the Lawrence Company, described the operatives' procession as an "amizonian [sic] display." He wrote further, in a letter to his company treasurer in Boston: "This afternoon we have paid off several of these Amazons & presume that they will leave town on Monday." The turn-out was particularly offensive to the agents because of the relationship they thought they had with their operatives. William Austin probably expressed the feelings of other agents when he wrote: "Notwithstanding the friendly and disinterested advice which has been on all proper occasions [*sic*] communicated to the girls of the Lawrence mills a spirit of evil omen . . . has prevailed, and overcome the judgment and discretion of too many, and this morning a general turn-out from most of the rooms has been the consequence."

Mill agents assumed an attitude of benevolent paternalism toward their female operatives, and found it particularly disturbing that the women paid such little heed to their advice. The strikers were not merely unfeminine, they were ungrateful as well.

Such attitudes notwithstanding, women chose to turn-out. They did so for two principal reasons. First, the wage cuts undermined the sense of dignity and social equality which was an important element in their Yankee heritage. Second, these wage cuts were seen as an attack on their economic independence.

Certainly a prime move for the strike was outrage at the social implications of the wage cuts. In a statement of principles accompanying the petition which was circulated among operatives, women expressed well the sense of themselves which prompted their protest of these wage cuts:

UNION IS POWER

Our present object is to have union and exertion, and we remain in possession of our unquestionable rights. We circulate this paper wishing to obtain the names of all who imbibe the spirit of our Patriotic Ancestors, who preferred privation to bondage, and parted with all that renders life desirable—and even life itself—to procure independence for their children. The oppressing hand of avarice would enslave us, and to gain their object, they gravely tell us of the pressure of the time, this we are already sensible of, and deplore it. If any are in want of assistance, the Ladies will be compassionate and assist them; but we prefer to have the disposing of our charities in our own hands; and as we are free, we would remain in possession of what kind Providence has bestowed upon us; and remain daughters of freemen still.

At several points in the proclamation the women drew on their Yankee heritage. Connecting their turn-out with the efforts of their "Patriotic Ancestors" to secure independence from England, they interpreted the wage cuts as an effort to "enslave" them—to deprive them of their independent status as "daughters of freemen."

Though very general and rhetorical, the statement of these women does suggest their sense of self, of their own worth and dignity. Elsewhere, they expressed the conviction that they were the social equals of the overseers, indeed of the mill owners themselves. The wage cuts, however, struck at this assertion of social equality. These reductions made it clear that the operatives were subordinate to their employers, rather than equal partners in a contract binding on both parties. By turning-out the women emphatically denied that they were subordinates; but by returning to work the next week, they demonstrated that in economic terms they were no match for their corporate superiors.

In point of fact, these Yankee operatives were subordinate in early Lowell's social and economic order, but they never consciously accepted this status. Their refusal to do so became evident whenever the mill owners attempted to exercise the power they possessed. This fundamental contradiction between the objective status of operatives and their consciousness of it was at the root of the 1834 turn-out and of subsequent labor protests in Lowell before 1850. The corporations could build mills, create thousands of jobs, and recruit women to fill them. Nevertheless, they bought only the workers' labor power, and then only for as long as these workers chose to stay. Women could always return to their rural homes, and they had a sense of their own worth and dignity, factors limiting the actions of management.

Women operatives viewed the wage cuts as a threat to their economic independence. This independence had two related dimensions. First, the women were self-supporting while they worked in the mills and, consequently, were independent of their families back home. Second, they were able to save out of their monthly earnings and could then leave the mills for the old homestead whenever they so desired. In effect, they were not totally dependent upon mill work. Their independence was based largely on the high level of wages in the mills. They could support themselves and still save enough to return home periodically. The wage cuts threatened to deny them this outlet, substituting instead the prospect of total dependence on mill work. Small wonder, then, there was alarm that "the oppressing hand of avarice would enslave us." To be forced, out of economic necessity, to lifelong labor in the mills would have indeed seemed like slavery. The Yankee operatives spoke directly to the fear of dependency based on impoverishment when offering to assist any women workers who "have not money enough to carry them home." Wage reductions, however, offered only the *prospect* of a future dependence on mill employment. By striking, the women asserted their actual economic independence of the mills and their determination to remain "daughters of freemen still."

While the women's traditional conception of themselves as independent daughters of freemen played a major role in the turn-out, this factor acting alone would not necessarily have triggered the 1834 strike. It would have led women as individuals to quit work and return to their rural homes. But the turn-out was a collective protest. When it was announced that wage reductions were being considered, women began to hold meetings in the mills during meal breaks in order to assess tactical possibilities. Their turn-out began at one mill when the agent discharged a woman who had presided at such a meeting. Their procession through the streets passed by other mills, expressing a conscious effort to enlist as much support as possible for their cause. At a mass meeting, the women drew up a resolution which insisted that none be discharged for their participation in the turn-out. This strike, then, was a collective response to the proposed wage cuts—made possible because women had come to form a "community" of operatives in the mill, rather than simply a group of individual workers. The existence of such a tight-knit community turned individual opposition of the wage cuts into a collective protest.

In October 1836, women again went on strike. This second turn-out was similar to the first in several respects. Its immediate cause was also a wage reduction; marches and a large outdoor rally were organized; again, like the earlier protest, the basic goal was not achieved; the corporations refused to restore wages; and operatives either left Lowell or returned to work at the new rates.

Despite these surface similarities between the turn-outs, there were some real differences. One involved scale: over 1,500 operatives turned out in 1836, compared to only 800 earlier. Moreover, the second strike lasted much longer than the first. In 1834 operatives stayed out for only a few days; in 1836, the mills ran far below capacity for several months. Two weeks after the second turn-out began, a mill agent reported that only a fifth of the strikers had returned to work: "The rest manifest *good 'spunk'* as they call it." Several days later he described the impact of the continuing strike on operations in his mills: "We must be feeble for months to come as probably not less than 250 of our former scanty supply of help have left town." These lines read in sharp contrast to the optimistic reports of agents following the turn-out in February 1834.

Differences between the two turn-outs were not limited to the increased scale and duration of the later one. Women displayed a much higher degree of organization in 1836 than earlier. To co-ordinate strike activities, they formed a Factory Girls' Association. According to one historian, membership in the short-lived association reached 2,500 at its height. The larger organization among women was reflected in the tactics employed. Strikers, according to one mill agent, were able to halt production to a greater extent than numbers alone could explain; and, he complained, although some operatives were willing to work, "it has been impossible to give employment to many who remained." He attributed this difficulty to the strikers' tactics: "This was in many instances no doubt the result of calculation and contrivance. After the original turn-out they [the operatives] would assail a particular room—as for instance, all the warpers, or all the warp spinners, or all the speeder and stretcher girls, and this would close the mill as effectually as if all the girls in the mill had left."

Now giving more thought than they had in 1834 to the specific tactics of the turn-out, the women made a deliberate effort to shut down the mills in order to win their demands. They attempted to persuade less committed operatives, concentrating on those in crucial departments within the mill. Such tactics anticipated those of skilled mule-spinners and loomfixers who went out on strike in the 1880s and 1890s.

In their organization of a Factory Girls' Association and in their efforts to shut down the mills, the female operatives revealed that they had been changed by their industrial experience. Increasingly, they acted not simply as "daughters of freemen" offended by the impositions of the textile corporations, but also as industrial workers intent on improving their position within the mills.

There was a decline in protest among women in the Lowell mills following these early strike defeats. During the 1837–1843 depression, textile corporations twice reduced wages without evoking a collective response from operatives. Because of the frequency of production cutbacks and lay-offs in these years, workers probably accepted the mill agents' contention that they had to reduce wages or close entirely. But with the return of prosperity and the expansion of production in the mid-1840s, there were renewed labor protests among women. Their actions paralleled those of working men and reflected fluctuations in the business cycle. Prosperity itself did not prompt turn-outs, but it evidently facilitated collective actions by women operatives.

In contrast to the protests of the previous decade, the struggles now were primarily political. Women did not turn-out in the 1840s; rather, they mounted annual petition campaigns calling on the State legislature to limit the hours of labor within the mills. These campaigns reached their height in 1845 and 1846, when 2,000 and 5,000 operatives respectively signed petitions. Unable to curb the wage cuts, or the speed-up and stretch-out imposed by mill owners, operatives sought to mitigate the consequences of these changes by reducing the length of the working day. Having been defeated earlier in economic struggles, they now sought to achieve their new goal through political action. The Ten Hour Movement, seen in these terms, was a logical outgrowth of the unsuccessful turn-outs of the previous decade. Like the earlier struggles, the Ten Hour Movement was an assertion of the dignity of operatives and an attempt to maintain that dignity under the changing conditions of industrial capitalism.

The growth of relatively permanent labor organizations and institutions among women was a distinguishing feature of the Ten Hour Movement of the 1840s. The Lowell Female Labor Reform Association was organized in 1845 by women operatives. It became Lowell's leading organization over the next three years, organizing the city's female operatives and helping to set up branches in other mill towns. The Association was affiliated with the New England Workingmen's Association and sent delegates to its meetings. It acted in concert with similar male groups, and yet maintained its own autonomy. Women elected their own officers, held their own meetings, testified before a State legislative committee, and published a series of "Factory Tracts" which exposed conditions within the mills and argued for the ten-hour day.

An important educational and organizing tool of the Lowell Female Labor Reform Association was the *Voice of Industry*, a labor weekly published in Lowell between 1845 and 1848 by the New England Workingmen's Association. Female operatives were involved in every aspect of its publication and used the *Voice* to further the Ten Hour Movement among women. Their Association owned the press on which the *Voice* was printed. Sarah Bagley, the Association president, was a member of the three-person publishing committee of the *Voice* and for a time served as editor. Other women were employed by the paper as travelling editors. They wrote articles about the Ten Hour Movement in other mill towns, in an effort to give ten-hour supporters a sense of the large cause of which they were a part. Furthermore, they raised money for the *Voice* and increased its circulation by selling subscriptions to the paper in their travels about New England. Finally, women used the *Voice* to appeal directly to their fellow operatives. They edited a separate "Female Department," which published letters and articles by and about women in the mills.

Another aspect of the Ten Hour Movement which distinguished it from the earlier labor struggles in Lowell was that it involved both men and women. At the same time that women in Lowell formed the Female Labor Reform Association, a male mechanics' and laborers' association was also organized. Both groups worked to secure the passage of legislation setting ten hours as the length of the working day. Both groups circulated petitions to this end and when the legislative committee came to Lowell to hear testimony, both men and women testified in favor of the ten-hour day.

The two groups, then, worked together, and each made an important contribution to the movement in Lowell. Women had the numbers, comprising as they did over eighty percent of the mill workforce. Men, on the other hand, had the votes, and since the Ten Hour Movement was a political struggle, they played a crucial part. After the State committee reported unfavorably on the ten-hour petitions, the Female Labor Reform Association denounced the committee chairman, a State representative from Lowell, as a corporation "tool." Working for his defeat at the polls, they did so successfully and then passed the following post-election resolution: *"Resolved,* That the members of this Association tender their grateful acknowl- edgements to the voters of Lowell, for consigning William Schouler to the obscurity he so justly deserves." Women took a more prom- inent part in the Ten Hour Movement in Lowell than did men, but they obviously remained dependent on male voters and legislators for the ultimate success of their movement.

Although co-ordinating their efforts with those of working men, women operatives organized independently within the Ten Hour Movement. For instance, in 1845 two important petitions were sent from Lowell to the State legislature. Almost ninety percent of the signers of one petition were females, and more than two-thirds of the signers of the second were males. Clearly the separation of men and women in their daily lives was reflected in the Ten Hour petitions of these years.

The way in which the Ten Hour Movement was carried from Low- ell to other mill towns also illustrated the independent organizing of women within the larger movement. For example, at a spirited meet- ing in Manchester, New Hampshire, in December 1845—one pre- sided over by Lowell operatives—more than a thousand workers, two- thirds of them women, passed resolutions calling for the ten-hour day. Later, those in attendance divided along male-female lines, each meeting separately to set up parallel organizations. Sixty women joined the Manchester Female Labor Reform Association that eve- ning, and by the following summer it claimed over three hundred members. Female operatives met in company boarding houses to in- volve new women in the movement. In their first year of organizing, Manchester workers obtained more than 4,000 signatures on ten-hour petitions. While men and women were both active in the movement, they worked through separate institutional structures from the outset.

The division of men and women within the Ten Hour Movement also reflected their separate daily lives in Lowell and in other mill towns. To repeat, they held different jobs in the mills and had little contact apart from the formal, structured overseer-operative relation. Outside the mill, we have noted, women tended to live in female boarding houses provided by the corporations and were isolated from men. Consequently, the experiences of women in "these early" mill towns were different from those of men, and in the course of their daily lives they came to form a close-knit community. It was logical that women's participation in the Ten Hour Movement mirrored this basic fact.

The women's Ten Hour Movement, like the earlier turnouts, was based in part on the participants' sense of their own worth and dignity as daughters of freemen. At the same time, however, it also indicated the growth of a new consciousness. It reflected a mounting feeling of community among women operatives and a realization that their interests and those of their employers were not identical, that they had to rely on themselves and not on corporate benevolence to achieve a reduction in the hours of labor. One woman, in an open letter to a State legislator, expressed this rejection of middle-class paternalism: "Bad as is the condition of so many women, it would be much worse if they had nothing but your boasted protection to rely upon; but they have at last learnt the lesson which a bitter experience teaches, that not to those who style themselves their 'natural protectors' are they to look for the needful help, but to the strong and resolute of their own sex." Such an attitude, underlying the self-organizing of women in the ten-hour petition campaigns, was clearly the product of the industrial experience in Lowell.

Both the early turn-outs and the Ten Hour Movement were, as noted above, in large measure dependent upon the existence of a close-knit community of women operatives. Such a community was based on the work structure, the nature of worker housing, and workforce homogeneity. Women were drawn together by the initial job training of newcomers; by the informal work sharing among experienced hands; by living in company boarding houses; by sharing religious, educational, and social activities in their leisure hours. Working and living in a new and alien setting, they came to rely upon one another for friendship and support. Understandably, a community feeling developed among them.

This evolving community as well as the common cultural traditions which Yankee women carried into Lowell were major elements that governed their response to changing mill conditions. The pre-industrial tradition of independence and self-respect made them particularly sensitive to management labor policies. The sense of community enabled them to transform their individual opposition to wage cuts and to the

increasing pace of work into public protest. In these labor struggles
women operatives expressed a new consciousness of their rights both
as workers and as women. Such a consciousness, like the community
of women itself, was one product of Lowell's industrial revolution.

The experiences of Lowell women before 1850 present a fascinating
picture of the contradictory impact of industrial capitalism. Repeated
labor protests reveal that female operatives felt the demands of mill
employment to be oppressive. At the same time, however, the mills
provided women with work outside of the home and family, thereby
offering them an unprecedented [opportunity]. That they came to
challenge employer paternalism was a direct consequence of the increasing opportunities offered them in these years. The Lowell mills
both exploited and liberated women in ways unknown to the pre-
industrial political economy.

15

Fifty-four Forty or Fight! Oregon Territory Becomes American at Last

ROBERT MADDOX

• American foreign policy has traditionally been rooted in two cardinal beliefs: the Monroe Doctrine and Manifest Destiny. Indicating that the United States would consider it a threat to itself if any European nation attempted to gain a foothold in the Western Hemisphere, President James Monroe's message to Congress in 1823 has been sanctioned by most Americans as having the effect of an international law. Manifest Destiny is a more indeterminate concept, but it might generally be defined as the belief that God has chosen us to do His will on earth. Whether Americans moved westward, booted the Indians off their ancestral lands, freed the Cubans from Spanish tyranny in 1898, took over the Philippines, entered World War I to make the world safe for democracy, or acted as leader of the free world to thwart Communist expansion, federal policymakers have usually justified their actions in moral terms. Thus, the United States seized almost half of Mexico (including most of what is now California, New Mexico, Arizona, Utah, and Nevada) during the 1840s while insisting that it was acting on behalf of democracy and justice. In actuality, the colossus of the North was stronger, richer, more populous, and more technologically advanced than its neighbor and hence able to enforce its will.

The dispute over the proper boundary of the Oregon territory, which included all or part of what would later become five separate states, was another matter entirely. In this instance, the competitor was not a weak and backward Latin neighbor but Great Britain, then the most powerful nation on earth. Indeed, the British Empire stretched around the

Reproduced through the courtesy of Historical Times, Inc., publisher of *American History Illustrated*.

globe, and its mighty Royal Navy had no serious competitor on any ocean. The nature of the "fifty-four forty" dispute and the peaceful way it was finally resolved not only reveals how the United States came to have its present boundary, but it also points out that powerful nations can settle strong disagreements in a permanent fashion without resorting to armed conflict.

The United States government granted territorial status to Oregon on August 14, 1848. The area then included what would become the states of Oregon and Washington, as well as portions of Idaho, Wyoming, and Montana. At one time or another most of the major European powers had laid claim to the region, and on several occasions came close to war. Indeed, in the mid-1840s there was talk of conflict between the United States and Great Britain over the Oregon question. How important was the region? South Carolina Senator McDuffie had said he would not give "a pinch of snuff for the whole territory" and thanked God "for his mercy" in placing the Rocky Mountains between it and the interior. Others thought differently. As one newspaper, the Washington *Madisonian*, put it, "*Oregon is ours*, and we will keep it, at the price, if need be, of every drop of the nation's blood." Fortunately, most Americans stood between these extremes and acquired the area—most of it, anyway—without shedding a drop of blood.

The first whites to reach the coast of the Pacific Northwest most likely were Spanish explorers during the middle of the sixteenth century. They were searching for the Strait of Aniàn, a mythical passageway which was supposed to connect the Atlantic and Pacific Oceans. Sir Francis Drake, during one of his raids against Spanish shipping a few decades later, may also have sailed as far north as Oregon, though the evidence is inconclusive. In any event, almost two hundred years passed before renewed explorations again created interest in the region—this time with implications for Americans.

In 1774, the year when the First Continental Congress met in Philadelphia, Spain sent an expedition to the coast of Oregon which, among other things, discovered Nootka Sound on the western side of what later became known as Vancouver Island. Several more Spanish probes followed, and in 1776 the great British explorer Captain James Cook set sail to explore the northwestern coast. Aside from particular findings, important in themselves, the most significant aspect of Cook's expedition was that its journals later were published and were widely read. What caused a sensation was the report that furs secured from the local Indians for a small amount later fetched as much as fifty to seventy dollars per skin when sold in China. "The rage with which our seamen were possessed to return," recorded one officer, ". . . to make their fortunes, at one time, was not far short of mutiny." The result of this news, according to one historian of Oregon, "was to send the first of a multinational flotilla to the Northwest coast," and to set in motion a train of events with far-reaching consequences.

Although Spain claimed sovereignty over the Pacific Northwest by virtue of a papal bull of 1494 and by her own explorations, her British rivals showed no inclination to back off. The matter came to a head during the summer of 1789 when Spanish authorities seized several British ships that had dropped anchor in Nootka Sound. The affair immediately took on international implications, especially for the new American government under George Washington, which had taken office only a few months earlier. If, as for a time seemed likely, war broke out between the two European rivals, Washington and his advisors assumed the British in Canada would strike at Spanish possessions in Louisiana and Florida. They could only do so by crossing American territory.

Washington was placed in a quandary. Agreeing to the anticipated British request to cross American soil might mean war with Spain; refusal might mean war with Great Britain. As became his habit, Washington placed the matter before his cabinet only to find it badly divided. Alexander Hamilton, the pro-British secretary of the treasury, favored granting the right of access. Secretary of State Thomas Jefferson suggested ignoring any such request. Fortunately, Washington did not have to decide. Spain was unable to stand alone against Great Britain, but when she turned to her ally, France, the latter nation was convulsed in revolution and unable to help. Spain had no choice but to capitulate and, in what became known as the Nootka Convention of 1790, recognized the right of British subjects to trade and settle

along the coast of the Pacific Northwest. This greatly strengthened future British claims on the region and signaled "the beginning of the
end of the Spanish Empire in America."

The Oregon country faded as a source of political friction among the
powers for the next several decadse, but explorations of its coastline
and harbors continued as did the trade in furs. Americans played an
active role in both activities. In 1792 Captain Robert Gray located the
mouth of the Columbia River, and by the mid-1790s Yankee traders
dominated the sea otter trade. During this period the first expedition
from the interior to reach the Pacific through Oregon was made by the
Canadian explorer Alexander Mackenzie.

Finally, a few years after the turn of the century, President Thomas
Jefferson authorized the historic expedition of Meriwether Lewis and
William Clark, the last great overland survey of the Oregon country.
Jefferson was motivated by several considerations in mounting this
project, not the least of which was to strengthen American claims on
Oregon for the future.

Oregon surfaced as a diplomatic issue several times during the decade following the War of 1812—and the United States profited in every instance. Most important was the Convention of 1818, negotiated
with the British by Albert Gallatin and Richard Rush. This agreement
settled a number of issues which had been hanging fire since the end
of the war, including the establishment of the Canadian-American border at the forty-ninth parallel between the Lake of the Woods and the
Rocky Mountains. Both parties claimed land west of the Rockies—
Oregon—and no boundary could be agreed upon. In a spirit of compromise, however, the negotiators decided to leave the territory "free
and open" to both Americans and Britons. Commonly referred to as
"joint occupation," this arrangement had the effect of bolstering subsequent claims by the latecoming Americans.

Negotiations with Spain during this period also bore fruit with regard to Oregon. Although the most pressing issue had to do with acquiring Spanish possessions in Florida, President Monroe's secretary
of state, John Quincy Adams, also sought to pressure Spain into relinquishing her claims on all territories lying north of the forty-second
parallel, the northern border of California. Spain, weak militarily and
beset with internal problems, had no wish either to knuckle under or

to fight. Instead she simply dragged the negotiations out for as long as she could.

The Spanish thought their delaying tactics might pay off when, in April 1818, General Andrew Jackson conducted a punitive raid in Spanish Florida in "hot pursuit" of Indians and renegades who had been plundering American settlements. In the process Jackson's forces captured two British subjects and quickly executed them on the ground that they had incited the Indians. Spain hoped to play upon the resultant British indignation to secure an ally against the United States. When cooler heads prevailed—British officials had no desire to risk hostilities over two such obvious blunders—Spain realized she had to capitulate to Adams. The Adams-Onis Treaty of 1819, among other things, turned over Spanish claims to the Oregon territory to the United States.

Yet another European nation bowed out of the picture a few years later. During the late eighteenth and early nineteenth centuries Russian traders had moved south of Alaska—or Russian America, as it was then known—to establish outposts almost as far as San Francisco. In 1821 the tsar issued a proclamation, prohibiting the ships of other nations from coming within a hundred miles of the coast north of the fifty-first parallel. The proclamation was unenforceable, but seemed to Americans to indicate a potential threat to the Oregon country.

Secretary Adams responded to this move in terms very similar to those later found in the Monroe Doctrine. The United States, he warned, considered this hemisphere closed to "any new European colonial establishments." Adams did not frighten the Russians very much, but they were diplomatically isolated in Europe at the time and had grave domestic ills as well. In any event, Adams negotiated a treaty with them in 1824, the terms of which provided that Russia lay no claims to territory south of 54°40'.

By the mid-1820s, therefore, only Great Britain and the United States were left to contest the territory between 42° and 54°40'. Britain's case for ownership rested upon the Nootka Convention of 1790, various explorations such as Captain Cook's, and the establishment of numerous fur trading posts then controlled by the mighty Hudson's Bay Company. The United States pointed to her own explorations, such as Gray's and the Lewis and Clark expedition, the acquisition of

Spanish rights via the Adams-Onis Treaty, and the fact that Oregon
was contiguous to American soil. Neither government thought the
matter was important enough to squabble over during these years, and
in 1827 the 1818 "joint occupation" agreement was extended indefinitely with the proviso that either party could terminate it by giving a
year's notice. This happy state of affairs lasted a decade and then began to disintegrate into an ominous situation.

The Oregon question became prominent during the early 1840s because of three developments, one of them potentially explosive. First,
business interests became increasingly enamored with the idea of ob-
taining ports on the Pacific Ocean. Trade with the Far East had always figured in American thinking, but now visionaries dreamed of
making the United States the center of world commerce by linking the
Atlantic and Pacific oceans by means of transcontinental railroads. Second, more and more Americans began crossing the Rockies to settle in
the Oregon territory. In 1841 there were about 500 Americans scattered throughout the region; by 1845 there were more than 5,000. And
more were on the way, as what the Independence, Missouri *Expositor*
called "Oregon fever" spread in the middle west.

Finally, a mood of militant expansionism was growing in the nation,
a mood characterized by the term "Manifest Destiny." Though in the
minority, more and more people began talking about America's right
to *all* of Oregon and bandied about slogans such as "fifty-four forty or
fight."

Over the years there had been several tentative efforts made to resolve the Oregon question diplomatically. Basically, the Americans
wished merely to extend the 49° boundary west to the Pacific. In offering such a solution the United States implicitly recognized British
claims to the area north of that line. The British, seeking to protect
the interests of the Hudson's Bay Company, wanted the boundary
drawn at the Columbia River, which meandered through Oregon to
the sea several hundred miles south of the forty-ninth parallel.

Such a position, of course, implicitly recognized American claims
south of the river. The crux of the issue, therefore, had been that triangle of land between the Columbia River and 49°. American settlers
posed no obstacle to peaceful adjustment since they located almost
exclusively in the lush Willamette Valley, which lay to the south of

the Columbia. The desire for port facilities raised a thornier question, for these lay north of the river. Still, the British were inclined to be flexible, provided a decent regard was paid to the interests of the Hudson's Bay Company, whose operations in any event were becoming less profitable as the years went by. But the demand for *all* of Oregon, aside from being completely without foundation, was an intolerable affront to the British and unacceptable whatever the costs. In 1844, unfortunately, the entire question became enmeshed in "the noisy arena of Presidential politics."

The Oregon question by this time was irretrievably linked with the matter of admitting Texas to the union. This in turn involved sectional disputes and the slavery issue, among others. The Whig candidate, Henry Clay, sought to avoid dividing his party by equivocating on Mexico and Oregon. The lesser-known James K. Polk, whom the Democrats nominated, did the opposite by proclaiming his determination to acquire *both* areas, and the Democratic platform specifically referred to the "whole" of Oregon. Contrary to myth, the party never used the slogan "fifty-four forty or fight," but it amounted to the same thing.

Polk was a short, slender man with a shock of long hair and a perpetually mournful countenance. If he had a sense of humor he concealed it with great success. Stubborn and intense, he had no experience in diplomacy and was temperamentally unsuited for it. His guiding principle, if it can be called such, was that above all one should never trust the British. "The only way to treat John Bull," he confided to his diary, "was to look him straight in the eye." He appeared to be doing just that when he referred to Oregon in his inaugural address. America's claim to Oregon, Polk stated, was "clear and unquestionable," a phrase taken directly from the belligerent Democratic campaign platform. On the other hand he did not refer to "all" of Oregon, and later in the address said that "meantime every obligation imposed by treaty or conventional stipulation should be sacredly respected."

Actually Polk had no intention of risking war with Great Britain over unsupportable claims, particularly at a time when trouble with Mexico was brewing over the Texas issue. His real goal was modest and traditional—to extend the line of 49° west to the Pacific—and he was prepared to concede all of Vancouver Island to the British even though the southern portion of it lay below the parallel. His "clear and unquestionable" statement was a clumsy ploy designed in part to impress the British with his firmness, and in part to placate the hawks in his own party. It failed to do either. The more jingoistic elements in the British government and press howled in indignation and loosed their own broadsides against American treachery. And the hawks, or "ultras" as they were called, rushed to the attack over his failure to insist upon American rights to the entire territory.

Polk blundered again a few months later. When the furor over his inaugural address died down, the British instructed their minister in Washington, Richard Pakenham, to reopen the Oregon question. The British were willing to accept the forty-ninth parallel boundary, but wished to retain navigational rights on the Columbia River. After a delay of several weeks, on July 12 Polk formally replied through Secretary of State James Buchanan. He proposed extending the 49° boundary with all of Vancouver Island going to the British, but refused to offer use of the Columbia. Most important, Polk had written into the message a statement the gist of which was that the United States was making this proposal even though its claims to *all* of Oregon were valid.

It was insulting, to say the least. British acceptance of such terms would have amounted to an admission that *their* claims were invalid, and such territory as they received would represent a gift made by the generous Americans. Pakenham rejected the proposal without even referring it back to his government. Polk, angered by such ingratitude, broke off negotiations.

The Oregon question simmered along until December when Polk heated it up again in his first annual message to Congress. Referring to what had taken place thus far, the president placed the entire blame for failure on the British. The United States, he said, had acted in "a spirit of liberal concession" and "will be relieved of all responsibility which may follow the failure to settle the controversy." He asked Congress to provide armed escorts for wagon trains heading there, and said it would be desirable to serve Britain the required one-year's notice that the joint occupation agreement would be terminated.

Polk then specifically referred to the Monroe Doctrine, and there was no question as for whom his warning was meant. Looking John Bull "in the eye" again, Polk hoped to pressure the British into re-opening negotiations on his own terms.

If the president hoped to obtain a show of national unity over Oregon, he was sadly mistaken. Instead his speech touched off a debate in and outside of Congress which lasted for months. The issue centered around terminating the joint occupation agreement. Moderates fought against serving any notice at all, while the more belligerent Democrats wished to accompany the notice with a defiant claim to all the Oregon territory. Finally a coalition of Whigs and administration Democrats secured for Polk a neutrally worded statement advising him to give notice of termination.

The belligerent language of Polk's annual message caused an up-roar in Great Britain. British Foreign Secretary Aberdeen, a longtime proponent of compromise, told the American minister in London that "the possibility of a rupture with the United States" had to be con-sidered. Fortunately, talk of war quickly faded as Great Britain at the time was wracked with internal disputes. Probably most Britishers wished to settle the issue provided it could be done with grace.

Finally, Aberdeen and the other moderates received a fortuitous break. Opponents of the 49° boundary had argued that the Columbia River was indispensable, not only for the Hudson's Bay Company, but for the western provinces of Canada. Now, however, news arrived in London that the Hudson's Bay Company had moved its main depot from the Columbia River to Vancouver Island. The company's volun-tary withdrawal undercut the idea that the Columbia triangle was significant and permitted Aberdeen to begin negotiations on the basis of extending the 49° boundary.

Polk's stubbornness once again threatened a successful settlement. The British proposal provided that the treaty would guarantee the Hudson's Bay Company—and those doing business with it—free navi-gation of the Columbia. The president balked at this, and it required the strong arguments of a majority of the cabinet to convince him to go along. The fact that the nation was now in the midst of war with Mexico no doubt helped. His cabinet members also persuaded Polk to take an unusual step with the proposed treaty.

The normal procedure is for a president to sign a treaty and then send it to the Senate for passage. To have done so in this case would have exposed the administration to charges by the "fifty-four forty or fight" elements of signing away American rights. Instead, a reluctant Polk submitted the treaty to the Senate for its *previous* advice, thereby dropping a very hot potato into other people's laps. On June 12, 1846, by a vote of 38 to 12, the Senate advised the president to accept the proposal as it stood. He signed the treaty on June 15, and three days later the Senate passed it.

Oregon, at least that portion of it up to the forty-ninth parallel, was American at last! Rarely in human history has so much effort been expended to make a settlement over which the two parties were so close in goals all along. Both nations repeatedly had offered terms almost identical with those finally embodied in the treaty, and both repeatedly had been spurned.

Polk's willfulness had almost caused a rupture with Great Britain over the inconsequential matter of navigation rights to the Columbia. History credits his administration with acquiring Oregon, but it is fair to say that he succeeded in spite of himself. And to some of his contemporaries he had not even succeeded. "Oh," cried Senator Thomas Hart Benton, "mountain that was delivered of a mouse, thy name shall henceforth be fifty-four forty."

16

The Underground Railroad

CHARLES L. BLOCKSON

• The story of the underground railroad in American history
is a popular one. Containing elements of fact, fiction, and
fantasy, it describes how terror-stricken, yet courageous, slaves
made their way North stopping at various "stations" along
their way to freedom. These tales often celebrate and em-
bellish the roles played by numerous white sympathizers and
abolitionists, such as the militant John Brown and the Quaker
Levi Coffin. And they suggest that the underground railroad
kindled enormous rage in the breasts of slave owners.

No one knows how many slaves escaped from bondage via
the "U.G." Most historians agree that the numbers were
small and that the secret organization has loomed larger in
reminiscence and propaganda than it ever was in reality.
Moreover, many fugitives either refrained from using the
"stations" of the underground railroad or made their escape
in ignorance of its existence. Professor Larry Gara has even
written that white politicians and wily businessmen used the
erstwhile bondsmen to serve their own purposes.

In the following essay, Charles L. Blockson argues that the
underground railroad was important even if as few as 30,000
slaves made use of it between 1830 and 1860. This legendary
escape route was vital for those whom it did help and, according to Blockson, it was "an epic of American heroism."

Though forty years have passed, I remember as if it were yesterday
the moment when the Underground Railroad in all its abiding mystery
and hope and terror took possession of my imagination. It was a Sunday afternoon during World War II; I was a boy of ten, sitting on a

Reprinted by permission from Charles L. Blockson, "Escape From Slavery:
The Underground Railroad," *National Geographic*, 166 (July 1984).

box in the backyard of our home in Norristown, Pennsylvania, listening to my grandfather tell stories about our family.

"My father—your great-grandfather, James Blockson—was a slave over in Delaware," Grandfather said, "but as a teenager he ran away underground and escaped to Canada." Grandfather knew little more than these bare details about his father's flight to freedom, for James Blockson, like tens of thousands of other black slaves who fled north along its invisible rails and hid in its clandestine stations in the years before the Civil War, kept the secrets of the Underground Railroad locked in his heart until he died.

So did his cousin Jacob Blockson, who escaped to St. Catharines, Ontario, in 1858, two years after my great-grandfather's journey to the promised land, as runaway slaves sometimes called Canada. But Jacob told William Still, a famous black agent of the Underground Railroad in Philadelphia, the reasons for his escape: "My master was about to be sold out this Fall, and I made up my mind that I did not want to be sold like a horse. . . . I resolved to die sooner than I would be taken back."

Years after that backyard conversation with Grandfather, I read Jacob's words in Still's classic book, *The Underground Rail Road*, and saw the name of my great-grandfather written there too—and thus authenticated my family's passage upon the Underground Railroad. In Still's book I found accounts of the heroism of the fugitive slaves and that of the men and women, black and white, North and South, who helped them flee from bondage at the risk of their own lives, fortunes, and personal liberty. For the Underground Railroad was no actual railroad of steel and steam. It was a network of paths through the woods and fields, river crossings, boats and ships, trains and wagons, all haunted by the specter of recapture. Its stations were the houses and the churches of men and women—agents of the railroad—who refused to believe that human slavery and human decency could exist together in the same land.

The scholar Edwin Wolf II captured the essence of my ancestors' experience when he wrote that *The Underground Rail Road* is filled "with tales of crated escapees, murdered agents, soft knocks on side doors, and a network as clandestine and complicated as anything dreamed up by James Bond."

As a historian attempting to research the Underground Railroad,

I have found, with a mixture of admiration and chagrin, that this atmosphere of secrecy endures. So much is uncertain. Even the origin of the term "Underground Railroad" is obscure. No one knows how many fled from bondage along its invisible tracks: As many as 100,000 between 1830 and 1860? As few as 30,000? Probably no one will ever know. What we do know is a mere fragment of the whole, but it is enough. Ordeals may have gone unrecorded and names may have been forgotten, but such records as have survived in the memories of men like my grandfather and in the memoirs of those who risked all for freedom and brotherhood make it clear that the flight to freedom on the Underground Railroad was an epic of American heroism.

The flight to freedom actually began long before the Underground Railroad was known by that name. George Washington wrote in 1786 about fugitive slaves in Philadelphia "which a Society of Quakers in the city (formed for such purposes) have attempted to liberate." Washington, a slaveholder himself, was probably referring to the Pennsylvania Abolition Society, which included among its members at various times such non-Quakers as Benjamin Franklin, Thomas Paine, Dr. Benjamin Rush, and the Marquis de Lafayette.

Ottawa Indians led by Chief Kinjeino were among the earliest friends of fugitives in western Ohio. Portuguese fishermen are said to have conspired with members of the Shinnecock tribe to transport fugitive slaves from the north shore of Long Island into ports of freedom in Massachusetts, Connecticut, and Rhode Island. The Seminoles harbored escaped slaves and fought a continuing war with the United States to preserve their refuge in Florida.

Most heroic of all were the slaves and free blacks who offered their churches and their homes to help the enslaved—and above all, the passengers themselves.

There were ingenious escapes. Henry "Box" Brown, a "model slave" from Richmond, had himself nailed in a box with a bladder of water and a few biscuits and shipped to the Philadelphia Vigilance Committee. Though he traveled upside down part of the way, he arrived safely. But the white Virginian who helped him, Samuel A. Smith, was sentenced to prison for a subsequent attempt to freight slaves to freedom.

In 1848 a slave from Macon, Georgia, named William Craft dressed his young wife, Ellen, who was possessed of a light complexion, in the top hat and well-cut suit of a planter. They contrived a bandage for a "toothache" and a sling for a "broken arm" to conceal her beardless-ness and her inability to write. Masquerading as master and slave, the two traveled northward with Ellen sleeping in first-class accommoda-tions in southern cities along the way, until they reached Philadelphia and relative safety.

The vast Dismal Swamp on the Virginia-North Carolina border was a refuge for many slaves and a magnet for slave hunters who disabled their human quarry with bird shot, so as not to damage such valuable flesh with heavier ammunition. A runaway slave belonging to Augustus Holly of Bertie County, North Carolina, when finally recaptured in the swamp, was found to be wearing "a coat that was impervious to shot, it being thickly wadded with turkey feathers."

Most simply walked to freedom. "Guided by the north star alone," wrote the great rescuer William Still, "penniless, braving the perils of land and sea, eluding the keen scent of the blood-hound as well as the more dangerous pursuit of the savage slave-hunter . . . [endur-ing] indescribable suffering from hunger and other privations . . . making their way to freedom."

Slaveholders, of course, looked upon the Underground Railroad as organized theft. Under the Constitution of the United States, it was. Slavery was lawful and slaves were property. Their bondage was up-held as a matter of economic necessity for the agricultural South. Buying and selling at slave auctions was a sort of human stock market and a major source of income for many. Not only the South benefited. Entrepreneurs in the industrial North were eager to purchase cheap, slave-produced raw materials.

If the Underground Railroad had a charter apart from the longing for freedom and the urgings of conscience, it was the Fugitive Slave Law of 1850, which greatly strengthened an earlier law dating from 1793 and gave slaveholders the right to organize a posse at any point in the United States to aid in recapturing runaway slaves. Courts and police everywhere in the United States were obligated to assist them.

As a result, slave hunters plied their trade under the protection of governmental authority in all the free states bordering on slave states

Thousands of people sought to aid slaves. The varied lot included former slaves, freeborn blacks, white reformers, and clergy. Some whites championed gradual emancipation, others a return to Africa or freedom without citizenship; few approved social integration.

JERMAIN LOGUEN (ca 1813–1872) "No day dawns for the slave, nor is it looked for. It is all night—night forever," said this fugitive, son of his Tennessee master and a slave woman. Underground agent and ordained minister, he helped 1,500 escapees and started black schools in New York State.

LUCRETIA COFFIN MOTT (1793–1880) A well-educated Quaker wife and mother, she preached eloquently for abolition, women's rights, and temperance. She stood with William Garrison for immediate emancipation.

FREDERICK DOUGLASS (ca 1817–1895) A fugitive slave, Douglass became a skilled abolitionist speaker, praised for "wit, argument, sarcasm and pathos." He urged blacks to pursue vocational education and the vote; his print shop in Rochester, New York, was a depot on the underground.

JOHN GREENLEAF WHITTIER (1807–1892) Remembered for bucolic verse, the Quaker poet gave powerful voice to the abolition movement. He early joined the Republican Party, founded partly to halt the spread of slavery.

ALLAN PINKERTON (1819–1884) Before founding a detective agency, this Scottish immigrant managed an underground depot at his cooper's shop near Chicago.

JOSIAH HENSON (1789–1883) So trustworthy a slave that his owner made him an overseer, Henson, while transporting slaves to Kentucky, resisted others' efforts to free them all. Harriet Beecher Stowe attributed a similar episode to Uncle Tom in her novel. Henson eventually escaped to Canada, led others to safety, and traveled as abolitionist and businessman.

THOMAS GARRETT (1789–1871) "Among the manliest of men, and the gentlest of spirits," wrote William Lloyd Garrison about the Wilmington businessman who aided more than 2,700 slaves to freedom.

MARY ANN SHADD (1823–1893) Daughter of a black agent in the Wilmington underground, the Quaker-educated teacher moved to Canada, where as a writer and editor she preached permanent emigration from the States.

WILLIAM LLOYD GARRISON (1805–1879) One of the earliest, most vitriolic abolitionists, he devoted full time to the cause, speaking against slavery and the Constitution that permitted it. By 1841 he was calling upon the North to secede.

SUSAN B. ANTHONY (1820–1906) Raised to be self-supporting by a Quaker father, the teacher spoke out for temperance, women's rights, and abolition, despite vehement prejudice against women in public affairs. Later she led the fight for women's suffrage.

JONATHAN WALKER (1799–1878) Imprisoned for helping seven slaves sail from Florida bound for the Bahamas, he was branded on the hand with SS for "Slave Stealer." After release he became a "conspicuous witness against slave power" for the abolitionists.

WILLIAM STILL (1821–1902) Indefatigable worker in the Philadelphia underground, Still kept rare day-to-day records, which were published in 1872. A successful coal merchant, he continued to campaign against discrimination.

and even far into New England. Fugitives were plucked from churches in Ohio, from ships in Boston harbor, from the bosoms of free wives and husbands whom they had married in the North. The runaways were not safe anywhere in the nation. Those who aided them faced criminal penalties of six months in jail and a $1,000 fine in addition to a civil liability to the owner of $1,000 for each fugitive.

Some who helped the runaways were important figures in American history: Thaddeus Stevens, Frederick Douglass, Allan Pinkerton, Henry David Thoreau, Harriet Beecher Stowe, William Lloyd Garrison. One among them is a colossus: John Brown.

Captain Brown, the Old Man, Osawatomie Brown, Brown of Kansas—called by whatever name, he was known to all. Among abolitionists, some of whom supported him with money, Brown was revered as a righteous warrior and martyr. Others, including the government, regarded him as a murderous insurgent.

Believing that slavery must be eliminated by force, Brown organized guerrillas to preserve Kansas from slavery, and at Pottawotamie, Kansas, on May 24, 1856, they killed five men in revenge for an earlier attack by proslavery forces at Lawrence. With a score of followers on October 16–18, 1859, he seized the government arsenal at Harpers Ferry, Virginia, in the hope of igniting a general uprising of slaves, but he was taken prisoner, convicted of treason, and hanged.

Like his stationmaster father before him, Brown supported the Underground Railroad body and soul. In December 1858 he and his guerrilla fighters undertook one of the boldest adventures in the history of the Underground Railroad. With 11 slaves, including men, women, and children, the group set out in wagons on a journey of a thousand miles from Missouri to Windsor, Ontario, in the dead of winter. In Chicago they met the celebrated detective and Underground Railroad agent Allan Pinkerton. Pinkerton helped the group on to Detroit, where they boarded a ferry to Canada.

Nestled in the woods on Hines Hill Road in Hudson, Ohio, is a house where John Brown once lived. Only the red chimney is visible from the road, and still existing somewhere under the barn floor is said to be a secret compartment where runaways hid.

Not far from there I came upon a surprising symbol of the Underground Railroad—an iron manikin of a young black groomsman, hand outstretched, which had been designed as an ornamental hitching post. Just such a lawn statue was used on the property of Federal Judge Benjamin Piatt, whose wife was an agent of the Underground Railroad, as a signal to fugitives and conductors. If the manikin held a flag, runaways were welcomed; if the flag was missing, the judge was at home and fugitives must pass on.

Invisible though it may have been, the railroad had many subsidiary routes and innumerable sidings and spurs. The great trunk routes led north from the slave states. The one my great-grandfather probably followed when he escaped from Seaford, Delaware, ran through Wilmington and Philadelphia to New York City and the Canadian border. Farther west, fugitives passed through Lancaster County and on up through central Pennsylvania to the Finger Lakes and Lake Ontario.

Eliza Harris, immortalized as a fictional character in Harriet Beecher Stowe's *Uncle Tom's Cabin*, is modeled on a real woman who crossed the ice of the Ohio River. Faced with the threat of being separated from her only child, Eliza planned to make her flight to freedom beyond the river. But when she reached its banks she discovered that the ice had broken up and was drifting in large cakes and floes. In desperation as her pursuers closed in, Eliza darted into the river, holding her child in her arms. Springing from one floe to another, she lost her shoes in the icy waters but struggled on with bleeding feet to the opposite shore and the safety of the Ohio underground.

Ohio was a broad field of escape; the rights-of-way to freedom led to the Great Lakes and friendly ship captains en route to Canada, as did the routes through Indiana and Illinois, Wisconsin and Minnesota.

Before publishing *Uncle Tom's Cabin*, Stowe kept an underground station in Walnut Hills, near Cincinnati. Another celebrated Cincinnati agent was Levi Coffin, sometimes called the president of the Underground Railroad. A birthright Quaker, Coffin was first active in the system in New Garden, North Carolina, and Newport (now Fountain City), Indiana. He and his wife, Catherine, assisted more than 2,000 fugitive slaves from their Newport home, later known as the Grand Central Station of the railroad.

In Ashtabula on Lake Erie I encountered Tim Hubbard, descendant of Colonel William Hubbard, an ardent abolitionist whose large brick house was an important refuge for fugitives. "No fugitive slave was ever retaken from Ashtabula County," Tim told me, with pride and tolerable accuracy. Every year Tim Hubbard helps conduct an Underground Railroad pilgrimage, retracing the northern portion of the route from Wheeling, West Virginia, to Ashtabula Harbor, onetime anchorage of abolitionist sea captains bound for Canada.

Oberlin, Ohio, has a unique tradition pertaining to blacks. John Brown's father was one of the trustees of Oberlin College, and the community was strongly abolitionist. In effect, the whole town was a station, and when, in 1858, a fugitive slave named John Price was seized on the outskirts of Oberlin, hundreds of her citizens followed him and his captors to nearby Wellington, stormed the hotel where he was confined, and freed him. Later they helped Price north toward Canada and safety.

The tradition lives on. In January 1980 David Hoard and eight other black Oberlin College students reconstructed the flight of escaping slaves from Kentucky to Oberlin. They covered about 420 miles on foot, crossing valleys and mountains, sleeping in barns, churches, and houses.

Crossing a starlit field in Kentucky, the students got a taste of the harsh realities faced by the fugitives. An officer of the law, seeing the group of black strangers marching out of the night, mistook their purpose and declared that he would have no demonstrations in his county. "You can't sleep here tonight," said the sheriff. "Get on across the [Ohio] river." But that, protested the young people, was a walk of 35 miles. "Fine—keep moving," said the sheriff.

A bit farther on the students found a friendly family who let them sleep in their barn. "We sang spirituals of the Underground Railroad, but it was a frightening night," David told me. "Sometimes it's too cloudy to see the North Star."

But there was safety across the Ohio and the Mason-Dixon Line. Thousands of fugitives passed to the North through the forests along the Appalachian range. Many from the Deep South hid on Mississippi River steamboats to northern ports. As Jefferson Davis observed: "Negroes do escape from Mississippi frequently, and the boats, constantly passing by our line of river frontier, furnish great facility to get into Ohio, and when they do escape it is with great difficulty that they are recovered.

Beyond Ohio one of the most important Underground Railroad sites may have been the Joseph Goodrich house at Milton, Wisconsin, where passengers escaped intruding slave catchers through a secret underground tunnel. Among the most ingenious of the Michigan agents were George De Baptiste and William Lambert, who created the Order of African-American Mysteries, with its system of secret signs. Such handshakes, passwords, and other signals were known and used by agents throughout the underground system.

Sojourner Truth, an unlettered black woman born a slave in New York State, is memorialized by a statue at Battle Creek, where she died in 1883. Alone and in company with her friend Frederick Douglass and other leading abolitionists, always in the plainest of clothes, she wandered the land, speaking with an orator's eloquence and a victim's rage against the institution of slavery.

Although most runaways reached the protection of the Free States and the underground on their own, abolitionists did daring work even in the heart of the South. Virginian John Fairfield conducted dozens across the Ohio. The son of a slaveholder in New Bern, North Carolina, secreted slaves aboard ships hauling lumber to Philadelphia. In Florida, the Seminole Indians welcomed slaves from Georgia and South Carolina as well as Florida who fled through swamps and wilderness into Seminole territory.

When the Seminoles were removed to Indian Territory starting in the early 1830s, 450 to 500 black members of the tribe, representing about 15 percent of its numbers, went with them. Ironically, some of these black Seminoles were formed into a special U.S. Army unit to fight the Comanches and Apaches. About 800 descendants of these fugitives, known as Seminole freedmen, now live in Seminole County, Oklahoma, as members of the tribe that harbored their ancestors.

The ghosts of fugitives and their collaborators linger in all these places. To me, the most vivid of all figures connected with the Underground Railroad was Harriet Tubman, who lived on the Eastern Shore of Maryland, just across the Delmarva Peninsula from my great-grandfather. Born a slave into an environment that is still harsh today, Harriet was one of ten or so children. As a woman in her twenties, she set off one dark summer night in 1849 from Bucktown, Maryland, to follow the North Star. From there the railroad route passed through country filled with fearful dangers: armed patrols on horseback, bloodhounds, placards advertising rewards for the capture of runaways posted at every tavern and crossroads. At length Harriet crossed the Mason-Dixon Line into free territory in Pennsylvania, penniless and "a stranger in a strange land," as she later remembered.

In Philadelphia she found employment and saved almost every penny she earned for the real work to come. Her own freedom was not enough for Harriet Tubman. Again and again she returned south through the nights, seeking passengers for her train, risking recapture and defying the wrath of slave hunters. The price on her head, by the time she conducted her final perilous journey as a liberator, reportedly reached $40,000. Among those Harriet brought north in her caravans were her parents, whom she conducted to Canada.

Dark of skin, medium in height, with a full broad face topped often by a colorful kerchief, Harriet developed extraordinary physical endurance and muscular strength as well as mental fortitude. John Brown so admired Harriet's character and prowess that he nicknamed her "General Tubman."

It was with Harriet Tubman, a famous heroine of the Underground Railroad, and my great-grandfather, one of its unknown passengers, linked in my mind that I began a pilgrimage of rediscovery along the old freedom rights-of-way.

As George Washington's letter suggests, the Quakers won an early and richly deserved reputation as friends to fugitive slaves. But the fellowship of the Underground Railroad was truly ecumenical, including Roman Catholics, Jews, and Protestants, as well as freethinkers, and if adherents of most other faiths were numbered among slaveholders, so (contrary to legend, alas!) were certain members of the Society of Friends.

Nevertheless, one cannot travel very far along the Underground Railroad without encountering a Quaker. In the graveyard of Longwood Meetinghouse, not far from my present home in Pennsylvania, sleep great conductors of the railroad: Darlington, Mendenhall, Taylor. All were members of this progressive Quaker meeting that concealed fugitive slaves and spirited them away from the meetinghouse under the very eyes of proslavery spies and informers who knew of their activity but could not prove or prevent it.

At Longwood Harriet Tubman, too, found sympathizers to welcome her into their homes in moments of danger.

Baltimore was a pivotal junction point on the railroad. A city with both an antislavery society and a slave auction block, it was divided in its allegiances. Here many a fugitive found friendship and aid. The eloquent Frederick Douglass labored as a slave at Fells Point, but met a friendly sailor who provided false papers and so obtained his freedom. He wrote a powerful autobiography and became one of the greatest of the black antislavery orators as well as U.S. minister to Haiti. In his lifetime and beyond, the connection of the term "statesman" to his name seemed a natural thing.

Douglass also served as a U.S. marshal for the District of Columbia, where, well into his manhood, manacled slaves had marched under the windows of the White House to the auction block at Decatur House on Lafayette Square, across Pennsylvania Avenue. Solomon

Northup, a free black kidnapped and on his way to slavery in New Orleans, recalled that "the voices of patriotic representatives boasting of freedom and equality, and the rattling of the poor slave's chains, almost commingled."

In Cambridge, Maryland, not far from Harriet Tubman's birthplace on the Edward Brodas plantation in Dorchester County, I encountered her kinswoman Addie Travers. Together we explored the crooked creeks of the Eastern Shore, where Harriet's route took her along the Choptank River and its many inlets.

This was perilous country, home ground on the slave hunter Patty Cannon and her merciless gang. A tall, striking woman whose salty language was her trademark, Mrs. Cannon ran her underground railroad in reverse. A letter to Philadelphia Mayor Joseph Watson in 1826 suggests that her gang was abducting blacks as far north as his city.

Sometimes she employed renegade blacks to entice fugitives into their homes as false station stops on the Underground Railroad. There the trusting runaways were entrapped by Patty's gang, who often tortured and murdered free blacks as well as escaped slaves and sold the survivors.

Finally captured and indicted for the murder of four fugitives— two of them children—Patty Cannon poisoned herself on May 11, 1829, in her prison cell at Georgetown, Delaware, cheating a public eager to witness her trial and execution.

According to family tradition, my great-great-grandfather Spencer Blockson occasionally saw Patty while living in slavery in Sussex County near the Nanticoke River where she operated. My great-aunt Minerva Blockson, born only nine years after Appomattox, was terrified as a child growing up on the Delmarva Peninsula by tales of this villainess. "We children would hide behind chairs while the big folks told how evil old Patty Cannon would catch us and sell us to slavers down south," she told me in a voice hoarse with age. And in Aunt Minerva's bright face the old terror rekindled, though she was then 102 years of age.

Through peril and wilderness, Harriet Tubman was a natural navigator. She did not keep a journal, but she described her various routes of escape to her biographer Sarah Bradford and others. Usually she followed the route from Cambridge along the Choptank toward Camden, Delaware. Harriet always carried a pistol to ward off pursuers. She didn't hesitate to raise it when slaves refused to travel on, crying, "You go or die." She carried tincture of opium to quiet crying babies and frightened and wounded fugitives.

At 227 Shipley Street in Wilmington, Delaware, stood the home of Quaker Thomas Garrett, Harriet Tubman's great collaborator and keeper of perhaps the most important Underground Railroad station on this right-of-way. It was Garrett who forwarded Harriet and her passengers on to William Still in Philadelphia; he is said to have aided about 2,700 fugitive slaves with assistance from Wilmington's free black community. In the early days of the Civil War these blacks protected Garrett's home, and he had need of their vigilance, for his activities earned him the hatred of many who wished to preserve the institution of slavery.

Friend Garrett was not deterred by physical threats or financial penalties. Ordered to pay $5,400 in damages for helping a family of fugitives to escape, Garrett defiantly told the court: "I had assisted over 1,400 in 25 years on their way to the North, and I now consider the penalty imposed might be as a license for the remainder of my life . . . if any of you know of any slave who *needs* assistance, send him to me."

Runaway slaves entering Philadelphia—as many as 9,000 of them before 1860—were forwarded to points along the Reading and Pennsylvania Railroads and put on trains to New York State and New England. As a great port and rail center, Philadelphia was a natural junction on the Underground Railroad. It was also an abolitionist center and had a large community of free blacks.

Yet even on the Underground Railroad, bigotry existed. William Wells Brown, a former slave and a celebrated orator, said of Philadelphia in 1854: "Colorphobia is more rampant there than in the proslavery . . . city of New York." Fugitives were sometimes banned from entering conductors' homes; some conductors were known to shackle fugitives for "control," and these fetters can still be seen in one former Pennsylvania underground station. Spies of both races abounded, ready to sell out escaped slaves.

A steadfast friend to the Underground Railroad in Philadelphia, Lucretia Mott, Quaker minister and leader in both the antislavery and women's rights movements, was threatened by an angry crowd in my hometown of Norristown in 1842 when she offended against politics and convention by leaving an antislavery meeting at the First Baptist Church arm in arm with Frederick Douglass. When the meeting reconvened that evening, the crowd outside stoned the church before being dispersed by antislavery sympathizers and members of the black community.

But Philadelphia's Mother Bethel African Methodist Episcopal Church hid hundreds of fugitive slaves. Although the original building had been replaced, the existing church stands on the oldest piece of ground continuously owned by blacks in the United States.

In nearby Plymouth Meeting, George Corson and others received the passengers forwarded north by Elijah Pennypacker of Phoenixville, another major terminal on the eastern railroad. Pennypacker and his Valley Forge neighbor Lewis Peart directed slaves on a route leading along property that once belonged to John James Audubon.

My friend Richard Mayhew tells of his Shinnecock Indian ancestors' conspiring with Portuguese fishermen to transport fugitive slaves from Long Island into New England ports. The Mayhews are connected with the family of the great conductor William Still, and at a reunion of the Still family in Lawnside, New Jersey, I found myself surrounded by members of this remarkable clan.

Its progenitors, Levin and Charity Still, were born as slaves, but they were able to buy Levin's freedom and he moved to Indian Mills, New Jersey, about 1810. Charity succeeded in escaping with two of their children and the Stills eventually raised a family of 18. One son, James, the "black doctor of the pines," treated patients both black and white with herbal remedies and became an ardent worker on the Underground Railroad from his Mount Holly home. Two of his sons were physicians. James's brother Peter, left behind in slavery, was the subject of *The Kidnapped and the Ransomed*, a dramatic account by Kate Pickard of Peter's forty years as a slave. He finally bought his own way to freedom, assisted by two benevolent Jewish brothers, Joseph and Isaac Friedman of Tuscumbia, Alabama.

Most famous of all the Stills, of course, was William, the legendary Philadelphia dispatcher and historian who forwarded hundreds— including Jacob Blockson—along the route to freedom. This is a family with a great will to be together. "The original Still's Day was celebrated in 1870," Clarence Still told me. "We have doctors, teachers, scientists, and military heroes. We have been able to accomplish so much because of our family's strength and stability."

At Columbia, Pennsylvania, along the Susquehanna River, spies and informers watched the bridges. A few miles from here, at Christiana, in September 1851, the first blood was shed in resistance to the Fugitive Slave Law of the previous year when a Maryland planter, Edward Gorsuch, with his son and a deputy U.S. marshal, tried to serve warrants for the return of some fugitives. Threats were exchanged at the home of a William Parker, who sheltered the runaways, while Parker's wife sounded a horn over and over again to summon help. A force of local free blacks, accompanied by a Quaker sympathizer named Castner Hanway, arrived. In the ensuing melee, afterward known as the Christiana Riot, the runaways escaped.

But shots were fired and Gorsuch was killed. Parker, charged with treason, became the object of a celebrated manhunt but escaped to Canada with the aid of the antislavery underground.

More than thirty Christiana blacks were arrested and jailed in Philadelphia. Friend Hanway, charged not with violation of the Fugitive Slave Law but with "wickedly and traitorously [intending] to levy war against the United States," went on trial in a federal courtroom in Independence Hall.

Lancaster's Thaddeus Stevens, member of the U.S. House of Representatives, the Old Commoner, the Great Leveler, led the defense. Stevens's hatred of slavery was matched by his genius for courtroom drama. When the blacks were led into the courtroom, each wore a red-white-and-blue scarf around his neck in a demonstration of support for Hanway. Lucretia Mott sat nearby in her plain Quaker dress, serenely knitting.

When even the federal judge, otherwise no friend to abolitionists, was forced to say that the charges against Hanway were absurd, a "not guilty" verdict was returned within 20 minutes. The Christiana Riot ranked with John Brown's raid on Harpers Ferry in the power of its symbolism to the antislavery movement before the Civil War.

During the Civil War, Confederate cavalry raiders led by Maj. Jubal A. Early sacked an ironworks owned by Stevens. Early remarked that he was sorry he had not found Stevens there: "I would hang him on the spot and divide his bones and send them to several states as curiosities."

The day after the raid Gen. Robert E. Lee issued a reproof. "We cannot take vengeance . . . without . . . offending against Him to whom vengeance belongeth," wrote the Confederate commander.

From central Pennsylvania one branch of the Underground Railroad passed through New York State to the Canadian border. In Rochester, Frederick Douglass published his newspaper *The North Star* and made friends with Susan B. Anthony and the abolitionist Elizabeth Cady Stanton. Miss Anthony's brother Merritt fought beside John Brown in a bloody skirmish with proslavery forces at Osawatomie, Kansas. Brother and sister had early imbibed the abolitionist spirit from their Quaker family.

In Buffalo, Professor Monroe Fordham of Buffalo State College, standing on the banks of Lake Erie, described the bitter local winter, and I pictured the lake then, frozen enough for fugitives to walk across to Canada and freedom. In other seasons, many got rides from ferryboat captains who were sympathetic toward the underground.

Had my great-grandfather struggled across the ice in a winter gale? Had he found a sympathetic ferryman to take him over this symbolic Jordan? It was just as possible that he had passed over by another route altogether—New England. If he passed through New Hampshire, he may have been regarded as something of a curiosity. As I ate lunch in Manchester, an elderly gentleman fixed me with a friendly wrinkled smile and said: "We don't see many colored people in our state." I explained that I was conducting a study of the Underground Railroad throughout New England. "I thought all that abolition business took place in Massachusetts," he replied.

A good deal of it did. In Concord, Massachusetts, on the night of my arrival, I heard the tolling of the town's bell. Here, on October 30, 1859, Thoreau had rung the great bell as John Brown was tried for treason. The Thoreau house was a hiding place for slaves traveling on the Underground Railroad.

In Boston, gaunt, fiery William Lloyd Garrison published his inflammatory newspaper, *The Liberator*. In the cause of immediate and complete emancipation, Garrison was willing to cast away the church, the Constitution, and the Union. He paid for his convictions in a way that defined his enemies and helped the cause. In 1835 Garrison was confronted by a proslavery mob shouting, "Kill him! Lynch him! Hang the abolitionist!" Seized and tied up, he was finally rescued by delegates of the mayor.

In 1838 a slave about twenty years old named Frederick Augustus Washington Bailey escaped from his owner in Maryland and was forwarded to the noted black conductor Nathan Johnson in New Bedford. Johnson suggested that the fugitive slave change his name to Frederick Douglass. In later life Douglass, a proponent of moderation, would oppose Garrison's extremist tactics.

New Bedford, an important port, welcomed many runaways, and the sea had its own story of the Underground Railroad; many agents and conductors were sea captains. My favorite underground sea story concerns a Massachusetts shipwright named Jonathan Walker, who went to Florida to salvage a wreck. One torrid day in 1844 seven slaves left Pensacola with Walker in his open boat, bound for a Bahamian island. As their craft approached Cape Florida, it was overtaken by another vessel. The fugitives were delivered to their owners, and Walker, sent back to Pensacola in chains, was placed in a pillory and pelted with rotten eggs.

By order of a federal court Walker's right hand was branded with the letters S S for "Slave Stealer." Eventually his fines were paid by abolitionist friends and he returned to New England, where he attracted large audiences on the antislavery lecture circuit as "the man with the branded hand."

My Pilgrimage took me, finally, across the Canadian border to St. Catharines, an Ontario city that Harriet Tubman once called home. Here too James Blockson and his cousin Jacob had briefly lived. Nearby, the trembling suspension bridge over the Niagara River had been the passage between slavery and freedom.

William Lloyd Garrison reported that there were 25,000 fugitives in Canada in 1852. No fewer than 3,000 had arrived there within three months after the Fugitive Slave Law of 1850 was passed. The Reverend William Mitchell, a black Underground Railroad conductor and historian, estimated that at the end of the decade at least 1,200 refugees were reaching Canada every year.

Josiah Henson, on whom the character of Uncle Tom is partly based, settled in Dawn, not far from St. Catharines, after escaping from slavery in 1830. In 1841 Henson and a group of abolitionists purchased 200 acres and established a vocational school for fugitive slaves known as the British-American Institute. Henson made numerous trips on the Underground Railroad, leading fugitives to Canada. It is a supreme irony that the name of this activist's fictional counterpart should have become synonymous with servility in the usage of a later generation.

In nearby Chatham, before John Brown marched to his apotheosis along a forest route long used by fugitive slaves, he had plotted the new government he dreamed would follow his attack on the Harpers Ferry arsenal.

Walking through this hushed Canadian town, I remembered that other quiet town—Harpers Ferry. In both places John Brown's tumultuous spirit seemed to reside. I found myself humming "The Battle Hymn of the Republic," of which the tune, of course, is "John Brown's Body."

A little time before, while visiting Harriet Tubman's home in Auburn, New York, I had attended her old church and with a group of friends sang the coded spirituals of the Underground Railroad: "Steal Away to Jesus" and "Wade in the Water, Children," songs doubtless sung by Harriet Tubman during her journeys through that vanished South where men would have taken her life because she had taken her freedom.

These coded songs had double meanings: "Follow the Drinking Gourd," for example, was a metaphoric allusion to the Big Dipper and North Star. And, as Frederick Douglass once said, "A keen observer might have detected [Canada] in our repeated singing of:

'O Canaan, sweet Canaan,
I am bound for the land of Canaan.' "

We also sang the soulful "Amazing Grace," whose origins amaze with their power, for the hymn was written by a former English slave trader, John Newton, after he was seized by the Lord and exchanged his slave ship for the ministry.

The spirituals, filled with secrets that perhaps could only be told in song, have not lost their power to join one heart to many others and to explain mysteries. Standing beneath the tall evergreen that guards the grave of Harriet Tubman, I felt close to this woman who was called the Moses of our people, and to the ancestors, those of blood and those of spirit, black and white, who had trod these rights-of-way to freedom and kept the stations of the Underground Railroad and kept the faith in the oneness of mankind.

We held hands in a circle. Gladys Bryant, seventy-seven-year-old great-great-grandniece of Harriet Tubman, told us that "Harriet would be proud of the gathering assembled here today. She would have supported the causes that brought us together."

Saying good-bye, we tightened our hands one upon the other and sang "Swing Low, Sweet Chariot," the song, beloved by Harriet and by each of us, that Harriet's friends sang on March 10, 1913, the evening that she died.

17

Women and Their Families on the Overland Trail
to California and Oregon, 1842–1867

JOHNNY FARAGHER AND CHRISTINE STANSELL

• The image of wagon trains crawling across vast plains has been entrenched in our minds by frequent movie and television westerns. Yet despite this popular treatment, the day-to-day reality of the way west remains shrouded in mystery. What impact those miles of desolation had on the minds and the lifestyles of families has rarely been explored in a serious way.

Each family that risked the dangerous trip brought with them not only physical reminders of home but in addition an entire way of viewing the world and their place in it. This viewpoint was necessarily based on a quite different reality from the one they would face during endless days of travel as well as in future places of settlement.

The frontier experience challenged in particular the basis of many of the values that characterized nineteenth-century "civilized society." An important part of this value system dealt with "the woman's place." From the 1840s on, the women's rights movement was making progress, and in that same decade the first settlers crossed into Nebraska to begin the trek to the Pacific. For the women who went west in the 1840s and thereafter, the new life was a mixture of incredible deprivation and quiet anticipation of the "great day a-comin.'" They literally put so many miles between themselves and their sisters and mothers back east that the established society of the settled country never fully caught up with them. Their very scarcity gave women a special prestige. The 1865 bylaws of Yellowstone City, Montana, for example, stated that death

This article is reprinted from *Feminist Studies*, 2, no. 2/3 (1975): 150–166, by permission of the publisher, Feminist Studies, Inc., c/o Women's Studies Program, University of Maryland, College Park, MD 20742.

was to be the penalty for "murder, thieving, or for insulting a woman." Not surprisingly, there were just fifteen women in the town and three hundred men.

Johnny Faragher and Christine Stansell explore not only how life on the Western trails affected the women's roles but also how the women themselves reacted to such changes. In addressing themselves to such issues, the authors raise an important question of historical writing. How effectively can you put yourself into the minds of people who lived more than a century ago? Does the fact that historians are usually limited to written records substantially affect the accuracy of their conclusions?

> *I am not a wheatfield*
> *nor the virgin forest*
>
> *I never chose this place*
> *yet I am of it now*
>
> —Adrienne Rich
> "From an Old House in America"

From 1841 until 1867, the year in which the transcontinental railroad was completed, nearly 350,000 North Americans emigrated to the Pacific coast along the western wagon road known variously as the Oregon, the California, or simply the Overland Trail. This migration was essentially a family phenomenon. Although single men constituted the majority of the party which pioneered large-scale emigration on the Overland Trail in 1841, significant numbers of women and children were already present in the wagon trains of the next season. Families made up the preponderant proportion of the migrations throughout the 1840s. In 1849, during the overwhelmingly male Gold Rush, the number dropped precipitously, but after 1851 families once again assumed dominance in the overland migration. The contention that "the family was the one substantial social institution" on the frontier is too sweeping, yet it is undeniable that the white family largely mediated the incorporation of the western territories into the American nation.

The emigrating families were a heterogeneous lot. Some came from farms in the Midwest and upper South, many from small Midwestern towns, and others from Northeastern and Midwestern cities. Clerks and shopkeepers as well as farmers outfitted their wagons in Independence, St. Louis, or Westport Landing on the Missouri. Since costs for supplies, travel, and settlement were not negligible, few of the very poor were present, nor were the exceptionally prosperous. The dreams of fortune which lured the wagon trains into new lands were those of modest men whose hopes were pinned to small farms or larger dry-goods stores, more fertile soil or more customers, better market prospects and a steadily expanding economy.

For every member of the family, the trip west was exhausting, toilsome, and often grueling. Each year in late spring, west-bound emigrants gathered for the journey at spots along the Missouri River and moved out in parties of ten to several hundred wagons. Aggregates of nuclear families, loosely attached by kinship or friendship, traveled together or joined an even larger caravan. Coast-bound families traveled by ox-drawn wagons at the frustratingly slow pace of fifteen to twenty miles per day. They worked their way up the Platte River valley through what is now Kansas and Nebraska, crossing the Rockies at South Pass in southwestern Wyoming by mid-summer. The Platte route was relatively easy going, but from present-day Idaho, where the roads to California and Oregon diverged, to their final destinations, the pioneers faced disastrous conditions: scorching deserts, boggy salt flats, and rugged mountains. By this time, families had been on the road some three months and were only at the midpoint of the journey; the environment, along with the wear of the road, made the last months difficult almost beyond endurance. Finally, in late fall or early winter the pioneers straggled into their promised lands, after six months and over two thousand miles of hardship.

As this journey progressed, bare necessity became the determinant of most of each day's activities. The primary task of surviving and getting to the coast gradually suspended accustomed patterns of dividing work between women and men. All able-bodied adults worked all day in one way or another to keep the family moving. Women's work was no less indispensable than men's; indeed, as the summer wore on, the boundaries dividing the work of the sexes were threatened, blurred, and transgressed.

The vicissitudes of the trail opened new possibilities for expanded work roles for women, and in the cooperative work of the family there existed a basis for a vigorous struggle for female-male equality. But most women did not see the experience in this way. They viewed it as a male enterprise from its very inception. Women experienced the breakdown of the sexual division of labor as a dissolution of their own autonomous "sphere." Bereft of the footing which this independent base gave them, they lacked a cultural rationale for the work they did, and remained estranged from the possibilities of the enlarged scope and power of family life on the trail. Instead, women fought *against* the forces of necessity to hold together the few fragments of female subculture left to them. We have been bequeathed a remarkable record of this struggle in the diaries, journals, and memoirs of emigrating women. In this study, we will examine a particular habit of living, or culture, in conflict with the new material circumstances of the Trail, and the efforts of women to maintain a place, a sphere of their own.

The overland family was not a homogeneous unit, its members imbued with identical aspirations and desires. On the contrary, the period of westward movement was also one of multiplying schisms within those families whose location and social status placed them in the mainstream of national culture. Child-rearing tracts, housekeeping manuals, and etiquette books by the hundreds proscribed and rationalized to these Americans a radical separation of the work responsibilities and social duties of mothers and fathers; popular thought assigned unique personality traits, spiritual capacities, and forms of experience to the respective categories of man, woman, and child. In many families, the tensions inherent in this separatist ideology, often repressed in the everyday routines of the East, erupted under the strain of the overland crossing. The difficulties of the emigrants, while inextricably linked to the duress of the journey itself, also revealed family dynamics which had been submerged in the less eventful life "back home."

A full-blown ideology of "woman's place" was absent in pre-industrial America. On farms, in artisan shops, and in town marketplaces, women and children made essential contributions to family income and subsistence; it was the family which functioned as the basic unit of production in the colony and the young nation. As commercial exchanges displaced the local markets where women had sold surplus dairy products and textiles, and the workplace drifted away from the household, women and children lost their breadwinning prerogatives.

In Jacksonian America, a doctrine of "sexual spheres" arose to facilitate and justify the segregation of women into the home and men into productive work. While the latter attended to politics, economics, and wage-earning, popular thought assigned women the refurbished and newly professionalized tasks of child-rearing and housekeeping. A host of corollaries followed on the heels of these shifts. Men were physically strong, women naturally delicate; men were skilled in practical matters, women in moral and emotional concerns; men were prone to corruption, women to virtue; men belonged in the world, women in the home. For women, the system of sexual spheres represented a decline in social status and isolation from political and economic power. Yet it also provided them with a psychological power base of undeniable importance. The "cult of true womanhood" was more than simply a retreat. Catharine Beecher, one of the chief theorists of "woman's influence," proudly quoted Tocqueville's observation that "in no country has such constant care been taken, as in America, to trace two clearly distinct lines of action for the two sexes, and to make them keep pace with the other, but in two pathways which are always different." Neither Beecher nor her sisters were simply dupes of a masculine imperialism. The supervision of child-rearing, household economy, and the moral and religious life of the family granted women a certain degree of real autonomy and control over their lives as well as those of their husbands and children.

Indeed, recent scholarship has indicated that a distinctly female subculture emerged from "woman's sphere." By "subculture" we simply mean a "habit of living"—as we have used "culture" above—of a minority group which is self-consciously distinct from the dominant activities, expectations, and values of a society. Historians have seen female church groups, reform associations, and philanthropic activity as expressions of this subculture in actual behavior, while a large and rich body of writing by and for women articulated the subcultural impulses on the ideational level. Both behavior and thought point to child-rearing, religious activity, education, home life, associationism, and female communality as components of women's subculture. Female friendships, strikingly intimate and deep in this period, formed the actual bonds. Within their tight and atomized family households, women carved out a life of their own.

At its very inception, the western emigration sent tremors through the foundations of this carefully compartmentalized family structure. The rationale behind pulling up stakes was nearly always economic advancement. Since breadwinning was a masculine concern, the husband and father introduced the idea of going west and made the final decision. Family participation in the intervening time ran the gamut from enthusiastic support to stolid resistance. Many women cooperated with their ambitious spouses: "The motive that induced us to part with pleasant associations and the dear friends of our childhood days, was to obtain from the government of the United States a grant of land that 'Uncle Sam' had promised to give to the head of each family who settled in this new country." Others, however, only acquiesced. "Poor Ma said only this morning, 'Oh, I wish we never had started,' " Lucy Cooke wrote her first day on the trail, "and she looks so sorrowful and dejected. I think if Pa had not passengers to take through she would urge him to return; not that he should be so inclined." Huddled with her children in a cold, damp wagon, trying to calm them despite the ominous chanting of visiting Indians, another woman wondered "what had possessed my husband, anyway, that he should have thought of bringing us away out through this God forsaken country." Similar alienation from the "pioneer spirit" haunted Lavinia Porter's leave-taking:

> I never recall that sad parting from my dear sister on the plains of Kansas without the tears flowing fast and free. . . . We were the eldest of a large family, and the bond of affection and love that existed between us was strong indeed . . . as she with the other friends turned to leave me for the ferry which was to take them back to home and civilization, I stood alone on that wild prairie. Looking westward I saw my husband driving slowly over the plain; turning my face once more to the east, my dear sister's footsteps were fast widening the distance between us. For the time I knew not which way to go, nor whom to follow. But in a few moments I rallied my forces . . . and soon overtook the slowly moving oxen who were bearing my husband and child over the green prairie . . . the unbidden tears would flow in spite of my brave resolve to be the courageous and valiant frontierswoman.

Her dazed vacillation soon gave way to a private conviction that the family had made a dire mistake: "I would make a brave effort to be cheerful and patient until the camp work was done. Then starting out ahead of the team and my men folks, when I thought I had gone beyond hearing distance, I would throw myself down on the unfriendly desert and give way like a child to sobs and tears, wishing myself back home with my friends and chiding myself for consenting to take this wild goose chase." Men viewed drudgery, calamity, and privation as trials along the road to prosperity, unfortunate but inevitable corollaries of the rational decision they had made. But to those women who were unable to appropriate the vision of the upwardly mobile pilgrimage, hardship and loss only testified to the inherent folly of the emigration, "this wild goose chase."

If women were reluctant to accompany their men, however, they were often equally unwilling to let them go alone. In the late 1840s, the conflict between wives and their gold-crazed husbands reveals the determination with which women enforced the cohesion of the nuclear family. In the name of family unity, some obdurate wives simply chose to blockbust the sexually segregated Gold Rush: "My husband grew enthusiastic and wanted to start immediately," one woman recalled, "but I would not be left behind. I thought where he could go I could and where I went I could take my two little toddling babies." Her family departed intact. Other women used their moral authority to smash the enterprise in its planning stages. "We were married to live together," a wife acidly reminded her spouse when he informed her of his intention to join the Rush: "I am willing to go with you to any part of *God's Foot Stool* where you think you can do best, and under these circumstances you have no right to go where I cannot, and if you do you need never return for I shall look upon you as dead." Roundly chastised, the man postponed his journey until the next season, when his family could leave with him. When included in the plans, women seldom wrote of their husbands' decisions to emigrate in their diaries or memoirs. A breadwinner who tried to leave alone, however, threatened the family unity upon which his authority was based; only then did a wife challenge his dominance in worldly affairs.

There was an economic reason for the preponderance of families on the Trail. Women and children, but especially women, formed an essential supplementary work force in the settlements. The ideal wife in the West resembled a hired hand more than a nurturant Christian housekeeper. Narcissa Whitman wrote frankly to aspiring settlers of the functional necessity of women on the new farms: "Let every young man bring a wife, for he will want one after he gets here, if he never did before." In a letter from California, another seasoned woman warned a friend in Missouri that in the West women became "hewers of wood and drawers of water everywhere." Mrs. Whitman's fellow missionary Elkanah Walker was unabashedly practical in beseeching his wife to join him: "I am tired of keeping an old bachelor's hall. I want someone to get me a good supper and let me take my ease and when I am very tired in the morning I want someone to get up and get breakfast and let me lay in bed and take my rest." It would be both simplistic and harsh to argue that men brought their families West or married because of the labor power of women and children; there is no doubt, however, that the new Westerners appreciated the advantages of familial labor. Women were not superfluous; they were workers. The migration of women helped to solve the problem of labor scarcity, not only in the early years of the American settlement on the coast, but throughout the history of the continental frontier.

In the first days of the overland trip, new work requirements were not yet pressing and the division of labor among family members still replicated familiar patterns. Esther Hanna reported in one of her first diary entries that "our men have gone to build a bridge across the stream, which is impassable," while she baked her first bread on the prairie. Elizabeth Smith similarly described her party's day: "rainy . . . Men making rafts. Women cooking and washing. Children crying." When travel was suspended, "the men were generally busy mending wagons, harnesses, yokes, shoeing the animals etc., and the women washed clothes, boiled a big mess of beans, to warm over for several meals, or perhaps mended clothes." At first, even in emergencies, women and men hardly considered integrating their work. "None but those who have cooked for a family of eight, crossing the plains, have any idea of what it takes," a disgruntled woman recalled: "My sister-in-law was sick, my niece was much younger than I, and consequently I had the management of all the cooking and planning on my young shoulders." To ask a man to help was a possibility she was unable even to consider.

The relegation of women to purely domestic duties, however, soon broke down under the vicissitudes of the Trail. Within the first few weeks, the unladylike task of gathering buffalo dung for fuel (little firewood was available *en route*) became women's work. As one traveler astutely noted, "force of surroundings was a great leveler"; miles of grass, dust, glare, and mud erased some of the most rudimentary distinctions between female and male responsibilities. By summer, women often helped drive the wagons and the livestock. At one Platte crossing, "the men drawed the wagons over by hand and the women all crossed in safety"; but at the next, calamity struck when the bridge collapsed, "and then commenced the hurry and bustle of repairing; all were at work, even the women and children." Such crises, which compounded daily as the wagons moved past the Platte up the long stretches of desert and coastal mountains, generated equity in work; at times of Indian threats, for example, both women and men made bullets and stood guard. When mountain fever struck the Pengra family as they crossed the Rockies, Charlotte relieved her incapacitated husband of the driving while he took care of the youngest child. Only such severe afflictions forced men to take on traditionally female chores. While women did men's work, there is little evidence that men reciprocated.

Following a few days in the life of an overland woman discloses the magnitude of her work. During the hours her party traveled, Charlotte Pengra walked beside the wagons, driving the cattle and gathering buffalo chips. At night she cooked, baked bread for the next noon meal, and washed clothes. Three successive summer days illustrate how trying these small chores could be. Her train pulled out early on a Monday morning, only to be halted by rain and a flash flood; Mrs. Pengra washed and dried her family's wet clothes in the afternoon while doing her daily baking. On Tuesday the wagons pushed hard to make up for lost time, forcing her to trot all day to keep up. In camp that night there was no time to rest. Before going to bed, she wrote, "Kept busy in preparing tea and doing other things preparatory for the morrow. I baked a cracker pudding, warm biscuits and made tea, and after supper stewed two pans of dried apples, and made two loaves of bread, got my work done up, beds made, and child asleep, and have written in my journal. Pretty tired of course." The same routine devoured the next day and evening: "I have done a washing. Stewed apples, made pies and baked a rice pudding, and mended our wagon cover. Rather tired." And the next: "baked biscuits, stewed berries, fried meat, boiled and mashed potatoes, and made tea for supper, afterward baked bread. Thus you see I have not much rest." Children also burdened women's work and leisure. During one quiet time, Helen Stewart retreated in mild defiance from her small charges to a tent in order to salvage some private time: "It exceeding hot . . . some of the men is out hunting and some of them sleeping. The children is grumbling and crying and laughing and howling and playing all around." Although children are notably absent in women's journals, they do appear, frightened and imploring, during an Indian scare or a storm, or intrude into a rare and precious moment of relaxation, "grumbling and crying."

Because the rhythm of their chores was out of phase with that of the men, the division of labor could be especially taxing to women. Men's days were toilsome but broken up at regular intervals with periods of rest. Men hitched the teams, drove or walked until noon, relaxed at dinner, traveled until the evening camp, unhitched the oxen, ate supper, and in the evening sat at the campfire, mended equipment, or stood guard. They also provided most of the labor in emergencies, pulling the wagons through mires, across treacherous river crossings, up long grades, and down precipitous slopes. In the pandemonium of a steep descent,

> you would see the women and children in advance seeking the best way, some of them slipping down, or holding on to the rocks, now taking an "otter slide," and then a run til some natural obstacle presented itself to stop their accelerated progress and those who get down safely without a hurt or a bruise, are fortunate indeed. Looking back to the train, you would see some of the men holding on to the wagons, others slipping under the oxen's feet, some throwing articles out of the way that had fallen out, and all have enough to do to keep them busily occupied.

Women were responsible for staying out of the way and getting themselves and the children to safety, men for getting the wagons down. Women's work, far less demanding of brute strength and endurance, was nevertheless distributed without significant respite over all waking hours: mealtimes offered no leisure to the cooks. "The plain fact of the matter is," a young woman complained,

> we *have no time for sociability*. From the time we get up in the morning, until we are on the road, it is hurry scurry to get break-

fast and put away the things that necessarily had to be pulled out last night—while under way there is no room in the wagon for a visitor, nooning is barely long enough to eat a cold bite—and at night all the cooking utensils and provisions are to be gotten about the camp fire, and cooking enough to last until the next night.

After supper, the men gathered together, "lolling and smoking their pipes and guessing, or maybe betting, how many miles we had covered during the day," while the women baked, washed, and put the children to bed before they finally sat down. Charlotte Pengra found "as I was told before I started that there is no rest in such a journey."

Unaccustomed tasks beset the travelers, who were equipped with only the familiar expectation that work was divided along gender lines. The solutions which sexual "spheres" offered were usually irrelevant to the new problems facing families. Women, for example, could not afford to be delicate: their new duties demanded far greater stamina and hardiness than their traditional domestic tasks. With no tradition to deal with the new exigencies of fuel-gathering, cattle-driving, and cooking, families found that "the division of labor in a party . . . was a prolific cause of quarrel." Within the Vincent party, "assignments to duty were not accomplished without grumbling and objection . . . there were occasional angry debates while the various burdens were being adjusted," while in "the camps of others who sometimes jogged along the trail in our company . . . we saw not a little fighting . . . and these bloody fisticuffs were invariably the outcome of disputes over division of labor." At home, these assignments were familiar and accepted, not subject to questioning. New work opened the division of labor to debate and conflict.

By mid-journey, most women worked at male tasks. The men still retained dominance within their "sphere," despite the fact that it was no longer exclusively masculine. Like most women, Lavinia Porter was responsible for gathering buffalo chips for fuel. One afternoon, spying a grove of cottonwoods half a mile away, she asked her husband to branch off the trail so that the party could fell trees for firewood, thus easing her work. "But men on the plains I had found were not so accomodating, nor so ready to wait upon women as they were in more civilized communities." Her husband refused and Porter fought back: "I was feeling somewhat under the weather and unusually tired, and crawling into the wagon told them if they wanted fuel for the evening meal they could get it themselves and cook the meal also, and laying my head down on a pillow, I cried myself to sleep." Later that evening her husband awakened her with a belated dinner he had prepared himself, but despite his conciliatory spirit their relations were strained for weeks: "James and I had gradually grown silent and taciturn and had unwittingly partaken of the gloom and somberness of the dreary landscape." No longer a housewife or a domestic ornament, but a laborer in a male arena, Porter was still subordinate to her husband in practical matters.

Lydia Waters recorded another clash between new work and old consciousness: "I had learned to drive an ox team on the Platte and my driving was admired by an officer and his wife who were going with the mail to Salt Lake City." Pleased with the compliment, she later overheard them "laughing at the thought of a woman driving oxen." By no means did censure come only from men. The officer's wife as well as the officer derided Lydia Waters, while her own mother indirectly reprimanded teen-aged Mary Ellen Todd. "All along our journey, I had tried to crack that big whip," Mary Ellen remembered years later:

> Now while out at the wagon we kept trying until I was fairly successful. How my heart bounded a few days later when I chanced to hear father say to mother, "Do you know that Mary Ellen is beginning to crack the whip." Then how it fell again when mother replied, "I am afraid it isn't a very lady-like thing for a girl to do." After this, while I felt a secret joy in being able to have a power that set things going, there was also a sense of shame over this new accomplishment.

To understand Mrs. Todd's primness, so incongruous in the rugged setting of the Trail, we must see it in the context of a broader struggle on the part of women to preserve the home in transit. Against the leveling forces of the Plains, women tried to maintain the standards of cleanliness and order that had prevailed in their homes back East:

> Our caravan had a good many women and children and although we were probably longer on the journey owing to their presence— they exerted a good influence, as the men did not take such risks with Indians . . . were more alert about the care of teams and seldom had accidents; more attention was paid to cleanliness and

sanitation and, lastly, but not of less importance, meals were
more regular and better cooked thus preventing much sickness
and·there was less waste of food.

Sarah Royce remembered that family wagons "were easily distinguished by the greater number of conveniences, and household articles
they carried." In the evenings, or when the trains stopped for a day,
women had a chance to create with these few props a flimsy facsimile
of the home.

Even in camp women had little leisure time, but within the "hurry
scurry" of work they managed to recreate the routine of the home. Indeed, a female subculture, central to the communities women had left
behind, reemerged in these settings. At night, women often clustered
together, chatting, working, or commiserating, instead of joining the
men: "High teas were not popular, but tatting, knitting, crochetting,
exchanging recipes for cooking beans or dried apples or swopping food
for the sake of variety kept us in practice of feminine occupations and
diversions." Besides using the domestic concerns of the Trail to reconstruct a female sphere, women also consciously invoked fantasy:
"Mrs. Fox and her daughter are with us and everything is so still and
quiet we can almost imagine ourselves at home again. We took out
our Daguerrotypes and tried to live over again some of the happy days
of 'Auld Lang Syne.' " Sisterly contact kept "feminine occupations"
from withering away from disuse: "In the evening the young ladies
came over to our house and we had a concert with both guitars. Indeed it seemed almost like a pleasant evening at home. We could none
of us realize that we were almost at the summit of the Rocky Mountains." The hostess added with somewhat strained sanguinity that her
young daughter seemed "just as happy sitting on the ground playing
her guitar as she was at home, although she does not love it as much
as her piano." Although a guitar was no substitute for the more refined instrument, it at least kept the girl "in practice with feminine
occupations and diversions": unlike Mary Ellen Todd, no big whip
would tempt her to unwomanly pleasure in the power to "set things
going."

But books, furniture, knick-knacks, china, the daguerrotypes that
Mrs. Fox shared, or the guitars of young musicians—the "various articles of ornament and convenience"—were among the first things discarded on the epic trash heap which trailed over the mountains. On

long uphill grades and over sandy deserts, the wagons had to be lightened; any materials not essential to survival were fair game for disposal. Such commodities of woman's sphere, although functionally useless, provided women with a psychological lifeline to their abandoned homes and communities, as well as to elements of their identities which the westward journey threatened to mutilate or entirely extinguish. Losing homely treasures and memorabilia was yet another defeat within an accelerating process of dispossession.

The male-directed venture likewise encroached upon the Sabbath, another female preserve. Through the influence of women's magazines, by mid-century Sunday had become a veritable ladies' day; women zealously exercised their religious influence and moral skill on the day of their families' retirement from the world. Although parties on the Trail often suspended travel on Sundays, the time only provided the opportunity to unload and dry the precious cargo of the wagons—seeds, food, and clothing—which otherwise would rot from dampness. For women whose creed forbade any worldly activity on the Sabbath, the work was not only irksome and tedious but profane.

> This is Sabath it is a beautiful day but indeed we do not use it as such for we have not traveled far when we stop in a most lovely place oh it is such a beautiful spot and take everything out of our wagon to air them and it is well we done it as the flower was damp and there was some of the other ones flower was rotten . . . and we baked and boiled and washed oh dear me I did not think we would have abused the sabeth in such a manner. I do not see how we can expect to get along but we did not intend to do so before we started.

Denied a voice in the male sphere that surrounded them, women were also unable to partake of the limited yet meaningful power of women with homes. On almost every Sunday, Helen Stewart lamented the disruption of a familiar and sustaining order of life, symbolized by the household goods strewn about the ground to dry: "We took everything out the wagons and the side of the hill is covered with flower biscut meat rice oat meal clothes and such a quantity of articles of all discertions to many to mention and childre[n] included in the number. And hobos that is neather men nor yet boys being in and out hang about."

The disintegration of the physical base of domesticity was symptomatic of an even more serious disruption in the female subculture. Because the wagon trains so often broke into smaller units, many women were stranded in parties without other women. Since there were usually two or more men in the same family party, some male friendships and bonds remained intact for the duration of the journey. But by midway in the trip, female companionship, so valued by nineteenth-century women, was unavailable to the solitary wife in a party of hired men, husband, and children that had broken away from a larger train. Emergencies and quarrels, usually between men, broke up the parties. Dr. Powers, a particularly ill-tempered man, decided after many disagreements with others in his train to make the crossing alone with his family. His wife shared neither his misanthropy nor his grim independence. On the day they separated from the others, she wrote in her journal: "The women came over to bid me goodbye, for we were to go alone, all alone. They said there was no color in my face. I felt as if there was none." She perceived the separation as a banishment, almost a death sentence: "There is something peculiar in such a parting on the Plains, one there realizes what a goodbye is. Miss Turner and Mrs. Hendricks were the last to leave, and they bade me adieu the tears running down their sunburnt cheeks. I felt as though my last friends were leaving me, for what—as I thought then—was a Maniac." Charlotte Pengra likewise left Missouri with her family in a large train. Several weeks out, mechanical problems detained some of the wagons, including those of the other three women. During the month they were separated, Pengra became increasingly dispirited and anxious: "The roads have been good today—I feel lonely and almost disheartened. . . . Can hear the wolves howl very distinctly. Rather ominis, perhaps you think. . . . Feel very tird and lonely—our folks not having come—I fear some of them ar sick." Having waited as long as possible for the others, the advance group made a major river crossing. "Then I felt that indeed I had left all my friends," Pengra wrote, "save my husband and his brother, to journey over the dreaded Plains, without one female acquaintance even for a companion—of course I wept and grieved about it but to no purpose."

Others echoed her mourning. "The whipporwills are chirping," Helen Stewart wrote, "they bring me in mind of our old farm in pensillvania the home of my childhood where I have spent the happiest days I will ever see again. . . . I feel rather lonesome today oh solitude how I love it if I had about a dozen of my companions to enjoy it with me." Uprootedness took its toll in debilitation and numbness. After a hard week, men "lolled around in the tents and on their blankets seeming to realize that the 'Sabbath was made for man,' " resting on the palpable achievements of miles covered and rivers crossed. In contrast, the women "could not fully appreciate physical rest, and were rendered more uneasy by the continual passing of emigrant trains all day long. . . . To me, much of the day was spent in meditating over the past and in forebodings for the future."

The ultimate expression of this alienation was the pressure to turn back, to retrace steps to the old life. Occasionally anxiety or bewilderment erupted into open revolt against going on.

> This morning our company moved on, except one family. The woman got mad and wouldn't budge or let the children go. He had the cattle hitched on for three hours and coaxed her to go, but she wouldn't stir. I told my husband the circumstances and he and Adam Polk and Mr. Kimball went and each one took a young one and crammed them in the wagon, and the husband drove off and left her sitting. . . . She cut across and overtook her husband. Meantime he sent his boy back to camp after a horse he had left, and when she came up her husband said, "Did you meet John?" "Yes," was the reply, "and I picked up a stone and knocked out his brains." Her husband went back to ascertain the truth and while he was gone she set fire to one of the wagons. . . . He saw the flames and came running and put it out, and then mustered spunk enough to give her a good flogging.

Short of violent resistance, it was always possible that circumstances would force a family to reconsider and turn back. During a cholera scare in 1852, "women cried, begging their men to take them back." When the men reluctantly relented, the writer observed that "they did the hooking up of their oxen in a spiritless sort of way," while "some of the girls and women were laughing." There was little lost and much regained for women in a decision to abandon the migration.

Both sexes worked, and both sexes suffered. Yet women lacked a sense of inclusion and a cultural rationale to give meaning to the suffering and the work; no augmented sense of self or role emerged from augmented privation. Both women and men also complained, but women expanded their caviling to a generalized critique of the whole enterprise. Margaret Chambers felt "as if we had left all civilization

behind us" after crossing the Missouri, and Harriet Ward's cry from
South Pass—"Oh, shall we ever live like civilized beings again?"—reverberated through the thoughts of many of her sisters. Civilization was
far more to these women than law, books, and municipal government;
it was pianos, church societies, daguerrotypes, mirrors—in short, their
homes. At their most hopeful, the exiles perceived the Trail as a hell-
ish but necessary transition to a land where they could renew their domestic mission: "Each advanced step of the slow, plodding cattle carried us farther and farther from civilization into a desolate, barbarous
country. . . . But our new home lay beyond all this and was a shining beacon that beckoned us on, inspiring our hearts with hope and
courage." At worst, temporary exigencies became in the minds of the
dispossessed the omens of an irrevocable exile: "We have been travelling with 25–18–14–129–64–3 wagons—now all alone—how dreary it
seems. Can it be that I have left my quiet little home and taken this
dreary land of solitude in exchange?"

Only a minority of the women who emigrated over the Overland Trail
were from the Northeastern middle classes where the cult of true
womanhood reached its fullest bloom. Yet their responses to the labor
demands of the Trail indicate that "womanliness" had penetrated the
values, expectations, and personalities of midwestern farm women as
well as New England "ladies." "Woman's sphere" provided them
with companionship, a sense of self-worth, and most important, independence from men in a patriarchal world. The Trail, in breaking
down sexual segregation, offered women the opportunities of socially
essential work. Yet this work was performed in a male arena, and
many women saw themselves as draftees rather than partners.

Historians have generally associated "positive work roles" for women
with the absence of narrowly defined notions of "woman's place." In
the best summary of literature on colonial women, for example, the
authors of *Women in American Society* write: "In general, neither
men nor women seemed concerned with defining what women were or
what their unique contribution to society should be. . . . Abstract
theories about the proper role of women did not stand in the way of
meeting familial and social needs." Conversely, the ascendancy of
"true womanhood" and the doctrine of sexual spheres coincided with
the declining importance of the labor of middle- and upper-class

women in a rapidly expanding market economy. On the Overland Trail, cultural roles and self-definitions conflicted with the immediate necessities of the socioeconomic situation. Women themselves fought to preserve a circumscribed role when material circumstances rendered it dysfunctional. Like their colonial great-grandmothers on pre-market subsistence farms, they labored at socially indispensable tasks. Yet they refused to appropriate their new work to their own ends and advantage. In their deepest sense of themselves they remained estranged from their function as "able bodies."

It could be argued that the time span of the trip was not long enough to alter cultural values. Yet there is evidence that the tensions of the Trail haunted the small and isolated market farms at the journey's end. Women in the Western settlements continued to try to reinstate a culture of domesticity, although their work as virtual hired hands rendered obsolete the material base of separate arenas for women and men.

The notion of subculture employed in this and other studies of nineteenth-century women is hazy and ill-defined. We need to develop more rigorous conceptions of society, culture, and subculture, and to clarify the paradoxes of women's position, both isolated and integrated, in the dominant social and cultural movements of their time. Nonetheless, the journals of overland women are irrefutable testimony to the importance of a separate female province. Such theorists as Catharine Beecher were acutely aware of the advantages in keeping life divvied up, in maintaining "two pathways which are always different" for women and men. The women who traveled on the Overland Trail experienced firsthand the tribulations of integration which Beecher and her colleagues could predict in theory.

18

Abraham Lincoln and the Idea of Equality

DAVID L. LIGHTNER

• The social and political upheavals that began with the Montgomery (Alabama) Bus Boycott in 1956 and subsided after the withdrawal of the United States from Vietnam and the resignation of President Richard Nixon in 1974 left few areas of American life untouched. One important conse- quence was a reappraisal of the nation's history from the per- spective of the black minority. Although the work never took the form of one unified school of thought, it effectively chal- lenged many of the assumptions in the standard texts.

The reappraisals reached such figures as Woodrow Wilson and Franklin D. Roosevelt, but even more importantly they touched Abraham Lincoln himself. No other American, liv- ing or dead, has ever won more universal respect or world- wide adulation than the man who epitomized the dream of "log cabin to White House," the man who in his words and actions seemed to represent all that was good and decent in the American character. As Don E. Fehrenbacher has noted, if the United States had a patron saint it would no doubt be the Illinois lawyer who could somehow mute the natural an- tagonism between strong leadership and vigorous democracy.

Yet the black power movement of the 1960s, which was understandably critical of patronizing, well-intentioned white liberals, noticed anew that even the Great Emancipator was a condescending savior. President Lincoln specifically affirmed that his desire was to save the Union, not to destroy slavery; and even when the famous Emancipation Proclamation was issued, it did not apply to the border states or to those sec- tions of the Confederacy that had already been overrun by federal troops. In other words, it did not immediately free even a single slave.

From *Journal of the Illinois State Historical Society* 74 (1982): 289–308.

Cooler heads have prevailed and have noted that to term Abraham Lincoln a "racist" is to take the man out of his time and place. In his own day, he was considered a radical on the race question, and his very election was sufficient to drive the Southern states to rebellion. David L. Lightner offers a reasoned analysis of the shifting view of Lincoln and points out that the Great Emancipator was indeed a firm believer in the egalitarian ideal.

In 1858 Abraham Lincoln stated publicly that he did not believe the Negro to be his equal, that he was not and never had been in favor of allowing Negroes to vote, and that he was not and never had been in favor of bringing about in any way the social and political equality of the white and black races. Although Lincoln opposed the spread of slavery into new territories, he denied any intention of interfering with the institution in those states where it already existed. After his election to the Presidency in 1860 precipitated Southern secession and civil war, Lincoln declared that he was leading a struggle only to preserve the Union and not to destroy slavery. Although he eventually proclaimed the emancipation of those slaves held within rebel territory, Lincoln justified that action solely as a matter of military necessity, and he coupled it with a call for colonization projects aimed at the ultimate removal of free black people from the United States.

When that historical record is viewed from a modern perspective, it is no wonder that Abraham Lincoln tends to be regarded with something less than reverence. No one denies that Lincoln disliked slavery, but some scholars do argue that his opposition was so moderate and so ineffectual that he hardly deserves his celebration in folklore as the Great Emancipator. And if Lincoln's record on slavery is found wanting, his position on the broader issue of racial equality seems hopeless. Lincoln, says Mark E. Neely, Jr., "did not make much of the Negro's abilities outside of slavery." "As is well known," writes Ludwell Johnson, "Lincoln was anything but an equalitarian." Don Fehrenbacher concludes that "in his attitude toward the wrongs of the free Negro, Lincoln had none of the moral conviction that inspired his opposition to slavery. He never seems to have suspected that systematic racial discrimination might be, like slavery, a stain on the national honor and a crime against mankind." Let us "admit once and for all," says Bruce Catton, "that Lincoln did not believe in racial equality." While Harold Hyman contends that at the close of his life Lincoln was edging toward a less benighted position on the race question, George Fredrickson disagrees, saying that "although no final answer can be given to the question of whether Lincoln changed his mind, the weight of evidence and logic seems to support the hypothesis that Lincoln died with the same basic views on black-white relations that he had held tenaciously throughout his public life."

Despite such evidence and scholarship, I am convinced that Abraham Lincoln was a far more enlightened individual than is commonly supposed and that he was genuinely devoted to the ideal of human equality—not only in the closing days of his life but throughout his years of prominence in American politics. I believe that if Lincoln's words and actions are understood within their specific historical context, it becomes evident that when Lincoln said or did things that were inconsistent with egalitarianism, he did so with the deliberate intent of misleading his countrymen with regard to his personal beliefs and ultimate aims. In our own day, it would make little sense for a politician aspiring to national leadership to conceal a personal commitment to equality. But Lincoln lived in a different age. In antebellum America, only the abolitionist minority dared to advocate racial equality. Had Abraham Lincoln joined those few voices crying out in the wilderness of pervasive racism, it is possible that he would have achieved notoriety as an outspoken idealist, but it is certain that he never would have been elected President of the United States. In order to combat slavery and to advance the cause of human equality, Lincoln was compelled to conceal from the electorate the full implications of his personal devotion to the egalitarian ideal. Yet of that devotion itself, he made no secret.

In the 1850s Lincoln repeatedly cited the Declaration of Independence as the touchstone of his political creed. For Lincoln, the principle that all men are created equal was indeed a self-evident truth. Although Lincoln liked to present himself as a devoted disciple of Henry Clay, it is clear that Lincoln's views on slavery found their inspiration in the unalloyed idealism of Thomas Jefferson, rather than in the pragmatic maneuverings of Henry Clay. In his eulogy following the death of the Great Compromiser in 1852, Lincoln pronounced Clay's day gone and past, thus indicating that he had no intention of binding himself to the doctrines of his fallen leader. Even as he eulogized Clay, Lincoln quoted Jefferson's prophetic words on the evil and the danger of slavery, and he lamented the growing tendency of politicians to ridicule the Declaration of Independence and its proclamation that all men are created free and equal. Two years later, in a series of speeches to Illinois audiences, Lincoln justified his opposition to the spread of slavery into the territories by citing the precedent of the Northwest Ordinance of 1787, which he credited to "Mr. Jefferson, the author of the Declaration of Independence[,] . . . who was, is, and perhaps will continue to be, the most distinguished politician of our history." In the debates with Stephen Douglas in 1858, Lincoln again and again reiterated his devotion to the Declaration and to the ideal of equality. Shortly before his inauguration as President in 1861, he declared that he had never had "a feeling politically that did not spring from the sentiments embodied in the Declaration of Independence." Finally, in the most memorable of all his speeches, the Gettysburg Address of November 19, 1863, Lincoln offered the ideals of liberty and equality as the moral basis for the Union cause; the American Revolution, he said, had given birth to a nation dedicated to the proposition that all men are created equal, and the Civil War was testing whether a nation so dedicated could endure.

Although Lincoln thus declared himself devoted to the egalitarian principle, he acknowledged that perfect equality was unattainable in an imperfect world. In an 1857 speech he explained that the framers of the Declaration had not meant to assert the "obvious untruth" that all men were actually enjoying equality; rather, "they meant simply to declare the *right*, so that the *enforcement* of it might follow as fast as circumstances should permit." Thus the Declaration stood not as a description of reality but rather as "a standard maxim for free society . . . constantly looked to, constantly labored for, and even though never perfectly attained, constantly approximated, and thereby constantly spreading and deepening its influence, and augmenting the happiness and value of life to all people of all colors everywhere." Making the same point a year later, Lincoln said, "The Savior, I suppose, did not expect that any human creature could be perfect as the Father in Heaven; but He said, 'As your Father in Heaven is perfect, be ye also

perfect.' . . . So I say in relation to the principle that all men are created equal, let it be as nearly reached as we can." Progress could be
made toward the fulfillment of the egalitarian ideal, but in a democracy the pace of that progress depended upon the growth of popular
enlightenment. During the debates with Douglas, Lincoln said, "public sentiment is everything. With public sentiment, nothing can fail;
without it nothing can succeed. Consequently he who moulds public
sentiment, goes deeper than he who enacts statutes or pronounces decisions. He makes statutes and decisions possible or impossible to be
executed."

Some scholars have questioned the depth of Lincoln's commitment
to the ideals that he espoused, noting how slowly and hesitantly he
moved toward the goal of emancipation. Yet Lincoln's caution is easily
understood, provided one takes into account his Jeffersonian respect
for public opinion and his tactical skill in the political arena. In his debates with Douglas, Lincoln portrayed himself as a moderate on the
slavery question, professing his willingness to allow slavery to endure
"for a hundred years, if it should live so long." No doubt he did not
intend any direct violation of the constitutional right of the slave
states to retain their peculiar institution. Lincoln did call for the repeal of the Dred Scott decision, however, and he firmly insisted that
slavery must not be permitted to expand into new territory. He drew
an analogy between the presence of slavery in the United States and
the presence of cancer in human tissue: "You may have a wen or cancer upon your person and not be able to cut it out lest you bleed to
death; but surely it is no way to cure it, to engraft it and spread it over
your whole body." Lincoln argued that the containment of slavery
would undermine the economic viability of the institution: "The plainest print cannot be read through a gold eagle; and it will be ever hard
to find many men who will send a slave to Liberia, and pay his passage [,] while they can send him to a new country . . . and sell him
for fifteen hundred dollars, and the rise."

Had the secession crisis not followed hard upon the heels of Lincoln's election to the Presidency, it is possible that he would have
taken at least one additional step to undermine the viability of slavery.
Those historians who do not believe that Lincoln's election posed any
real menace to slaveholders might ponder an incident in the debates of
1858. When Douglas asked Lincoln whether he would favor the aboli-

tion of the interstate slave trade, Lincoln refused to commit himself. He claimed that he had not given the issue the "mature consideration" that would enable him to decide whether Congress had the power to take such action. But if Congress did have the power, he said, then he would oppose using it, "unless upon some conservative principle" comparable to the compensated emancipation that he had long advocated for the District of Columbia. Lincoln's evasiveness here is noteworthy. Although the actual use of the interstate commerce power as a weapon against social evil is a twentieth-century phenomenon, the idea existed in antislavery circles in Lincoln's day. Clearly both Douglas and Lincoln were familiar with the concept. Indeed, in a later debate Lincoln confronted Douglas with the example of an antislavery Democrat who in 1850 had taken the position that "so long as the slave States continue to treat slaves as articles of commerce, the Constitution confers power on Congress to pass laws regulating that peculiar *commerce*, and that the protection of Human Rights imperatively demands the interposition of every constitutional means to prevent this most inhuman and iniquitous traffic."

Douglas posed his question on the slave trade a week before Lincoln answered it, and thus the latter should have had time to make up his mind, if he had not done so already. Throughout his political career, Lincoln had taken a broad view of congressional powers under the Constitution, defending the legitimacy of a national bank and of federal aid for internal improvements. On the latter issue, Lincoln had based his constitutional argument squarely upon a broad construction of the interstate commerce clause.

In the midst of the secession crisis, Lincoln did indicate his willingness to compromise on the slave trade question, but we can only speculate as to the course that he would have followed had his mere election not provoked the secession of the Southern states. But clearly those Southerners who chose the drastic course of sundering the Union were expecting the worst from Abraham Lincoln, and historians should not be too quick to assume that they were wrong.

The outbreak of civil war afforded President Lincoln the opportunity of moving against slavery by a means that could not be contemplated in time of peace: the war powers of the Presidency. In order to hold the border states within the Union and to win the widest possible public support for the Northern cause, Lincoln at first insisted that his only aim was to preserve the nation and not to do battle against slavery. Yet even as he publicly assured Horace Greeley that his "paramount object" was to save the Union and not either to save or to destroy slavery, Lincoln had in fact already determined upon the latter course, had already drafted the Emancipation Proclamation. In that Proclamation, Lincoln justified the freeing of slaves solely as a military necessity. Some historians have taken him at his word, but to do so is naive. The argument of military necessity was calculated to appeal to those white citizens who continued to spurn the moral arguments against slavery but who could, however reluctantly, accept emancipation as a weapon against treason. Also, describing emancipation as a military necessity provided the only possible constitutional sanction for a presidential initiative that would have been unthinkable under normal circumstances. The Emancipation Proclamation, applying as it did only to areas held by the enemy, did not immediately free a single slave. But it did mean that the Civil War was now a war against human bondage as well as against Southern secession and that a Union victory would mean the annihilation of the slave power.

Lincoln's struggle to win popular acceptance of the Emancipation Proclamation explains his public preoccupation in 1862 with colonization experiments. Since the days of Jefferson, the dream of removing free Negroes from the United States had served as a convenient "out" for those persons who detested the idea of slavery but who could not accept the necessary alternative of envisioning a biracial, egalitarian society. Lincoln's support for colonization has sometimes been seen as evidence of racial prejudice, but it seems more likely that it was the overwhelming racism of his white countrymen rather than his own feelings that prompted him to hail colonization as the solution to the American dilemma. In the 1850s there had always been an unreal quality to Lincoln's remarks about colonization, for he virtually acknowledged the impossibility of removing the entire black population yet continued to speak of his "high hope" that somehow that objective could be achieved "in the long run." In 1862 President Lincoln instigated a flurry of colonization experiments, but these efforts were so minuscule that it is difficult to escape the conclusion that they were staged primarily for their psychological effect upon the white citizenry. When Lincoln met with a black delegation in August, 1862, he said that free blacks who saw no merit in colonization were being selfish, for they ought to realize that merely making a start to colonization would "open a wide door for many to be made free," and that the departure of one hundred, or fifty, or even twenty-five blacks would be sufficient for a successful beginning. In order to win white acceptance of emancipation, Lincoln thus conjured up the illusion that Negro removal was underway. Once colonization had served that purpose, Lincoln's interest in the subject evaporated. After issuing the Emancipation Proclamation, he never again made a public appeal for colonization.

If the political context of his actions is taken into account, Lincoln's record with regard to slavery and colonization is easy to reconcile with his egalitarian principles. Lincoln's words and actions with respect to the status of the free Negro in American society are a more complex matter, however. While in speech after speech he denounced slavery as an unmitigated evil, he never acknowledged that the denial of civil equality to free black people constituted a similar, if less horrendous, contradiction of the egalitarian ideal. But we must not be too quick to assume that in his private thoughts Lincoln was as blind to this lesser evil as he appeared to be in his public pronouncements. There was, after all, nothing to be gained politically, and perhaps a great deal to be lost, from advocating racial equality at a time when the great mass of white Americans recoiled at such a prospect and when the greater demon of slavery had yet to be exorcised.

Defenders of the peculiar institution always tried to maximize support for their cause by equating opposition to slavery with advocacy of racial equality. In championing his idea of popular sovereignty, Douglas in 1858 used this same tactic against Lincoln. Douglas openly appealed to the racial prejudice of white Illinoisans and tried as hard as he could to convince the voters that Lincoln believed in racial equality. "If you, Black Republicans, think that the negro ought to be on a social equality with your wives and daughters, and ride in a carriage with your wife, whilst you drive the team, you have perfect right to do so," cried Douglas. "Those of you who believe that the negro is your equal and ought to be on an equality with you socially, politically, and legally, have a right to entertain those opinions, and of course will vote for Mr. Lincoln."

If it is recognized that during the 1858 senatorial campaign Abraham Lincoln was battling for his political life within the social climate of antebellum Illinois and against that kind of rhetoric from his opponent, what seems remarkable is not that Lincoln made some racist-sounding statements of his own, but rather that in doing so he used language so equivocal as to imply a deliberate effort to deceive his audience. Lincoln never said that he believed black people to be of an inherently inferior race. The closest he came to making such a pronouncement was in the debate at Ottawa when he said, "I agree with Judge Douglas [that] he [the Negro] is not my equal in many respects—certainly not in color, perhaps not in moral or intellectual endowment." That sounds like a racist statement, but is it? By inserting the word "perhaps," Lincoln removed all force from his reference to black inferiority in morals and intellect. He did state for certain that the Negro was not his equal in color, but that affirmation conveys no clear meaning other than the truism that black people are not white. That Lincoln was trying to mislead his audience as to his true beliefs seems likely if we compare the equivocal comments that he made during the debates with a forthright statement that he had uttered only weeks before his bouts with Douglas got underway. "Let us discard all this quibbling about this man and the other man—this race and that race and the other race being inferior," Lincoln had said at Chicago in July. "Let us discard all these things, and unite as one people throughout this land, until we shall once more stand up declaring that all men are created equal."

While Lincoln succeeded in muddling his position on the subject of inherent racial inferiority, he could not similarly finesse the practical question of whether civil rights should be afforded to free blacks. As early as 1854, in a speech at Peoria, Lincoln had confessed his uncertainty as to that question. Since immediate colonization was impracticable, and since keeping free blacks as underlings would not necessarily have been an improvement over slavery, Lincoln rejected those possibilities. "What next?" he said.

> Free them, and make them politically and socially, our equals? My own feelings will not admit of this; and if mine would, we well know that those of the great mass of white people will not. Whether this feeling accords with justice and sound judgment, is not the sole question, if indeed, it is any part of it. A universal feeling, whether well or ill-founded, can not be safely disregarded. We can not, then, make them equals.

Here Lincoln claimed that his own feelings would not allow equal rights for Negroes. Yet the words that follow make it clear that for Lincoln the real barrier to equality was not his own feelings but rather those of his white countrymen. Just as significant, Lincoln had as much as said that the denial of equality to black people was based solely on white prejudice and that it accorded with neither justice nor good judgment.

Later in his Peoria speech, Lincoln justified his opposition to allowing the expansion of slavery into new territory by attacking bondage as a violation of the Declaration of Independence statement that all governments derive their just powers from the consent of the governed. Douglas had insisted that popular sovereignty was a logical exercise of the right of self-government. Lincoln replied:

> The relation of masters and slaves is, *pro tanto,* a total violation of this principle. The master not only governs the slave without his consent, but he governs him by a set of rules altogether different from those which he prescribes for himself. Allow *all* the governed an equal voice in the government, and that, and that only is self-government.
>
> Let it not be said that I am contending for the establishment of political and social equality between the whites and blacks. I have already said the contrary. I am not now combating the argument of *necessity*, arising from the fact that the blacks are already amongst us.

In that curious passage, Lincoln's use of the word "government" was ambiguous, for he transferred it from a political to a social context, but in maintaining that the unequal relationship of master and slave violated the right of self-government, Lincoln strongly implied that the Declaration of Independence also required that all people, including blacks, possess full political equality. In refusing to endorse such equality, despite the weight of his own logic, Lincoln conceded again that only expediency, not principle, could underlie the denial of equal rights to the Negro.

For a person who had claimed that his own feelings would not permit equality for blacks, Lincoln reacted to the Dred Scott decision of 1857 in a manner that is in one respect peculiar. In a speech at Springfield in June, 1857, Lincoln noted that Chief Justice Roger B. Taney had erred in asserting that Negroes were "no part of the people who made, or for whom was made, the Declaration of Independence, or the Constitution of the United States," for, in a dissenting opinion, Justice Benjamin R. Curtis had pointed out that in five of the original thirteen states free Negroes had voted and had a role in the making of the Constitution. Since that time, Lincoln said, the condition of the free Negro had deteriorated: "In two of the five States—New Jersey and North Carolina—that then gave the free negro the right of voting, the right has since been taken away." Lincoln went on to enumerate other respects in which the condition of the Negro had worsened since the days of the Founding Fathers, and then he concluded: "In those days, our Declaration of Independence was held sacred by all, and thought to include all; but now, to aid in making the bondage of the negro universal and eternal, it is assailed, and sneered at, and construed, and hawked at, and torn, till, if its framers could rise from their graves, they could not at all recognize it."

A year later, in another address at Springfield, the famous "House Divided" speech of June 16, 1858, Lincoln again commented on the Scott case, noting among other things that Taney had declared that a Negro could not be a citizen of the United States. "This point," Lincoln said, "is made in order to deprive the negro, in every possible event, of the benefit of that provision of the United States Constitution, which declares that 'The citizens of each State shall be entitled to all privileges and immunities of citizens in the several States.' " When Douglas later pounced upon this statement as evidence that Lincoln endorsed Negro citizenship, Lincoln replied that he had merely repeated what the Supreme Court had said "without making any complaint of it at all." Lincoln's rejoinder was effective, for certainly Douglas had misrepresented Lincoln when he asserted that the latter actually had endorsed Negro citizenship. Yet doubt lingers as to just why Lincoln had chosen to talk about the deteriorated civil status of the free Negro and about Taney's bar to Negro citizenship if he was in fact truly opposed to any future improvement in the status of free blacks. Even as Lincoln denied Douglas's charge and scoffed at this "beautiful fabrication—of my purpose to introduce a perfect, social, and political equality between the white and black races," he also, in the same speech, defended the abstract principle of human equality and protested its opponents' tendency "to dehumanize the negro—to take away from him the right of ever striving to be a man."

In his first three debates with Douglas in 1858, Lincoln merely quoted his own remarks of 1854 and declined to be more specific about his position on the cvill status of free blacks. In the third debate, held at Jonesboro on September 15, however, Lincoln did quote the opinion of a newspaper editor who thought that "it would be best for all concerned to have the colored population in a State by themselves" and interjected the comment that he agreed with the editor on that point. While Lincoln did not specifically say that he agreed with the editor's further opinion that such a state should be properly represented in Congress, it is difficult to see how that consequence could have been avoided had a separate black state been created. Therefore, whether he realized it or not, Lincoln's remark implied that he was open to the idea of blacks voting and holding political office.

It was only after relentless hounding by Douglas and after having been strongly advised to take a clearer stand that Lincoln suddenly announced his adherence to a hard-line position against equal rights for blacks. In the fourth debate, held at Charleston on September 18, Lincoln said:

> I am not nor ever have been in favor of making voters or jurors of negroes, nor of qualifying them to hold office, nor to intermarry with white people; and I will say in addition to this that there is a physical difference between the white and black races which I believe will forever forbid the two races living together on terms of social and political equality. And inasmuch as they cannot so live, while they do remain together there must be the position of superior and inferior, and I as much as any other man am in favor of having the superior position assigned to the white race.

There was no ambiguity in this pronouncement, as even Douglas conceded. "I am glad that I have at last succeeded in getting an answer out of him upon this question of negro citizenship and eligibility to office," said Douglas, "for I have been trying to bring him to the point on it ever since this canvass commenced." But if Lincoln's words were clear, it is equally apparent that political necessity had here compelled him to adopt a position that is impossible to reconcile both with his earlier comments on the subject and with the egalitarian ideal that he continued to extol.

Lincoln's 1858 disavowal of any desire to allow black people to vote contrasts markedly with statements that he made years later, in the closing months of the Civil War. In March, 1864, Lincoln intimated to Michael Hahn, the newly elected loyalist governor of Louisiana, that the upcoming constitutional convention in that state should consider admitting some Negroes to the franchise: "I barely suggest for your private consideration, whether some of the colored people may not be let in—as, for instance, the very intelligent, and especially those who have fought gallantly in our ranks." Although Louisiana did adopt a constitution that empowered the state legislature to enfranchise Negroes, the lawmakers of the state kept the polls closed to blacks, and Lincoln did not press the issue.

A year passed before Lincoln again took up the question of Negro suffrage, but then for the first time he announced publicly rather than privately that he favored voting rights for blacks. On April 11, 1865, a crowd gathered in front of the White House in celebration of the news of Lee's surrender at Appomattox. Lincoln addressed the throng, noting that the nation now faced the difficult task of reconstruction. Lincoln said that he would prefer that Louisiana give the vote to the "very intelligent" Negroes and also to those who had served the Union as soldiers. But despite Louisiana's failings, Lincoln said:

> The colored man too, in seeing all united for him, is inspired with vigilance, and energy, and daring, to the same end. Grant that he desires the elective franchise, will he not attain it sooner by saving the already advanced steps toward it, than by running backward over them? Concede that the new government of Louisiana is only to what it should be as the egg is to the fowl, we shall sooner have the fowl by hatching the egg than by smashing it?

Lincoln added that what he said about Louisiana would apply generally to other Southern states and that it might soon become his duty to make some new announcement to the people of the South. "I am considering," he said, "and shall not fail to act, when satisfied that action will be proper." Four days later, at the hands of an assassin, Abraham Lincoln was dead.

What are we to make of Lincoln's muted call for Negro suffrage? Not all historians are convinced that much significance can be attached to this final episode. George Fredrickson argues that in calling for voting by the very intelligent Negroes, Lincoln may have been thinking only of those freeborn, educated mulattoes who were unique to Louisiana, and therefore his words would not have applied to other Southern states. And, according to Fredrickson, giving the vote to black veterans may have been aimed at pacifying that potentially dangerous element in society, making the veterans "contented and willing to forgo strenuous agitation on behalf of their voteless brothers." But that interpretation of Lincoln's motivation is implausible. Surely admitting any blacks to the franchise would have set a momentous precedent for the South and would have tended to increase rather than decrease black agitation for full equality. Other historians see Lincoln's final actions as evidence of his educability. Originally a convinced opponent of equal rights for the Negro, Lincoln had gradually outgrown his prejudices—so those historians have it—until, on the eve of his death, he had at last glimpsed, however dimly, the vision of a biracial, egalitarian America. That second interpretation is entirely reasonable only if it is assumed that Lincoln's earlier stand against equal rights had accurately reflected his heartfelt beliefs. But we have seen that such an assumption is not warranted.

If we reject both the argument that Lincoln's actions were not significant and also the view that Lincoln was a prejudiced man who was slowly becoming educated, the way is opened to a wholly different explanation for his conduct. In 1864 and 1865 Abraham Lincoln called for limited Negro suffrage not because his own convictions had changed but rather because public sentiment had changed. As the Civil War drew to a close, most white Americans, even in the South, were becoming reconciled to the impending doom of slavery. Therefore, the time had come for Lincoln to prepare public opinion for one more step toward the distant goal of equality.

By this point some of Lincoln's severest critics had come to see the wisdom of his cautious approach. Early in 1864 Frederick Douglass gave the following account of a meeting with Lincoln:

> He told me . . . that I had made a little speech somewhere in New York, and it had got into the papers, and among the things I had said was this: That if I were called upon to state what I

regarded as the most sad and most disheartening feature in our present political and military situation . . . it would be the tardy, hesitating and vacillating policy of the President of the United States; and the President said to me, "Mr. Douglass, I have been charged with being tardy, and the like"; and he went on, and partly admitted that he might seem slow; but he said, "I am charged with vacillating; but, Mr. Douglass, I do not think that charge can be sustained; I think it cannot be shown that when I have once taken a position, I have ever retreated from it." . . . That I regarded as the most significant point in what he said during our interview. I told him that he had been somewhat slow in proclaiming equal protection to our colored soldiers and prisoners; and he said that the country needed talking up to that point. . . . He knew that the colored man throughout this country was a despised man, a hated man, and he knew that if he at first came out with such a proclamation, all the hatred which is poured on the head of the negro race would be visited on his Administration. He said that there was preparatory work needed, and that that preparatory work had been done. . . . I thought it was reasonable."

William Lloyd Garrison was another convert. Garrison had been highly critical of the Lincoln administration, characterizing the President as "a dwarf in mind" and "a wet rag" and complaining that Lincoln had "not a drop of anti-slavery blood in his veins." But after meeting with the President on June 10, 1864, Garrison reported that he no longer doubted "Mr. Lincoln's desire to do all that he can see it right and possible for him to do to uproot slavery, and give fair play to the emancipated." One month later Garrison wrote: "Mr. Lincoln has seemed exceedingly slow in all his emancipatory measures. . . . Yet what long strides he has taken in the right direction, and never a backward step!"

We can never know how fast or how far Lincoln would have moved had he lived to guide the nation into the postwar era. He would have tempered his pace according to the progress of public enlightenment, and no doubt that progress would have been slow and halting at best. Yet, considering that the attempt of the Radical Reconstructionists to revolutionize the social and political structure of the South eventually failed, it is arguable that in the long run the cautious approach of Abraham Lincoln would have produced more rather than less permanent progress toward the egalitarian ideal. Had black suffrage come about only slowly and gradually, in a reconstruction program genuinely motivated by malice toward none and charity for all, then perhaps the opposition of white Southerners to black enfranchisement would have subsided, equally slowly and gradually, instead of boiling into violent resistance to the so-called "Negro rule" of the prostrate South. It seems more likely, however, that any reform policy, no matter how gradual, would have met with implacable resistance from white Southerners. How Lincoln would have reacted to Southern intransigence is impossible to guess. For all its failure, Radical Reconstruction did produce the Fourteenth and Fifteenth Amendments, and it is not certain that a Lincolnian policy would have left that important legacy, which has been so vital to the civil rights movement of our own times.

Living as we do in a different age, it is understandable that we should be disappointed to learn that Abraham Lincoln compromised so much with the evils of slavery and racism. We should realize, however, that in the complex process of historical change, there are legitimate roles to be played both by prophets, who adhere to their principles with absolute purity, and by politicians, who accept the constraints of their historical environment and press only for what is attainable at a given time. We need to dispel the myth of "Honest Abe," for Lincoln was more devious and manipulative than is commonly acknowledged. But we need only to qualify rather than reject the old heroic view of Lincoln as the Great Emancipator and harbinger of a racially egalitarian society. Lincoln did free the slaves, and he was guided by egalitarian idealism. Political circumstances sometimes compelled Lincoln to say things that were inconsistent with his commitment to the egalitarian ideal, but in his actions he displayed an overall consistency of purpose. However slow and cautious his pace, Lincoln never lost his direction and he never looked back. What explains this consistency if not an underlying commitment to a chosen goal? The Founding Fathers, Lincoln once said, had not by the stroke of a pen made all men equal. But they had set up "a standard maxim . . . constantly looked to, constantly labored for, . . . and thereby constantly spreading and deepening its influence and augmenting the happiness and value of life to all people, of all colors, every where."

19

Jefferson Davis—Leader Without Legend

FRANK E. VANDIVER

• Jefferson Davis was the only President the Confederacy ever had. In April 1865, when General Robert E. Lee informed him that Richmond could no longer be held, Davis fled southward with his cabinet in hopes of reaching Texas and continuing the fight west of the Mississippi River. While disguised as a woman, he was captured by the Union Army, placed in irons, and imprisoned for two years in Fort Monroe. The former chief executive was indicted for high treason against the United States but never actually brought to trial. Almost alone among Southern leaders he never asked for amnesty and was never restored to American citizenship. (Congress finally restored him to citizenship in the 1970s.) An unreconstructed Confederate who never gave up his belief in the Lost Cause, Davis died in New Orleans in 1889 as a man without a country.

Historians have been deeply divided about Davis's effectiveness as Confederate President. Everyone agrees that the tall, slender, and handsome West Point graduate was strong-willed and articulate. Some add that he was nation-minded and world-minded, a natural leader of integrity, virtue, and high principle who was misunderstood because of the prejudice of Northerners and because of the need of Southerners to find a scapegoat. Others argue that his reputation as a bungler and incompetent is well-deserved and that his constant interference in military matters undermined his generals and seriously compromised the effectiveness of his armies. Frank Vandiver, a noted military analyst who has written of many Civil War campaigns, traces the popular and

Frank E. Vandiver, "Jefferson Davis—Leader Without Legend," *Journal of Southern History*, XLIII (1977), 3–18. Copyright 1977 by the Southern Historical Association. Reprinted by permission of the Managing Editor. Footnotes have been omitted.

professional assessments of Davis and concludes with a generally favorable estimate of the tragic figure who has been
called "the most misunderstood man in history."

No saintly aura buffers Jefferson Davis from the barbs of judgment.
Precious little that he did as President of the Confederate States of
America is sanctified. So he stands from the past as the most curious
of chieftains—a man without legend in the *Oxford English Dictionary*
sense of legend as the life of a saint. He is not, to be sure, a man
without account. More cold dissection, carping, rebuke, harsh study,
critical interpretation, has been aimed at him than at perhaps any
other leader of the modern era. He is worn by analysis beyond reality.
Minute scrutiny has denied legend and has wrought a Davis of myth
and mystery. Something of his mythic future might have been
glimpsed forming during the war, especially in the first of the "histories" of the Confederacy.

Edward Alfred Pollard, curmudgeon extraordinary, Richmonder,
editor of the *Examiner*, early rejected hope for Davis and prophesied
doom for a cause trusted to him. Dislike and suspicion poisoned Pollard's eye and cost some of the impact of his occasionally valid criticism. But things he saw wrong with the President had the power of
popularity and the ring of repetition. Davis clearly aimed at des-
potism; his judgment erred everywhere; as a diplomat he lacked
suavity; as an administrator, reality; as a war leader, sense; as a man,
charity. Pollard's convictions grew as the war progressed, and he
advanced them beyond his newspaper. In 1862 his *First Year of the
War* appeared, followed by annual volumes, each more anti-Davis than
the last. In 1866 Pollard culled his multivolume diatribe into one,
The Lost Cause. Now the world could read of a cause elevated by the
sacrifices of southern women, by the heroism of all gray-clad soldiers
and lost by the perfidy of Jefferson Davis.

Pollard carried his indictment further in 1869 with his *Life of
Jefferson Davis, with a Secret History of the Southern Confederacy,
Gathered "Behind the Scenes in Richmond,"* Jefferson Davis should
have a truthful and acute biographer," Pollard allows in his preface,
and then boasts of his impartiality. Once accused of "hostility" to

Davis, he now "is able and willing to do exact justice" to his subject. In addressing the main question of *"Who were responsible for the failure of the Southern Confederacy?"* Pollard argues that "Responsibility must rest somewhere in hsitory" and sees it rising naturally to higher officials. Consequently, "in regarding Mr. Davis as the prime cause of the failure of the South in the late war, the author has but simply recognized and submitted to the great law of logic in historical composition:—that, in political affairs, where a certain result is clearly not an accident or misadventure, but must have come from a well defined cause, that cause ultimately and inevitably rests in the head of the government." Never had logic been so convenient. Davis led the Confederacy and lost; ergo, he engineered defeat. The interpretation stuck.

Later students who approached Davis favorably were finally engulfed by Pollard's lingering prejudice. Elisabeth Brown Cutting's *Jefferson Davis, Political Soldier* is an example. Cutting writes almost sentimentally about much of Davis's life, maintains a casual detachment amid some of the thornier Confederate problems, waxes almost maudlin at the end of her story. Davis's courage, his willed triumph over pain, his constancy under stress all find echo in her pages. And yet, at the end, there is an eight-page "Epilogue" which rejects sympathy and calls up once more all the faults and flaws, the lapses and misdeeds, in the manner of Pollard redivivus. "Loyalty" and "devotion" were allowed Davis. "Affairs of state were his occupation," Cutting asserts, "but only in a restricted sense was he a statesman."

> He was not a great executive. He could not delegate power, but he could heed the representations of the man who best understood that his vanity must be fed. . . . Davis was neither resourceful nor foresighted in his capacity of Commander-in-Chief of his army. He was unequal to dealing in large figures for the magnitude of the task demanded. . . . He had always the recourse of the egoist, an immovable faith in his own decisions. . . . His vanity admitted of no rebuke, and he recognized a mental equal only when their ideas coincided. . . . He was a leader of a cause but not of men.

Cutting suffered divided sentiments throughout her book. Good things somehow had to be balanced against "objective" things lest Davis loom beyond the dim confines of his reality. Her struggle and her perception show some growth beyond Pollard's simple venom. Yet her try for scholarly impartiality worked its own distortion. The illusion of new fairness gave added credence to old criticisms. The chilly near-statesman made reckless by ambition and aloof by hauteur stood revealed now by records, a creature made real by research.

As any scholar could have guessed, research revealed a fuller man than Pollard's shabby mannequin. Details of Davis's life fleshed him for history and offered glimpses of a nimble mind and a curiously difficult personality. Davis's character obviously had vast impact on the Confederacy, but his soul lacked some evoking spark—he was an incomplete man, flawed beyond success. That discovery was to prove crucial in carving Davis's special niche in history.

Cutting's work had added importance since it was based not only on new research in foreign archives, but also on three earlier books— William E. Dodd's near classic *Jefferson Davis*, Hamilton J. Eckenrode's strange Nordic polemic, *Jefferson Davis, President of the South*, and Allen Tate's *Jefferson Davis: His Rise and Fall*. Dodd's still rings truer than most studies of Davis in its unadorned try for the truth. Dodd ground no axes, simply tried to see the man lurking in the dusty myths of losing. In that quest he came close to giving Davis a history. Both Eckenrode and Tate use Davis for their own purposes. Eckenrode sees Davis as the leader of a failed racial crusade and hence as bearing guilt far beyond his time. All the old charges are leveled and an old conclusion reached: "Jefferson Davis was a great man, even if he was not great enough to triumph." Tate, too, sees the end of the Confederacy as the end of the original America; out of the cauldron of Civil War came a new alignment of Union, one different in tone and temperament, in soul and substance from the hope of the Founding Fathers. Tate assigns Davis less perfidy in engineering the loss of American innocence. He glosses his criticism—which reads familiarly —in kindness. Yet it was Davis who lost a world he lacked the vision to grasp. Pollard's old stamp prevailed; Cutting followed in a well-cut scholarly wake.

Robert McElroy, in his two-volume *Jefferson Davis: The Unreal and the Real*, labeled the role historians were giving Davis—"The Scapegoat." McElroy's impressive sifting of Dunbar Rowland's ten-volume collection of Davis letters, papers, and documents seemed to confirm an awful sterility of achievement. In an episodic, oddly discur-

sive book McElroy gives Davis a new patriotism—that of defender of an
older Union. Davis's views of America, of the right of secession, were
of lasting value in McElroy's eyes; the defeat of the South damaged
the ideas not a whit. The war McElroy treats almost as an anticlimax.
He believes that the scapegoat's mantle was thrown over Davis by a
frustrated Southland unable to accept reality. This perception, doubtless, is partly sound, but McElroy misses an important point of his
own work: he, too, makes Davis a scapegoat, makes him the stout
champion of dying ideals dear to McElroy. Davis's postwar life
stretched in dusty tedium as he guarded the ghosts of the past.

What makes Davis so ready a scapegoat? What makes him so
malleable a subject for historical role-givers? The fact that his cause
was lost? Possibly. But the most likely reason is his utter lack of
legend. Lincoln suffers from "picklock biographers" more fearsomely
by far than Davis, yet his legend only increases his identity. Davis
has lost his identity—he is virtually a historical nonperson. So he easily
fits any role historians may devise for him.

Pollard and most of his successors have allowed Davis scarcely even
a loser's mite. They dissect the dry bones of his Confederate administration, the symmetry of his prewar years, to find out how he lost
the war, the South, Camelot, the future—whatever they happen to
lament. They have, of course, made him more than a scapegoat—he
is a kind of southern Barabbas. Sharp analysis of his poor humanity
simplifies history. Davis's contemporaries, represented by Pollard,
needed to fix blame on the President lest they confront their own
failures.

Historical fads change. In the cascades of good, bad, and indifferent
studies emerging during the Civil war Centennial, a new Jefferson
Davis made a shadowy appearance. Simplistic symbolism, simplistic
causation, eroded under the impact of the consensus school of historical studies. Davis as a single cause of defeat no longer seemed
reasonable. He might well have contributed to the South's losing, but
he was surely just one of multiple causes. This view gained some head-
way in the works of Allan Nevins and David M. Potter. Some historians still recall the old Davis—Bell I. Wiley and Clifford Dowdey
come to mind—but Shelby Foote's monumental *Civil War* pretty well
sets the new Davis mold. In this mold he ceases to be a surrogate of
failings and begins to stand for himself. Thomas B. Alexander and

Richard E. Beringer's important *Anatomy of the Confederate Congress* tends to confirm the new image of Davis.

Fortunately, the emerging Davis appears to escape mawkishness. The idolatry of early Civil War days, when he was heroically distorted in schoolbooks for little Rebels, the cloying regret of a thousand funeral orations, the venom of Pollard, all are fading in a new awareness of complex causes of behavior. There is, to be sure, the ne'er-do-wrong view of Hudson Strode, but his work has become almost a benchmark of excess. The new Davis is a flawed man, too finely haughty for charisma, who holds his opinions too well for fair argument, and who stands too lofty for affection. But he comes now as a real leader, even a strong President. David Herbert Donald, in the most recent edition of his and James Garfield Randall's admirable *Civil War and Reconstruction*, gives the new Davis full play and concludes that "much of the criticism of the Confederate President fails to take into account the insuperable difficulties of his position and to realize that no other Southern political leader even approached Davis in stature."

A conviction that Davis somehow failed of fair treatment at history's hands led the late Allan Nevins to support a proposal to collect and publish the papers of the Confederate President anew. True, Dunbar Rowland had published ten volumes of papers in the 1920s, but a careful check of his pages against originals in the Huntington Library convinced Nevins that deliberate distortion marked the earlier collection; and he believed also that much new material must have been discovered since Rowland's work. He was right. The Jefferson Davis Association, a nonprofit organization chartered in Texas, started collecting in 1964, has developed sources of collections beyond Rowland's, and has issued two volumes of what may well be an endless series. This new Davis scholarship, focused as it is on sources, is beginning to take Davis on his own terms and reinforces the recent imagery. The man he thought he was is sometimes the man of his critics, but not often; nor is he often the man of his admirers. He shows early some irritating qualities that would have pleased Pollard. A whiff of legalism tinges his West Point career, but his vaunted prissiness is softened by troubles at Benny Haven's tavern. Legalism tinges his early army service, legalism infected by a love of regulations—Davis may even have liked filling out forms! His early Mississippi political career shows growing interest in issues, a flair for public speaking, and a tendency toward rigid conviction. Honesty and a fair mind are hallmarks from the start.

From the early evidence, what are likely to be the full lineaments of this newer Davis? Documents already on hand tend to confirm his punctilio, his statesman's dismissal of petty politicking, his finely tuned sense of constitutionalism, his complex nature. These documents, from far-scattered hoards, dimly show a Davis different from any yet revealed. This emerging Davis may force a legend of his own. Its full outline cannot be predicted, but some elements may be guessed from established evidence.

Old flaws will be granted. Davis will stand aloof, restive, above the haggling of part-time patriots, yet "sensitive" to critics who failed to see devotion in every act and screed. Misplaced friendship he will still hold beyond the public good, and his brittlely legalistic arguments will continue to alienate men of goodwill and many future historians.

Much of the new Davis will have to come from shadings, from analyses of things he did that were untypical, either of himself or of his fellow southrons. Throughout the years of his presidential service he ranked as a "doer." Business came first with him; hours were spent in his office in the Confederate White Houses, in the executive offices, reading the whelm of correspondence, reports, summaries, orders, which daily cascaded across his desks. The Confederate President found, as did Lincoln, that Americans had little hesitation in bombarding their leader with wartime's every problem. Davis probably spent too much time wrestling with trivia better handled by a cabinet member or by some other functionary. Awkwardness in delegation made up a good deal of Davis's business. But much that came to him did require presidential notice. Military and legal matters claimed most of his attention. A Pollard might suggest that Davis's fetish with details led him to sign commissions even for second lieutenants, but the charge ignores duty.

Business of the President came often from constitutional obligation. Matters of strategy, logistics, important personnel questions, all filtered to his office. Each item received at least a glance, often a long endorsement which might analyze complex constitutional issues. Hours were spent simply seeing people. Again, some Pollards suggest that Davis

shut himself away from the citizenry, even from Congress, that he hid
in his book-strewn "snuggery" to cherish the portents of fame—but
the stream's of casual callers, the crowds of congressmen trooping to
his office or to the White House belie the accusation. Special-interest
groups visited in numbers; special pleaders often arrived alone. Cabinet
members were at least weekly visitors to the White House. Those who
saw Davis in relative privacy saw an executive different from the marble man of Pollard's projection. In the comfort of a closed circle
Davis waxed warm, witty, and charmed visitors into zealots. In his
special diction Davis made pure reason into patriotism.

Something of that witchery Davis worked in extemporaneous remarks before large audiences—it was a talent he scarcely knew he had
until the inaugural trip to Montgomery, Alabama. In countless talks
from his railroad car Davis found a different oratory and the people a
different man—fire from such calm touched hearers with hope. But
before Congress, where events so much demanded suasion, Davis stood
often like a preacher. Why? Did the Confederate Congress overawe
a longtime United States senator? No, he was not overawed. He simply
expected quick support and understanding from fellow patriots. And
he went to Congress filled with an anguished love for his country and
his cause, a love as deep as Lincoln's for the Union, a love that somehow parched his eloquence and made him a strangely muffled leader.
He learned much in office; the need to cajole Congress he could not
bring himself to learn.

Davis and the Confederate Congress came to an unfortunate mutual disbelief—they stared at each other across a widening gulf of
troubles. Distrust grew in direct ratio to bad news about the war.
Davis thought congressmen should do what was right simply because
it was right; congressmen thought the President should explain himself and his program of emergency nationalism so that state-rights
constituents would know the need for temporary revolution. Instead
of communication—to use a modern word—both sides got declamations.

Davis could persuade individual congressmen; he should have
brought small groups to the White House on a regular basis—for
discussions, briefings, for mutual complaint. This smacked too much
of politicking to a statesman who knew his country's needs. Articulate
with a few, even with many, Davis seemed dumb to his Congress. It
was a grievous fault, surely, but his willingness to go to the people of

the Confederacy, his increasingly passionate correspondence, his public exhortations, were marks of growth in a highly private person. They were hallmarks, too, of a working President, who realized he had to grow into a different man to fill a different role.

Evidence of Davis's hard work came in every facet of his job. If southerners were indolent, as so many Yankees said, Davis seemed hardly a southerner. In his role as chief administrator of the government he lavished hours on filling offices, setting precedents, hearing plans and programs, dictating policy. Early he confronted the cabinet problem. Ability he wanted as the foremost quality of cabinet members, but politics dictated state representation as the first consideration in cabinet making. Even so, Davis picked men better than his critics admit. Far from a cranky lot of marplots, the cabinet was made of men of goodwill and competence, who managed a far-flung line, a disparate country, a tiny fleet for four years. Changes came in the membership, but mainly men of accomplishment aided Davis. Much administrative success came from lower-level management in each of the departments. A civil service, which relied only slightly on experienced exiles from Washington, developed early. Davis, like Lincoln, found energetic bureaucrats vital to the war. He managed them well enough, or rather, he allowed his cabinet to manage them. Clusters of government workers moved into Montgomery, thence to Richmond, and their numbers grew with war's complexities.

These workers, ferreting papers in all bureaus, did the daily business of government. Their doings pretty well prove that Davis did not supervise everything—too may details were attended to by too many people for the President's total comprehension. Many good and bad things were done by the burgeoning bureaucracy. Goaded by the apparent need for security in a city teeming with every kind of human, including Yankees, Richmond at length took on some trappings of a police city-state. Special detectives under General John Henry Winder imposed varying degrees of martial and kangaroo law. The whole country suffered restrictions on civilian travel. Complaints spilled through the national press, and Davis reaped some of the blame. All misdeeds of the administration were his own; few of the good deeds went to his credit.

Davis deserves praise as an executive. His government, organized from nothing, ran midst alarms, emergencies, crises of every kind; the machinery groaned and shuddered often, but it ran for four years well enough to hold the armies and the country together.

As a war leader Davis showed courage, considerable flexibility and imagination. Contrary to long-held notions, Davis did evolve and keep a war plan consistent with southern circumstance and with sound strategic theory: the "offensive-defensive." He groped for his plan, made a serious error early in advocating state and area defense, but learned from that mistake. His strategic ideas were bold enough for Confederate practice. His organizational ideas reflected growing awareness of the different nature of mass war. Quickly he appreciated the relative isolation of Richmond and the communication problems which resulted. He sought ways to delegate management of operations. First, he tried the familiar scheme of departmental commands designed along geographical lines. When this system proved inadequate, Davis devised a novel adaptation which showed his capacity to adjust to emergencies—the idea of a theater command. Twice he sought to apply his concept; twice it failed. He was undone by the human element. General Joseph Eggleston Johnston, first offered a vast satrapy from western Georgia to the Mississippi and from the Gulf to whatever northern boundary he could reach, missed the fullness of his opportunity and sought instead traditional army command. Later Pierre Gustave Toutant Beauregard, too, missed the opportunity—strange, for so vast a chance should have piqued his Gallic verve. If either Johnston or Beauregard had grasped the chance the President offered, a bold conception in command might have shown something of the strength it gathered in the Second World War. Human frailty ruined an idea ahead of its time, an idea which shows Davis's martial innovativeness at its best.

Innovation could be seen in his earliest military notions expressed to the Confederate Congress. Asserting that "all we ask is to be let alone," the President prophesied trouble. Hints of a coming storm Davis glimpsed in Lincoln's inaugural address and thought there was every chance for a "war of extermination on both sides." Supporting his expectations, Davis asked for an impressive folio of military laws. Congress accepted his lead and created staff departments for the army and navy, authorized regular land and naval establishments, and went so far as to agree with Davis's demand for provisional forces.

The provisional force notion had merit. An army of twelve-month volunteers would have flexibility for command experiments and would avoid the problem of a large standing army. Davis urged, too, the acceptance of volunteers organized by the states, the acceptance of militia units, even on short enlistment terms, and the control by his government of all military property in the states. Congress agreed to all these requests and also gathered to Confederate control all military operations in the country.

Familiarity with martial matters gave Davis a special interest in creating the Confederacy's army. In the early weeks of nationhood he worked to push organized units to points of concentration and have them ready for shipment to threatened points on southern borders. The government had thousands, even possibly half a million, men ready for the colors—and had barely two hundred thousand arms. Davis realized that time worked against the hasty patriotism everywhere apparent. While he struggled with diplomacy in Washington to solve the touchy issue of Forts Sumter and Pickens, he worried that diplomacy lacked excitement. Zealots for war would lose interest in protracted tranquillity. By mid-April 1861 the Sumter crisis rested not only on Federal intentions but also on Rebel enthusiasm. The solemn cabinet decision to fire on the Charleston fort was forced as much by the pressure of apathy as by sovereignty. General Beauregard's first shell launched a train of events which proved quickly Davis's wisdom in military legislation. Lincoln called for 75,000 volunteers; Davis for the 100,000 authorized by Congress.

War sparked a new enthusiasm; men trooped in from the far reaches of the Confederacy. Davis, concerned especially for the border areas, funneled men northward as Virginia joined the new nation. He thought the Old Dominion would be the coming battleground. It was, and the early battles were encouraging. First Manassas in July brought a triumph with dismal results. Southerners were now convinced that latter-day minute men could lay aside the plow, take up the musket, and run the Yankees off. Victory brought happiness and dangerously lowered guard. The President, fully aware of defeat's probable effect in the North, urged redoubled efforts—but his sobriety found few adherents in the South. By winter troubles ringed the Confederacy. Bad news came in batches; curious failures dulled southern martial sheen. Early in the new year, 1862, Forts Henry and Donelson on the Tennessee and Cumberland rivers fell; next went Roanoke

Island in a clutch of ill omens. Twelve-month enlistments were about to expire; tedium and defeat eroded patriotism. How many men would reenlist? Prognostications by the War Department were not good. Volunteering yielded to anxiety. The armies might well dissolve. That looming possibility demanded the firmest executive leadership. As the permanent government went to work in Richmond in February 1862 the new Congress found the administration increasingly urging some kind of conscription law. Davis pushed hard for drafting all white men between eighteen and thirty-five, and especially for extending the service of men already in the ranks. It was a tough stand, one likely to be extremely unpopular in a laissez-faireist, extremely loose Confederacy. But the President pressed his needs, and in April the first draft law in American history was enacted—to remarkably light opposition.

As the war continued and manpower dwindled Davis increased his efforts to sustain the armies. The use of Negroes as laborers, then as special auxiliaries to the armies, he advocated, and, at last, he openly urged the drafting of blacks into Confederate ranks. His persistence in the matter of arming the slaves illustrates something of his perception in leadership. A discussion among generals of the Army of Tennessee in January 1864 centered on filling depleted legions with Negroes—and the discussion erupted into charges and countercharges of treason, subversion, and other heinous intents. Davis, who received a bulky package of these protests, quashed the argument, refused to penalize anyone, and soothed ruffled social sensibilities. Why blacks should not be drafted for national defense he could not see, especially when the enemy used them in war against the South. In a perceptive passage to Congress he suggested that Negroes were more than chattels. "The slave . . . bears another relation to the State—that of a person. . . . In this respect [army service] the relation of person predominates so far as to render it doubtful whether the private right of property can consistently and beneficially be continued, and it would seem proper to acquire for the public service the entire property in the labor of the slave." Taking over the national slave supply would bring special confusions. "Should he [the slave] be retained in servitude," Davis asked, "or should his emancipation be held out to him as a reward for faithful service?" Davis advocated freedom after service as trained auxiliaries in supply and medical services. He went on to suggest that it might be necessary to put blacks in the ranks and explained his thinking: "A broad moral distinction exists between the use of slaves as soldiers in defense of their homes and the incitement of the same persons to insurrection against their masters. The one is justifiable, if necessary, the other is iniquitous and unworthy of a civilized people." Quietly he kept the debate going, urged discussion as he could in correspondence, and hoped that realities would change customs.

In the last months of the war he got his way as a few companies of Negroes drilled in gray uniforms and under the Stars and Bars. Their debt to servitude worried Davis, and he urged a reluctant Congress to grant freedom to every black Rebel soldier. Some of the states agreed with this highly revolutionary notion, and so did General Robert Edward Lee.

Radical change had been part and parcel of Davis's experience from his earliest days in the Confederate White House. When first he came to Montgomery he saw clearer than most the absurdity of southern circumstance. To wife Varina he noted in February 1861 that "We are without machinery, without means, and threatened by a powerful opposition." Refusing to "despond," he sought to build strength in unity—and unity seemed uncommon in a cause of confederation.

Next, certainly, to girding for war, Davis faced the task of nation-making. He had to do it almost alone—the various states pranced in high fettle, talked of the Confederacy, but acted with a truculent sense of new sovereignty.

He began the call for a country shortly after arriving in Montgomery, Alabama, on February 16, 1861. Summoned by a cheering throng to the Exchange Hotel's balcony, he spoke of a new brotherhood. "Brethren of the Confederate States of America," he labeled his listeners, "for now we are brethren, not in name, merely, but in fact—men of one flesh, one bone, one interest, one purpose." That theme he echoed again in his first inaugural address two days later. "To increase the power, develop the resources, and promote the happiness of the Confederacy," he prescribed "so much of homogeneity that the welfare of every portion shall be the aim of the whole. When this does not exist, antagonisms are engendered which . . . result in separation."

Unity ran through most of his public utterances. Stressing "common cause," Davis welcomed new states, preached the need for cohesion as he increased his private correspondence, and in several "swings around the Confederacy" he argued for nationalism. A group of western congressmen, harping on the need for separate state protection during the hectic campaigns of 1863, got the national catechism in blunt words from the President. It was a "fatal error" he said, to suppose "that this great war can be waged by the Confederate States *severally* and not *unitedly* with the least hope of success."

Just as William Gladstone could proclaim at Newcastle, England, in October 1862 that Jefferson Davis had made a country, Davis could proclaim in December 1863 that adversity had made Confederates out of southerners. "We have been united as a people never were united under like circumstances before," he boasted to Congress, and added that "the patriotism of the people has proved equal to every sacrifice demanded by their country's need."

But through the grinding year 1864—"the year the war broke up" as one anonymous Rebel put it—Davis fought growing despair from all corners of his country. Governors, influential citizens, generals, soldiers, people with boundless advice, all received presidential exhortations. Davis's eloquence grew with crisis; his letters to carpers were measured rebukes; his replies to state executives still prating state rights read like primers of federalism; his thanks for praise and comfort ran deep and sincere. But criticism mounted as the cause declined. He bore criticism poorly in the best of times; as disasters gathered his patience thinned until, at least, his acerb reaction transformed into a kind of acceptance of martyrdom—witness some sad words to General Lee on April 1, 1865: "The distrust is increasing and embarrasses in many ways." Against such old foes as Governors Joseph Emerson Brown of Georgia and Zebulon Baird Vance of North Carolina he turned almost at bay. These men were aware of the trending and still fought unity. Baffled by disloyalty he combatted it with logic—and logic rang hollowly in the dark Wilderness and was lost in the angry sieging at Petersburg. Davis became a kind of conscience of his country as he watched its substance ebb. The congealed calm so long preserved cracked at the end, and an unexpected passion spilled into his last shining vision of a future in which the South would win and be free. It was pitiful and human, and it lent nobility

to his last public message. Lee had gone from Richmond, the government fled to nameless places, the enemy swarmed everywhere—and
yet "Let us but will it, and we are free; and who, in the light of the
past, dare doubt your purpose in the future? . . . Let us not, then,
despond, my countrymen, but, relying on the never-failing mercies
and protecting care of our God, let us meet the foe with fresh defiance,
with unconquered and unconquerable hearts."

In the avalanche of enmity that came with defeat, most of Davis's
own substance was lost. His enemies, Union and Confederate, used his
errors as the stuff of myth. He symbolized everything tawdry the times
and the Pollards required—sinful southern arrogance, haughty Confederate incompetence. An image he had carefully fashioned throughout his life was ignored by northerners needing a traitor and by southerners needing a scapegoat. Who cared that he wanted to be the
epitome of the Southern Gentleman; who cared, for that matter,
about Southern Gentlemen in the wreckage of their era? He wrapped
the guise of Southern Gentleman around him, though, a cloak against
fate—it was a guise he began building after Sarah Knox Taylor
Davis's death. In grief and guilt, he sought to make himself something she would cherish, something his hating father-in-law might
admire. The role took form in Congress, in Pierce's cabinet, especially
in the United States Senate years, until, at last, Davis could stand in
that forum as the full embodiment of a class. In those comfortable
years he championed state rights with fiery rhetoric and firm belief.
As Confederate President he turned against state rights and became
a Rebel nationalist; still, though, the Gentleman incarnate.

Historians have recently noted Davis's move to nationalism—some
as a sign of growth, others as a sign of expediency. But none have so
far noticed the unusually revolutionary nature of Davis's shift in
loyalty.

If Davis comes to have a legend it may be as a gentleman revolutionary. Traditionally pictured as a constitutionalist trapped in a
revolutionary moment, he is often berated for sticking too closely to
the law. He stuck to the law all right, but in his hands the constitution became a revolutionary document.

Let me try to illustrate the point by first mentioning a recent paper
by my colleague, Professor Harold M. Hyman, in which he asserts
"that until the American Revolution is understood more clearly as a

revolution in government *procedures* and *institutions* rather than as
an overturning of class, economic, racial, or sex relationships, its
applicability to the present will be limited."

Davis's revolution must be seen first as one of procedures before
it can be understood as one of institutions and as, finally, a full rend-
ing of a people and a way of life. He took the Confederate constitutions for what they said they were: the supreme law of the land.
Under that conviction he turned the law against the states, first by
creating a national army out of state forces, an army loyal to the Confederacy. Next he worked to build a sense in the southern people of
a higher loyalty than state rights—a sense of Confederateness. In
doing this he fought the governors on economic, military, and political issues, even, at last, on social issues; he fought, too, the natural
independence of fellow southrons to devise a war plan consistent with
reality and with theory; he fought himself to change his ideal Southern
Gentleman into a Confederate.

Far from being a slave to the constitution, Davis early schemed to
rise above it or go around it. In a message to Congress on November
18, 1861, Davis urged the building of a railroad between Danville,
Virginia, and Greensboro, North Carolina. If the military necessity
was accepted by Congress, Davis had no doubt that "the action of
the Government will not be restrained by the constitutional objection
which would attach to a work for commercial purposes." If the war
demanded rationalizing the constitution, Davis rationalized. The
clearest example concerns finances and came in a message to Congress
in December 1863. Reviewing the general failure of war taxation to
that time, Davis bluntly said that land and slaves made up roughly
two-thirds of the Confederacy's taxable property, and they ought to
be taxed. Constitutional objections had prevented it, he thought,
objections with some validity. Taxes on land and slaves were considered direct taxes, and the constitution forbade such levies without a
census on which to apportion the burden. There had been no census,
and there was not likely to be one. Should the government, as a
consequence, not tax land and slaves? To that question Davis aimed
his nimblest analysis. "The general intent of our constitutional
charter is unquestionably that the property of the country is to be
taxed . . . for the common defense, and the special mode provided
by levying this tax is impracticable from unforeseen causes. It is in my

judgment our primary duty to execute the general intent expressed
. . . , and we cannot excuse ourselves for the failure to fulfill this
obligation on the ground that we are unable to perform it in the
precise mode pointed out." By that later stage of the war Davis's
priorities were coming into clear focus. Nothing mattered save victory.

That certainty sparked the President's attitude toward using slaves
in the army, even if slavery went as a result, and toward reconstruct-
ing the country along industrial lines. With uncommon boldness
Davis sponsored such tough policies as the tax in kind, direct war
taxation, the full-scale use of impressments, government control of
the railroads, commandeering of cargo space on blockade runners.
He even offered to trade slavery for recognition in February 1865. He
did these things because they were necessary for the war effort. He
knew what the war was about—independence. And he knew that
old-style gentlemen were yielding to a new breed of businessmen
whose sights were on the future. He was one of them.

What substance can there be to a Davis legend? To have substance, a legend ought to be based on some kind of remarkable
achievement, some kind of heroic deed. Was he a man who rose to
challenge—as do so many American Presidents? Certainly, he rose
to crises, and they increased daily into an unrelieved wave of woe.
He bore the burden with unwavering calm. Personal and official
tragedy never induced panic in the President—in travail he found
personal triumph.

Is personal triumph sufficient for legend? Probably not, but there
is another dimension for measure. Did Davis succeed in making a
Confederate nation? If so, then he deserves rank with a handful of
legendary Americans who changed history. Gladstone thought Davis
had succeeded in 1862, and Davis himself had no doubts of success
by 1863. The world noted Confederate deeds for four years. The
Confederacy's fate was sealed in battle. Its history, though, Davis
helped preserve in the hard years after the war, and its history is re-
written afresh by each generation. Persistent history is best proof of
success. About his own role in making that lasting legacy, Davis might
say, as he once said to Beauregard, "Enough was done for glory, and
the measure of duty was full."

What more does legend need?

20

The Metamorphosis of Slavery After Emancipation

PETE DANIEL

• The institution of slavery started on the North American
continent as an attempt to cope with severe labor shortages.
The first boatload of Africans arrived in 1619, and for the
next forty years blacks were sometimes treated as indentured
servants—workers who toiled for a fixed period of time and
who were then free to pursue their own lives—and sometimes
kept forever in bondage. Not until the 1660s did the custom
develop to keep all Afro-Americans in permanent servitude.
Thereafter the African slaves provided the bulk of the labor-
ing force in the southern colonies. Slavery existed in the
North also during this period but the institution was generally curbed, and the bondsmen released, well before the
Civil War. In the South, by contrast, the invention of the
cotton gin in 1793 created an enormous need for slaves to
support an essentially agricultural economy, and it took a
terrible conflict and many hundreds of thousands of battle
deaths before the "peculiar institution" was finally abolished.

The need for cheap farm labor remained, however, particularly in a section as ravaged by war as the Old South. The
result was a new form of involuntary servitude that was based
upon the contract system, the law, violence, and illiteracy,
and it trapped some whites as well as the vast majority of
blacks in a form of peonage. In recent years, historians have
done valuable work on the nature of racist thought, on the
conditions of plantation life, on the effect of bondage upon
personality, and on the profitability of slavery. Alex Haley has
pioneered in the effort to discover the ancestral roots of black
Americans, while other authors have turned to the efforts at
resistance by the oppressed. Less well-known to the general

Reprinted by permission of the author and the editor from Pete Daniel,
"Commentary/The Metamorphosis of Slavery, 1865–1900," *Journal of American History*, 66 (June 1979), 88–99.

08   PETE DANIEL

> public is the economic system of the South that evolved after
> the Civil War and deprived so many "citizens" of the full
> enjoyment of their constitutional guarantees. Pete Daniel is
> the nation's leading authority on sharecropping and tenant
> farming, and the following essay summarizes his judgments
> about the harsh labor contracts that were typical for two
> generations after the surrender at Appomattox.

The shock of emancipation, coming as it did during an unsuccessful
war, hardened the hearts of southern whites; defeated, they were un-
vanquished. From nearly every street corner and manor house, wrote
observers, southern whites threatened to reenslave blacks as soon as
northern occupation ended. Meanwhile, landlord and tenant entered
into contracts sharing land and labor, and blacks discovered that
emancipation did not signal equal rights—or even in some cases freedom. Like a patchwork quilt, the new labor system in the South was
varied and complex, an unpatterned blend of illiteracy, law, contracts,
and violence, confusing, if not incomprehensible, even to those closest
to it. The complexity of economic adjustment was eclipsed by the violence and corruption associated with politics, and the era of Reconstruction became, for those who lived through it and for historians who
wrote of it, too emotionally charged to explain rationally. Perhaps
agreeing with Albion Tourgée that Reconstruction was "a fool's er-
rand," northerners gradually lost interest in policing the South and allowed white southerners, within bounds, to handle the race problem.
Spokesmen as varied, at least in color, as Booker T. Washington and
Henry Grady gave their benedictions to the New South; in an age that
glorified progress, they accepted it warts and all.

   It came as a shock, then, in 1901, when a new kind of slavery was
discovered. It was called peonage after the labor practice in Mexico
and through an unlikely set of circumstances violated an 1867 federal
statute in the United States. The law lay dormant for thirty-four years,
but peonage was widespread in the South by the turn of the century,
and it was especially virulent in the cotton belt, the Mississippi Delta,
and the turpentine belt. A. J. Hoyt, a federal investigator, estimated in
1907 that one-third of the larger plantations in the cotton belt had

peons working the crops, and other estimates corroborate his figures. Those threats of 1865, then, had been partially fulfilled; slavery had indeed ended for some blacks, but for others it had endured, metamorphosed.

Definition of involuntary servitude is both crucial and difficult. First of all, chattel slavery, that peculiar institution, ended in 1865. It was replaced by sharecropping, a labor system that seemed, under the circumstances, well suited for landlords and tenants. Yet sharecropping arrangements varied—from state to state, crop to crop, county to county, and farm to farm—and changed subject to the passage of time and the passage, enforcement, and understanding of laws. Three general divisions of agricultural labor emerged in the South after the war. Most agricultural laborers were free, moving about and selling their labor as best they could; but at the other extreme, at the bottom of the agricultural ladder, were peons, laborers who were bound in debt from year to year and who were coerced to work out what they owed. The third category was simply the twilight zone between freedom and involuntary servitude. It was in this middle ground between slavery and freedom that the post-Civil War labor system metamorphosed. For example, a worker who ended the year in debt and who voluntarily remained with a landlord and worked off his debt was free, but when any element of coercion entered, he became a peon. The line was that thin. No doubt many workers drifted from freedom to peonage often in their lifetimes, never realizing that they had crossed the line.

This third category raises the question of how viable traditional terms such as freedom and slavery are when discussing post-Civil War agricultural labor. Coercion, the crucial element in involuntary servitude, came from sources other than the words of the landlords and merchants. It came from the law, which increasingly tightened its grip on workers; from the contract, which became a year sentence on a few acres; from violence, which gave object lessons to those who objected to the system; and from illiteracy, which placed the worker at the mercy of the literate elite and kept him from seeking jobs that required more skill than plowing, hoeing, and picking. All of these tentacles reached out toward those laborers who were technically free and embraced them in a system that was certainly, as Roger Ransom and Richard Sutch have suggested, only "one kind of freedom." In the moiling confusion of the post-Civil War South, debt visited most houses in the hinterland; it did not discriminate by race.

The origin, development, and institutionalization of involuntary servitude in the post-war South remains unclear, for historians have seldom asked the questions that would reveal it. And as novelist Thomas Pynchon has reminded us, "If they can get you asking the wrong questions, they don't have to worry about answers." The evolving post-war labor system can be likened to an unfinished patchwork quilt; year by year the design would change—a contract law added here, a lien law there, while lynchings, beatings, vagrancy laws, and illiteracy eventually pieced it out. Yet the quilt transcended the patches; its ultimate pattern was greater than its parts. There was a strength in its design that may well have been esthetically pleasing to the people who sewed it, but to those it covered, it was stifling.

The quilt was constructed on the frame of chattel slavery. To begin with, southern planters were almost struck dumb by emancipation, for nothing in their experience had prepared them for dealing with free blacks. "Emancipation was a rolling barrage that enveloped every plantation by 1865," James Roark has written recently. "For the planter class, slavery's destruction became the central experience of the Civil War." Planters were reluctant to inform blacks that slavery was over, and they were careful not to tell them how over it was. When blacks found out they were free, it was seldom because a southern white told them. Carpetbagger Albert T. Morgan wrote that around Yazoo City, Mississippi, "we afterward learned that fully half of the colored population did not know they were free." The report prepared by Carl Schurz often noted that blacks away from the coast were kept in slavery long after it legally ended and that "planters endeavored and partially succeeded in maintaining between themselves and the negroes the relation of master and slave, partly by concealing from them the great changes that had taken place, and partly by terrorizing them into submission to their behests." Even after blacks were freed, they often were not paid. As Thomas W. Knox observed before the war ended, "The difference between working for nothing as a slave, and working for the same wages under the Yankees, was not always perceptible to the unsophisticated negro." Correspondent Sidney Andrews, traveling through the Carolinas and Georgia, summed up the despair that many people felt in the summer of 1865 as blacks fell under the sway of the old regime. "The viciousness that could not overturn the nation is now mainly engaged in the effort to retain the substance of slavery," he observed. "What are names if the thing itself remains?" As Roark concluded, "The dominant theme in the planters' lives became the search for a substitute for slavery."

Freedmen, however, did not cooperate with the plans to reenslave them. Immediately, planters and whites in general were struck by the change in attitude among freedmen. Deference largely disappeared, respect for whites dwindled, and even the more patient whites found it difficult to work with free blacks. Paternalism no longer worked, and whites came to hate freedmen, projecting on blacks the defeat in battle, economic ruin, and the occupation by Union troops. Violence replaced paternalism. For the first time whites glimpsed the extent of the cultural gap that separated the races; the blinders of slavery fell away.

Yet a kind of paternalism emerged once again during the violence of Radical Reconstruction, during the rides of the Ku Klux [Klan]. Planters, sizing up the situation, gave tenants on their plantations protection in exchange for regular work and a general compliance with the new order. Willard Warner, a native of Ohio who served both in the Ohio state senate and in the Alabama legislature before being elected to the United States Senate in 1871, testified in 1883 to the new paternalistic arrangement. "And, to a great extent, as in the days of slavery the master was the first man to protect his negro—partly, of course, from motives of interest; partly, also, it is due to him to say, from a feeling of humanity and affection for him so—now the planter is disposed to protect his negro laborer, or his negro tenant, because it is his interest to do so, and also because of his kindly feeling toward him."

Surely the new arrangement differed from antebellum paternalism, but exactly how has not yet been explained. Tourgée gave another example of the relationship between violence and labor control. After a brutal lynching, Tourgée's character Comfort Servosse observed, "He saw at once how this potent instrumentality might be used so as to effectually destroy the liberty of the newly enfranchised citizen, and establish a serfdom more barbarous and horrible than any on earth, because it would be the creature of lawless insolence." It was all the more dramatic to Tourgée, for he believed that before the rides of the

Klan, "the negro manifested a most inveterate and invincible repug-
nance and disinclination towards allowing his former masters to define, regulate, and control his liberties."

Southern planters were desperate to maintain as much force as possible. Broken by the war and alarmed at the new mood of independence
among blacks, they expected the plantation system to disintegrate
quickly into chaos. After all, they had studied Haiti, which within
a generation after emancipation sank into economic chaos and poverty
as compulsory labor ended. In the West Indies free labor rarely performed as well as slave labor, and in some cases where freedmen refused to work, coolies supplemented the labor force. In Jamaica even
laws could not force freedmen back to the cane fields, but while Ja-
maican planters eventually threw up their hands in desperation at the
disintegration of the economy following the Morant Bay riot, southerners lost and then regained their power, and having vowed to continue slavery, they did not go back on their word. Replacing paternalism with violence which led back to paternalism, utilizing customs
from the past and the freedmen's illiteracy, relying on contracts and
northern sympathy with the work ethic, and mouthing laws and threats,
southern planters shaped a labor system that preserved the larva of
slavery in the evolution of freedom.

To historians familiar with other post-emancipation societies, the
continuation of slavery in the American South comes as no surprise,
for in no slave society did masters passively submit to freedom. H. J.
Nieboer, Willemina Kloosterboer, Harry Hoetink, and C. Vann Woodward all suggest a broader approach in studying the Reconstruction
era. Their works propose a theoretical model to explain what social,
political, demographic, legal, and economic conditions most contributed to a continuation of forced labor. Kloosterboer, whose study is the
most wide-ranging, reveals that in no case did planters willingly surrender their power over slaves. The weight of forced labor practices
was too heavy to be dragged away by a proclamation of emancipation.
"Freedom," William A. Green explained about the British West Indies, "was grafted upon an exclusive system which was ill-equipped in
sentiment and character to administer a free society."

With the exception of Haiti, the old planter classes continued as
the exploiters; their attitude changed little from slavery days. Nearly
all plantation areas emerged from slavery with parallel ideas and laws

that perpetuated forced labor. To continue disciplined labor, vagrancy laws appeared. To guarantee steady work from planting to harvest, contracts bound workers to the soil. Supply merchants or planters encouraged workers to become indebted to them and bound them tighter to the land with peonage. Throughout the plantation areas of the world, involuntary servitude continued after slavery was legally abolished.

Nieboer, Kloosterboer, Hoetink, and Woodward address themselves to the theory that open and closed resources determined the destiny of plantation systems in areas emerging from slavery. The Nieboer thesis posits that where resources were open, that is, where there was still available land for people to move to, slavery would continue, for only by enslavement could freedmen be kept off the land. In societies where the resources were closed, on the other hand, there was no option but to work, and slavery was not needed. Green showed that this theory worked well in the British West Indies. In Barbados, Antigua, and St. Kitts, where resources were closed, slavery ended and a wage system emerged. In Jamaica, as in other areas where there were open resources that would provide a subsistence living, it was impossible to keep the freedmen off the land. "There was extra land in the South," wrote Woodward, "but that which was most available was quickly snatched from their grasp by the frustration of the Freedmen's Bureau plans for the distribution of abandoned lands, and the less available land was beyond their reach for lack of capital." This generalization offers a tremendous challenge to demographers, for historians have not tested this theory for the United States.

There is a need for a comparative account of emancipation in the British West Indies and in the United States (as well as in all post-emancipation societies), for there are instructive parallels. The major differences, of course, were that West Indian planters were compensated for their slaves and that emancipation there came peacefully, but there were many similarities after freedom. There was a debate whether Parliament or the colonial legislatures would make the crucial decisions regarding vagrancy and contract laws, much as the period of Presidential Reconstruction saw the same conflict in the United States over whether Congress would allow state black codes. Unlike the United States, Great Britain tried a period of apprenticeship to prepare for complete freedom and, suggestive of the Freedmen's Bureau, sent stipendiary magistrates to supervise the transition. Like planters in the

United States wooing Freedmen's Bureau agents, West Indian planters tried to win the favor of the magistrates and in many cases did, but
Parliament sent far too few magistrates to supervise the vast slavehold-
ing areas of the Indies. There was a struggle for power between colonial governors and legislatures, especially in Barbados, and, as in the
South under radical rule, many opportunities for compromise were lost
because of intransigence. The apprenticeship period did ease the way
to freedom, but, like the effort of the Freedmen's Bureau, it ultimately
failed in what it set out to do. "Submissive and disciplined labour was
the pivot upon which the whole apparatus of planter power depended,"
Green concluded. "West Indian oligarchs intended to perpetuate their
exclusive control over the political, judicial, and law-enforcement machinery of the colonies as a means of regulating the lives and labours
of former slaves." Change a few words and the description fits the
South.

Yet West Indian planters were not as successful as were southern
planters in perpetuating involuntary servitude among freedmen. Despite vagrancy and contract laws in Jamaica, compulsion did not work.
"Even freedmen who lived on the estates refused to work under contract, and the planters had no satisfactory means of forcing them to,"
Green concluded. In the United States the legal machinery and violence were more successful in forcing plantation laborers to work. Yet
the British faced the same dilemma that the southern planters did.
"Finding a workable arrangement which permitted the survival of the
plantation system without sacrificing the liberty of freedmen was clearly
the most difficult and elusive problem of the free society," Green observed. While planters turned to immigrant labor to boost the labor
force in Jamaica and let the closed resources create a wage labor pool
in Barbados, in the United States a network of laws, violence, and custom kept blacks working; grandiose plans of importing immigrants
never materialized. Certainly a careful analysis of the West Indies and
the United States will show options, successes, and failures in post-
emancipation policies. The comparison certainly shows the tendency
for involuntary servitude to continue despite the best intentions of the
abolitionists in England and in the United States.

After slavery certain methods of labor control seemed almost prede-
termined. As Kloosterboer concluded, vagrancy laws emerged universally. "Penal sanction on breach of contract," she added, "was another

practically universal phenomenon, and the regulations covering it did not differ much in content in all the countries in which it was applied." Peonage emerged primarily in areas where there were tenant farmers, for example, in Latin America, the United States, and Madagascar. These and other countries used advances to bind laborers in debt, and it is well known that laws in the South hedged laborers this way. Immigrants to plantation areas in the West Indies were lured into debt to keep them from leaving after their contracts were fulfilled. Abolitionists and their reforming successors were unable to stem this drift back to forced labor. Indeed, in the South, despite widespread publicity and Supreme Court rulings, peonage and other forms of forced labor continued to be widespread until technological factors, the tractor and the picking machine, for example, eased the demand for a large and disciplined labor force. Certainly historians of the American South, utilizing a comparative model, should look more closely at the demographic and labor peculiarities of the South.

Perhaps the most challenging peculiarity was the presence in the South of white agricultural workers whose economic lives were subsumed under the same factors as blacks. Whereas blacks were moving from slavery to freedom, whites were passing them heading in the opposite direction. Rural workers of both races were caught in the exchange between freedom and slavery, and frictions generated from exploitation, social adjustment, and racism often sparked violence. Sharecroppers lived at the center of concentric circles of oppression—the law, contracts, violence, and illiteracy. The circumstantial evidence that these factors led to peonage is overwhelming.

Certainly illiteracy made workers vulnerable to manipulations in contracts and settlements. Since black illiteracy ran 75 to 80 percent in the 1870s and 1880s, there was little chance that sharecroppers could successfully contest their accounts. Neither could they move to more skilled jobs.

As in other post-emancipation societies, it was the law that was at the center of compulsion. Though it is impossible to state with certainty where freedom ended and slavery began, William Cohen goes a long way in documenting the tentacles of law that grasped laborers. Enticement laws, emigrant agent restrictions, contract laws, vagrancy statutes, the criminal-surety system, and convict labor laws snared laborers. Planters translated their immediate postwar demand for compliant labor into black codes, and as soon as they regained power after Radical Reconstruction reinstituted, even refined those codes. "Once the Redeemers took power, however," Cohen argued, "the former Confederate states began to resurrect the labor controls established from 1865 to 1867." After a thorough examination of the labor laws of the post-Reconstruction South, Cohen concluded that the legal net was formidable. But the new labor system, like the patchwork quilt, was more than that. "Transcending peonage as it transcended the legal structure which partially defined it," observed Cohen correctly, "the system of involuntary servitude was a unique blend of slavery and freedom which gave whites the option of limiting black movement while leaving Negroes otherwise free to come and go as they pleased." Cohen is also correct to treat the laws as a continuum from 1865 to 1940, as the legal history of peonage illustrates.

The yearly contract was one of the most important elements in the landlord's control over labor—not what the contract stated explicitly, but what it implied and how it was executed. The pattern emerged immediately after the war. With encouragement from the Freedmen's Bureau, blacks signed up for a year's work, and the vigilant eyes of federal officials noted that many contracts resembled slavery. Schurz in his report on the conditions in the South wrote that in South Carolina some contracts contained provisions to ensure that blacks would be in debt at the end of the year, and "the employer might thus obtain a permanent hold upon the person of the laborer." He observed that "it was something like the system of peonage existing in Mexico." The contracts were refused in this case, but other observers noticed the same trend. Correspondent Whitelaw Reid reported that contracts "seemed to be such as would virtually establish the Mexican peonage instead of Southern slavery." Planters encouraged blacks to run into debt, for this "would hold them forever by a constantly strengthening chain." The army often aided planters by returning workers who broke contracts still owing work or money.

Booker T. Washington, who settled in Black Belt Alabama in 1881 to begin educating blacks, described in 1889 as well as he could the shackles of the contract system. Responding to a letter of inquiry from George Washington Cable, Washington explained the contract system of advances, interest, and the inevitable way the farmers who could not pay out were cleaned up; the credit merchant or planter "takes every thing, mules, cows, plows, chickens, fodder—every thing except wife and children." He noted that four-fifths of the farms in Alabama had "fences tumbling down, animals poorly cared for, and the land growing poorer every year." Most people had lost hope, he concluded. "One of the strongest things that can be said in favor of the colored people is, that in almost every community there are one or two who have shaken off this yoke of slavery and have bought farms of their own and are making money—and there are a *few* who rent land and 'mortgage' and still do something." W. H. Gardner, a cotton broker from Mobile, agreed. "These shark storekeepers compel them to waive the right of exemption where supplies are wanted for the family, and the result is that in the end the whole thing is swallowed up by the storekeeper." As W. E. B. Du Bois concluded, "The slave went free; stood a brief moment in the sun; then moved back again toward slavery."

While much has been written about southern violence, the impact of violence on the economic options of blacks has not been fully explained. Random violence was often used to discourage political participation, but much as whipping in slavery days, it was also a method of labor control. To question a planter's books, to complain about a settlement, to shirk work became excuses for violence. "It was pretty clear that the negroes were often cheated out of their wages, and that they were sometimes roughly and severely treated on the plantations; while they, in turn, were restless in various portions of the State, and somewhat turbulent, idle, and dishonest," explained an *Atlantic Monthly* reporter in 1882.

As Roark has observed, "the more the freedmen resumed the habits and postures of slaves, the better the planters were able to accept the new system." In the 1870s and afterward there was an unsettling change in race relations. Blacks realized that they had lost the momentum of freedom, that they were more and more at the mercy of their former masters, and that they came to resemble slaves. As Andrews noted, "What are names if the thing itself remains?"

In some cases there was little difference between the involuntary servitude in the 1880s and chattel slavery. An *Atlantic Monthly* correspondent touring the South in the winter of 1882–1883 talked to a northern man who had taken to southern ways, and who admitted that blacks often ran off to the woods. "But what can they do?" he asked. "Their families are here, and they don't know where to go. Besides, I should n't let 'em go, if I didn't want to. The dogs would soon find 'em." As the senate investigation on capital and labor moved across the South, it recorded many instances of the ills of the credit and sharecropping system. The North Carolina Department of Labor Statistics collected reports in 1890, and many farmers complained about high fertilizer costs, high interest rates, and subsequent debts. "While it is generally understood that men can't be imprisoned for debt, I think I can give several instances in which men have been imprisoned for debt for fertilizer to raise tobacco when the tobacco didn't bring enough money to pay for fertilizer used under it," wrote one discouraged farmer. Even Nate Shaw, who continually worked to stay free of debt, admitted that it was rough going. "I had men turn me down, wouldn't let me have the land I needed to work, wouldn't sell me guano, didn't want to see me with anything."

As Washington observed, a fraction of the rural black population managed to buy land and prospered. Shaw lived in both worlds, the one of debt and the one of ownership, but he always remembered that it was his strength that led him out of debt, that and his wife's ability to figure—but Shaw was atypical. In the same county and one abutting it, federal agents filed ninety-nine indictments for peonage in 1903. When freedom came, Shaw remembered, the freedmen "knew that what they got wasn't what they wanted, it wasn't freedom, really."

If emancipation did not result in freedom, what was the status of blacks? No label seems to fit. Some peonage existed, but unless debt and overt coercion of word or deed entered the equation, it was not legally peonage. Neither were workers completely free to sell their labor or to contract as sharecroppers. Defining and documenting this vague twilight zone between freedom and slavery presents the historian with a difficult task. Competitive and monopolistic models, the proper mix of corn and cotton, coercion and competition, and other econometric questions inform us how the South adjusted to free or semifree labor systems, yet the number of blacks, or whites for that matter, who were working involuntarily remains a part of the equation that has not been measured.

The experience of the American South following the abolition of slavery was not unique in world history; a form of involuntary servitude continued. Evidence suggests that a peculiar form of involuntary servitude did persist and that it was based primarily upon illiteracy, the law, the contract system, and violence. The chains of compulsion were forged from all these factors, and their coercion remained largely invisible, like a bed of quicksand. This complex labor system put most blacks, and an increasing number of whites, under a subtle form of control. To discuss the postwar economic adjustment without taking involuntary servitude into consideration is to miss an important question, just as ignoring other post-emancipation adjustments is to miss an opportunity to gain insights into the southern settlement. The intricacies of this metamorphosis call for an interdisciplinary effort to explain the economic and social evolution of the post-Civil War agricultural labor system.